Before Wilde

The publisher gratefully acknowledges the support
of the Humanities Endowment Fund of the University
of California Press Foundation.

Before Wilde

Sex between Men
in Britain's Age of Reform

Charles Upchurch

UNIVERSITY OF CALIFORNIA PRESS
Berkeley · Los Angeles · London

University of California Press, one of the most
distinguished university presses in the United
States, enriches lives around the world by advancing
scholarship in the humanities, social sciences,
and natural sciences. Its activities are supported
by the UC Press Foundation and by philanthropic
contributions from individuals and institutions.
For more information, visit www.ucpress.edu.

University of California Press
Berkeley and Los Angeles, California

University of California Press, Ltd.
London, England

First paperback printing 2013

© 2009 by The Regents of the University of California

Library of Congress Cataloging-in-Publication Data

Upchurch, Charles, 1969–.
    Before Wilde : sex between men in Britain's age of
reform / Charles Upchurch.
        p.   cm.
    Includes bibliographical references and index.
    ISBN 978-0-520-28012-0 (pbk.: alk. paper)
    1. Gay men—Great Britain—History.   2. Gay
men—Great Britain—Social conditions.   3. Men—
Sexual behavior—Great Britain—History—19th
century.   4. Homosexuality—Great Britain—
History—19th century.   5. Sex—Great Britain—
History—19th century.   6. Great Britain—
History—19th century.   7. Great Britain—Social
conditions—19th century.   I. Title.

    HQ76.2.G7U63   2009
    306.76'62094109034—dc22   2008034391

Manufactured in the United States of America

18   17   16   15   14   13
10   9   8   7   6   5   4   3   2   1

This book is printed on Natures Book, which contains
30% post-consumer waste and meets the minimum
requirements of ANSI/NISO Z39.48–1992 (R 1997)
(Permanence of Paper).

For Fred

Contents

Tables

Acknowledgments

This work has benefited from a number of readers whose comments and suggestions have made it a markedly better book than it would have otherwise been. John Gillis's encouragement to think about this material within the framework of family, class, and community was the single greatest influence on what was originally a much narrower project. His suggestions were reinforced by the community of scholars at Rutgers University, where Bonnie Smith, Jennifer Jones, and Ed Cohen provided the comments that helped link the implications of this study to questions that were originally outside my area of interest. Randolph Trumbach's close readings of many chapters over the years and insistence on the importance of eighteenth-century precedents improved this work in numerous ways, as did my participation in the New York Gay and Lesbian History Seminar, which he ran for four years.

The final stages of this project were carried out with the funding and support of the Florida State University Department of History, during which time George Robb, Anna Clark, Ed Gray, Sean Brady, Niels Hooper, and Erika Büky each gave insightful comments on the final drafts of the work. Research assistance was provided by the staffs of the National Archive in London, the British Library, Bobst Library in New York, and Perkins Library in Durham, North Carolina. This work is also indebted to Bruce Kinzer, Kathleen Berkeley, Andy Dowless, Max Likin, and Joe Merieux, each in different ways.

Fred Bernstein provided invaluable help in the final stages of this project, as well as at many other points along the way.

Introduction

This book explores how sex between men was understood within British society in the first half of the nineteenth century. It does so by examining hundreds of public reports, many from newspaper and courtroom accounts, of sex between men in the years 1820 to 1870. Analysis of these narratives calls into question key elements of earlier scholarship on how these acts (real or alleged) were understood and discussed in early-nineteenth-century Britain.

It has long been assumed that the discussion of sex between men in the public sphere in mid-nineteenth-century Britain was minimal. A shift in public morals beginning in the late eighteenth century had severely limited official documentation of this behavior and its legal repercussions, as the state curtailed its record-keeping of trials involving sexual crimes. Overt and even oblique references to sex between men also disappeared from literature and popular writing. The silence on this issue began in the late Georgian period and is generally thought to have continued with only limited interruptions until the late nineteenth century.

In the late Victorian period, public anxiety over sex between men was fueled by fears of declining middle-class values and perceived threats to Britain's place in the world. A series of sensational trials—including those related to middle-class cross-dressers in 1870, upper-class men paying for sex with telegraph delivery boys in 1889–90, and an internationally known playwright defending his honor against

charges of sodomy in 1895—made sex between men a topic of sensational newspaper reporting. This material was often read in the context of the contemporary effort by some European physicians to define
the nature and origins of male same-sex desire in medical terms, and
together these factors have spawned a great deal of work by modern
scholars on the origins of the modern homosexual identity. Almost all
the secondary literature and most guides to the nineteenth-century
British sources, including both print and electronic newspaper indexes,
leave the impression that sex between men was not a topic of regular
public discussion.

But mainstream newspapers ran hundreds of articles pertaining to
sex between men in the years after 1820. The coverage was not primarily of sensational court cases but rather of the legal tribulations of
ordinary men. Statements from the time indicate that men who read the
newspapers regularly were assumed to be aware of this reporting, and
the scope of this newspaper coverage makes it clear that sex between
men, and its fallout, was a part of regular public discourse.

Uncovering much of this material has meant using the names, trial
dates, and trial locations preserved in nineteenth-century state records
in conjunction with the full text of multiple newspapers, as opposed
to relying on indexing terms that mask the extent of coverage. The
material located in this manner in turn led to further source material
both within and outside state collections. Taken together, this evidence,
pertaining to hundreds of cases, provides the opportunity to construct
a social history not only of the men who felt same-sex desire but also
of the men and women in their families and communities who were
affected by their actions. It shows how reactions varied according to
class, demonstrating that understandings of this behavior were largely
determined by material resources and the cultural texts available for
the interpretation of desires.[1] There was no single, unified understanding of sex between men in the early to mid-nineteenth century, and
analyzing the differences across class divisions is the first goal of this
book.

Achieving this goal requires focusing greater attention on the
examples of individuals like Frederick Samuel Lea, the sixteen-year-old
servant of a London bookseller who, in January 1840, fended off three
separate unwanted sexual advances from a male customer of the store.
Lea had not told anyone after the first or even the second advance, but
at the time of the third, which occurred outside the store, he confided
in a fellow servant and asked for her assistance. It was not until several

days later that Lea first told his story to a policeman, and then the officer did not act on Lea's accusation; instead he told Lea to take up the matter with his master. The young man's employer likewise did not want to act on the boy's story, and instead told him to speak with his father. The father's reaction was not recorded, but it had little bearing on the eventual arrest of the man making advances on his son. It was only when Lea saw the man walking down Great Russell Street at night in the company of another young man that he was able to convince a nearby police officer that he had a serious charge to make. The officer's willingness to believe Lea was bolstered when the man ran away once he noticed he was being observed.[2]

Both Lea and the man making unwanted sexual advances toward him exhibited behaviors typical of men of their class. Lea's economic status tied him to the public space of the bookshop in a way that made him vulnerable to an unwanted advance, and although Lea himself was not tempted by the offer of money for sexual acts, other working-class men in similar situations were. The individuals whom Lea asked for advice knew that they could resort to the law, but they also knew that this approach could be difficult and even dangerous, as prosecutions were expensive and the man making the unwanted advances was from an upper-class family. The newspapers regularly showed the many advantages that men of property could employ when confronted with charges of unnatural assault by poorer individuals, and Lea could easily find himself facing countercharges of attempting to extort money by making a charge of "an infamous crime."[3] Younger men like Lea could often ask their working-class fathers or brothers to accompany them in confronting a wealthier individual who had made an unwanted advance, and although Lea did not get this level of support, his willingness to seek help from his family and community network, facilitated by the fact that he had not instigated the contacts, was typical.

The class background of George Dawson Lowndes, the twenty-six-year-old man making the unwanted advances, also structured his engagement with the situation. His understanding of his desires was at least partially mediated by the texts he knew from his education. The first two advances began with Lowndes speaking to Lea in a secluded part of the store and showing Lea sexually suggestive material in the books of the collection.[4] That Lowndes aggressively pursued an individual ten years his junior and of lower social status also showed him to be following a rakish form of masculinity typical of the upper-class men who ended up in the courtroom on these charges. Lowndes was also typical of the men of his class in his efforts to gain special consideration: he wrote multiple letters to the Home Office after his eventual conviction, in which he seems certain that he will be released once the right personal connection is made and in which he presents a version of the story formulated to discredit his lower-class accuser. Unlike Lowndes, most men who tried this approach were successful.

Working with hundreds of court cases provides the ability to discern the behaviors typical of upper-, working-, and middle-class men and to track those behaviors through the social, economic, and political changes that occurred in the first half of the nineteenth century and led to a distinctly new pattern of regulating sex between men. The years between 1815 and 1850 were some of the most tumultuous in modern British history: the threat of revolution was never more acute, and the economic hardships stemming from industrialization and urbanization were never more intense. The second goal of this book, and another not previously achieved in the secondary literature, is to connect the shift in how sex between men was regulated and understood in the early nineteenth century to these larger historical events.

Given that the evidence of sex between men from the eighteenth and late nineteenth centuries was so much more sensational and readily accessible, it is little wonder that historians initially neglected the intervening period. The exploration of the eighteenth-century cases was begun by historians in the 1970s, in part because the details of most of the eighteenth-century sodomy trials were readily accessible in the published Session Papers of the Old Bailey.[5] The resulting scholarship established the association of certain public spaces in London with sex between men, indicating that some men strongly identified with their sexual desires for other men and were able to construct communities with other men of similar feelings. In addition, individuals such as John Cooper, the cross-dressing "Princess Seraphina," were shown to have been visible over long periods in the working-class communities where they lived. The work of organizations, including the Societies for the Reformation of Manners, was also examined, as scholars demonstrated how occasional raids on molly houses were staged by private organizations beginning in the early 1700s, and reported in the press along with the stories of indignant crowds lining the streets to taunt the convicted men.[6] The 1810 prosecution of the Vere Street Coterie, which met at the White Swan public house, is one of the most often recounted of these molly-house raids, and one of the last incidents to be cited in works that focus on the patterns associated with the eighteenth century.

Even more scholarly attention has been focused on the late nineteenth century. Almost from the time academics first began to turn
their attention to issues of homosexuality in history, a handful of cases
and events beginning in 1870 have been in the foreground. The popular work of H. Montgomery Hyde helped ensure that the Boulton and
Park trial, the Cleveland Street Scandal, and the Dublin Castle Affair
were known to modern scholars. Hyde also provided one of the most
important early accounts of the Oscar Wilde trials and the Labouchère
Amendment to the Criminal Law Amendment Act of 1885, although
many other writers, beginning with individuals such as Holbrook
Jackson, had long kept Wilde's story current.[7] The first and most significant of the academic books to offer a broader historical interpretation of these trials was Jeffrey Weeks's *Coming Out*, which historicized
the development of homosexual identity and distinguished it from the
more common and ahistorical phenomenon of homosexual behavior.[8]
The infamous trials of the later nineteenth century became important
markers in the work of many scholars, and not simply because of the
sustained level of national attention they received in their own day.
Occurring at a time when middle-class values were increasingly challenged politically, socially, and intellectually by the working class,
women's organizations, avant-garde artistic experimentation, and new
intellectual movements—including the growth of sexology as a scientific discipline—these trials were rightly seen by scholars as reflecting
cultural transformations, and they became the subject of an increasing number of wide-ranging interpretations in a variety of disciplines.[9]
Assumptions about the links between middle-class social anxiety and
the increased visibility of homosexuality in the late nineteenth century
have become commonplace, and the connection is often invoked even
in textbook accounts of the period.[10]

A great deal of important interpretative work came from the study
of these cases, but the degree of attention focused on them brought its
own problems. Because much of the work on these trials was outside
the discipline of history, archival research and the search for precedents
were not a priority. Moreover, contemporary statements in newspaper
and trial documents reinforced the impression that such scandals were
rare and that there were long periods of public silence between them.[11]
This pattern of silence and rupture seemed to be similar to the periodic
eruption of the eighteenth-century sodomy prosecutions. It also seemed
to coincide with a metaphor of the closet, of the open secret rarely
discussed, and of a language of periodic discovery and forgetting that

steadily gained momentum over the decades in scholarly work focused on sex between men and same-sex desire.[12]

The seeming similarity between the public discussion of sex between men at both ends of the nineteenth century led to a neglect of the serious study of the early to mid-nineteenth century, resulting in a distorted view of the period as a whole. This pattern is evident in books as diverse as those produced by Alan Sinfield, Neil Bartlett, and Jeffrey Weeks, each of which claims to account for patterns throughout the nineteenth century. Each of these works has played an important and influential part in moving the historiography forward in different ways. Weeks largely established the study of homosexuality within the academy. Bartlett's work provided an engaging, influential, and highly personalized interpretation of the periodic "discovery" of male same-sex desire by the society at large, and Sinfield addressed the important and often-neglected task of separating the cultural understanding of effeminacy from that of sex between men. All three authors make claims about the nineteenth century, but very little of their information is focused on the years 1810–70. None of these authors emphasizes any significant break, rupture, or discontinuity during this time. Instead, a number of events are used to connect the Vere Street molly-house raid of 1810 and the more heavily analyzed period beginning in 1870.

Works as recent as Matt Cook's 2003 study of homosexuality and the urban environment of London also replicate this pattern to some extent.[13] Cook's work focuses on the period between 1885 and 1914, but he opens his narrative with a survey of the British material related to sex between men from the Renaissance to the late nineteenth century. His account also moves rapidly from the eighteenth- and early nineteenth-century material to the 1870 trial of Boulton and Park. Other recent works on male homosexuality in nineteenth-century Britain, by Sean Brady and Morris Kaplan, have also kept their focus on the final decades of the century and largely overlook events before the 1860s.[14]

The work that offers the most detailed examination of the first half of the nineteenth century is H. G. Cocks's *Nameless Offences: Homosexual Desire in the Nineteenth Century*. Cocks was the first scholar to call attention to the imposition of the two-year sentence for prosecutions of sex between men and the first to use parliamentary papers and court records to demonstrate the frequency of unnatural-assault and attempted-sodomy prosecutions throughout the nineteenth century. More than any other researcher, Cocks has helped to correct one of the most persistent and distorting misinterpretations in the secondary literature over the frequency of prosecutions for sex between men.[15] Yet although Cocks discusses the changes in the law and patterns of prosecution in the 1820s early in his book, the subsequent chapters draw most of their examples from the later nineteenth century. Cocks uses his more fully developed view of the early nineteenth century primarily as a ground for developing his analysis of the later nineteenth century, providing both new interpretations of familiar material, such as the Cleveland Street Scandal and the Dublin Castle Affair, and extended analysis of new archival discoveries, including an exploration of desires and identities within a circle of male friends known among themselves as the Bolton Whitman Fellowship, who met at the end of the nineteenth century.

Because of Cocks's greater interest in the later period, important changes that occurred between 1820 and 1850 are only lightly sketched. A survey of the extent of newspaper reporting of trials involving sex between men was not a part of Cocks's project, and therefore the increase in unnatural-assault reporting from the 1820s through the 1860s, and what that reporting indicated about the public perceptions of sex between men, remains largely unexplored in his study. Although only a fraction of the thousands of court cases in these earlier decades left more than statistical information behind, taken together and combined with other sources, these fragments provide a unique picture of these transitional decades and demonstrate not only how men who had sex with men interpreted and acted on their desires, but also how members of their families and communities understood those behaviors.[16]

A better understanding of attitudes toward sexual behavior in these decades is especially important because the early nineteenth century witnessed a profound shift in the practice of law enforcement, from a system reliant on relatively rare but brutal displays of punishment on the offender's body to one that sought to reform behavior through a system of observation and regulation. Part of this shift entailed a move away from the public use of death penalty and the pillory and toward more frequent and consistent punishment with lesser sentences. Over time this shift influenced how individuals thought of the relationship between the law and the regulation of individual behavior, including behaviors related to sex between men. This change must be explored not only through statistical analysis but also at a social and cultural level.[17] Cultural context is just as important for explaining transitions in the understandings of sex between men for the early nineteenth

century as it is for the final decades of the nineteenth century. For all
the strengths of both the "new" and the "old" gay history, no work
has yet paid sufficient attention to the changes of the early nineteenth
century.[18]

Closer analysis of events in the earlier nineteenth century is also necessary in order to provide a link between the discordant narratives of
the two ends of the nineteenth century. In both style and substance as
well as in descriptive vocabulary, there is a substantial divide between
the representation of the molly-house culture and general Georgian
bawdiness of the eighteenth and early nineteenth centuries and the
descriptions of conduct in the public and private spaces of London
from 1870 onward. The degree to which the transformations of urban
life influenced the availability of sex between men needs to be better
defined, in relation to both the men who felt same-sex desire and those
who engaged in such acts for other reasons. We know of a handful of
men in the eighteenth and nineteenth centuries who were identified as
"buggers by nature," but what relationship do these men have to "the
homosexual," a type defined by his choice of sexual object?[19] How
did some men interpret their sexual acts with other men so as not to
profoundly affect how they perceived themselves? Finally, with respect
to controlling sexuality between men, how did the goals of the family,
the law, and, eventually, medical theorists complement, conflict with,
and shape one another?

Given the common assumptions about the role of economic and social
change in the development of sexuality as social category, it is interesting that the understandings of sex between men in Britain in the first
half of the nineteenth century have remained so understudied. David
Halperin has noted that both before and after Foucault, scholars have
argued that "something new happens to the various relations among
sexual roles, sexual object-choices, sexual categories, sexual behaviors,
and sexual identities in bourgeois Europe between the end of the seventeenth century and the beginning of the twentieth. Sex takes on new
social and individual functions, and it assumes a new importance in
defining and normalizing the modern self." Halperin also observes that
many scholars take it "as established that a large-scale transformation
of social and personal life took place in Europe as a part of the massive
cultural reorganization that accompanied the transition from a traditional, hierarchical, status-based society to a modern, individualistic,
mass society during the period of industrialization and the rise of a
capitalist economy."[20] For Britain, the most critical years in that trans-

formation, and the years during which the threat of outright political revolution stemming from these changes seemed most acute, occurred between the end of the Napoleonic wars in 1815 and the European revolutions of 1848.

For any other topic in British society, attention to changes between 1815 and 1850 would be commonplace rather than controversial. The period overlaps what has been known to generations of British historians as the "Age of Reform," and if the nature of the changes during this period has been called into question in recent years, most historians still agree that it saw fundamental alterations in the way the state, the society, and the economy were organized.[21] The change in governing institutions especially was abrupt because fear of revolution at home had led the governing class to resist deviations from traditional political arrangements. An expansion of the franchise had been seriously considered in the 1780s, but most talk of such experiments was stifled after the September massacres of 1792 in France, which seemed to confirm that bloodshed and anarchy might accompany the modification of traditional institutions. Not until the 1820s, during the more liberal phase of Lord Liverpool's long administration, did the government begin seriously to confront the task of realigning state institutions with the society and economy that had changed around them. The delay in reform often led to stark contrasts between the previous arrangements and the new methods proposed to modify or replace them.

The wars with France also exacerbated the tensions stemming from the industrial and demographic changes that had been building in England in the second half of the eighteenth century. The displacement of rural farm labor associated with the commercialization of agriculture combined with rapid overall population increase from the mid-eighteenth century onward to create a class of displaced and desperate laborers. The mass migration of labor to urban and industrial centers disrupted previous patterns of rural social organization, with new systems to take their place in the ever-expanding cities at best improvised and at worst nonexistent.[22] Over these years Britain went from being primarily a rural to primarily an urban society, and yet the historic British reluctance to create state institutions that could impinge on British liberty meant that many problems associated with urbanization were not addressed until they became acute. Britain's path to industrialization and urbanization was thoroughly unplanned, with no foreign model to copy as a positive example, to learn from as a negative example, or even to prove that society could weather such upheavals.

Benjamin Disraeli was only the most famous of the many authors and social commentators who grappled with the "condition of England" question in these decades, seeking solutions to the urgent and fundamental question of how society might be reorganized.

The shift to a capitalist industrial economy involved an ideological shift in moral values as well as physical relocation. Institutions such as wage labor and the factory system were initially denounced by many in the upper ranks as well as in the lower orders as shocking innovations that ignored the mutual obligations inherent in the relationship between property owners and those who worked for them. The idea that employers dispatched all their obligations to workers simply with a cash payment, regardless of the short-term or long-term needs of those workers or their families, might be one means by which the middle class was increasing its wealth, but it was not a value held by the gentry or the aristocracy.[23] In arguing against such a system and for the reciprocal responsibility inherent in the relationship between workers and employers, the lower class was seemingly on solid ground. They could claim not only the sanction of religion but also that of long-standing upper-class practices that had governed much of rural life.

And yet, in this struggle over the fundamental economic relationship among the classes, the middle class succeeded in claiming the language of morality as its own. The crisis of the French Revolution and the need to maintain both public order and economic production over a decades-long period of social upheaval were credited with helping to ease upper-class objections to middle-class economic and social innovations. But it was the growth of the Evangelical movement within the Church of England, and the strong identification of the middle class with this rigorous version of the official faith, that allowed them to establish the ground of morality as their own. Although there were many working-class Evangelicals, and the movement within the Church of England was pioneered by many powerful members of the upper class, such as William Wilberforce, in its emphasis on personal morality, responsibility to family, and loyalty to established authorities, Evangelical religion was well suited to the economic and social interests of the middle class, and over time it became most strongly identified with that group. For Evangelical men, the test of a man's character was his personal morality and his success at supporting his family, rather than his fulfillment of obligations to the community at large, and in this way Evangelical religion helped create the first generations of Britain's industrial middle class.[24] The Evangelical movement had been growing in strength even before the outbreak of the French Revolution, yet it was the fundamental threat that the revolution represented that increased the influence and power of Evangelicals within English governing circles. Evangelical religion proved a successful vehicle for shoring up a greater base of support for the aristocratic government in England and was a substantial factor in the English upper class's weathering the challenges of the wars intact and in control.[25]

The growing power of Evangelicals in society had implications for personal as well as economic morality. Michael Mason, Roy Porter, Lesley Hall, and Linda Colley have discussed the reformation of manners that British society underwent during the French Revolutionary and Napoleonic wars and how it affected individual behavior at all class levels.[26] Modes of public behavior associated with the upper class in the eighteenth century defined individual propriety differently. Men and women in the upper classes had latitude for indiscretions within marriage, so long as certain rules of etiquette and decorum were observed, and this period in general is associated with greater freedom of expression on sexual topics.[27]

Although these patterns were suppressed in the nineteenth century, the manners and morals at the highest levels of British society remained different from and often antagonistic to those of the middle class. Upper-class masculinity, especially, retained its distinct character, tolerating activities such as gambling, the consumption of alcohol, and the enjoyment of violent physical sports. Although some upper-class men attempted to better justify their privileged position in society through the adoption of aspects of the middle-class work ethic, it was equally acceptable to emphasize that only those who did not have to earn their fortunes had the leisure and broad perspective necessary for the governance of society as a whole. The upper-class dandy of the early nineteenth century did not fit a middle-class man's definition of an individual of good character, but the dandy's conviviality and manners could secure his reputation among his upper-class peers: reputation was more central to an upper-class man's status than was the more middle-class concept of character.[28] The distinctions and antagonisms between upper- and middle-class men's ideas of morality and masculinity remained sharp.

Also affected by the changing moral climate at the start of the century, even working-class individuals strongly influenced by Methodism drew the lines of responsibility governing relations within the family and the community differently from members of the middle and upper classes. Among the working class, for example, greater tolerance was displayed toward premarital sexual relations, provided a couple intended to marry, and a higher value was placed on obligations to the local community.[29] Increasingly in the nineteenth century, these and other working-class values came under attack as not only different from middle-class understandings of morality but also as inferior to them and the cause of the economic distress of the working class.

Middle-class notions of economic and personal morality combined in the reform of the Poor Law in 1834. One result for the working class was the abolition of a previous system of "outdoor" assistance on which many periodically depended and which many considered integral to the system of mutual obligations between the classes. The New Poor Law also stigmatized working-class women who became pregnant out of wedlock, making a woman solely responsible for the maintenance of her illegitimate children. Yet in an age when divorce was attainable only through an act of Parliament, pregnancy before marriage served an important function for the working class. Because the labor of children was vital to the survival of the working-class household, pregnancy before marriage offered evidence that a couple could have children together; it was therefore compatible with working-class morality and often seen as an economic survival strategy. Without a voice in Parliament, the working class had no opportunity to articulate the logic and morality of such practices in Westminster. The final legislation, which affected the lives of millions of Britons for generations, was framed around Evangelical notions of morality and middle-class economic imperatives.

The Poor Law reform was only one of many examples of the nineteenth-century reworking of institutions of government and the implementation of new ideas about its responsibility and scope. The state's new authority in shaping the role of the individual in society was also evident in the modest protections offered by the first Factory Acts and in the development of new systems of policing and new experiments in incarceration designed to modify behavior through surveillance and discipline. Underpinning these changes were newly ascendant ideologies stemming from liberal political and economic philosophy and the Evangelical revival, and the new concentrations of wealth and state power stemming from industrialization and wartime government expansion made such experiments possible. In an era when many felt that the old ties of local community and deference were fast coming undone, the search for new systems that might replace them and stabilize society were of paramount importance.[30]

None of those reforms, including those that affected the regulation of sexual acts between men, were carried out with the stated goal of affecting such sexual behavior. The changes relevant to the regulation of sex between men were only small components of much broader programs of reform. In this respect there is much evidence to confirm the cliché that throughout the nineteenth century, men avoided publicly discussing this topic.[31] The difficulty, though, was that many individual officials became involved in situations where such discussion could not be avoided, just as many individuals were likewise compelled to speak publicly about this behavior as laws were rewritten and a more intrusive level of policing was established. The moral injunction against sex between men remained in place in the early nineteenth century, but changes in the state and in society meant that the potential consequences of such acts shifted, sparking both public and private debates and discussions. One such debate, and one example of grappling with the potential consequences, was carried on between Frederick Samuel Lea and his father, his employer, and his fellow employee; the results were shared with the nation, as mediated through the newspapers and the courts. This book explores the cumulative effect of hundreds of such debates, and what they reveal about the social, political, and economic changes of the early nineteenth century.

Because the state's efforts in this area intruded on terrain previously considered the prerogative of the family, part 1 of this book explores families and their responses to the issue of sex between men. Although in no case do the records show that family members treated the discovery of sex between men with any form of acceptance or even indifference, their reactions are more complex than the vitriolic denunciations and instant ostracisms that seem to be implied by the public statements associated with the better-known trials of the later nineteenth century. The discovery of sex between men was treated as a crisis by families of all classes, but the nature of that crisis, and the form of response it required, differed significantly according to class. Although almost all responses sought to punish the individual or individuals responsible for instigating the behavior, they also more often than not allowed for the reincorporation of the men into the family. The severity of the transgression that such an act represented and the degree to which it might or might not be considered "the worst of crimes" were open to debate.

Chapter 2 turns to the question of how the men engaging in sex with other men understood those acts. Sex between men was condemned by all men in their public lives, although social class and geographic space could affect a man's perception of what it meant to privately have sex with another man. Upper- and working-class men's understandings of masculine identity might allow for sexual contact between men under some conditions. Within the middle-class understanding of respectability and character, such behavior was more problematic. The distinction between the desire for sex and the desire for sex with a man was central to these justifications, as were the types of physical acts engaged in, an individual's age, and the individual's active or passive role in those acts. Locations such as the Mediterranean, the public school, and the urban environment of London could all be associated with sexual acts between men, with the same act having different meanings and different consequences depending on the location. At least a few men in this period left records indicating that they did structure part of their personal identity around such desires. For other men, however, understanding the multiple possible attitudes toward sex between men is crucial to comprehending the nature of the changes that occurred in the nineteenth century.

The three chapters of part 2 examine the institutional forces that influenced understandings of this behavior throughout society. All three areas examined—the laws, policing, and the newspapers—were, not for the first time, influencing the regulation of sex between men in the early nineteenth century. In England the laws against sodomy and attempted sodomy date back to the sixteenth and seventeenth centuries respectively.[32] The early watch system facilitated arrests of men on charges of sex between men, just as the later Metropolitan Police would. Private pamphlets and Old Bailey Session Papers published the details of sodomy and attempted-sodomy trials before the newspapers eclipsed them in this role. Yet despite these precedents for punishing and publicizing acts of sex between men, each one of these three broad areas underwent significant transformations in the early nineteenth century.

These shifts are shown most clearly in chapter 3, which assesses the changes in the relevant laws. It begins by considering the revision of the laws against sodomy, attempted sodomy, unnatural assault, and "threatening to accuse of an infamous crime" in the context of Robert Peel's effort to consolidate English criminal law. The penalties and evidence requirements for cases involving sex between men were altered in statute law, although this change did not always affect what had been occurring in practice under common law. Some examples, such as the imposition of a two-year prison sentence for attempted sodomy and unnatural assault, suggest little real change beyond the increased frequency of application of the law. Other changes in statute law, such as those related to the threat to accuse another man of attempting an infamous crime, had real consequences in the courtroom. I argue here that the need to modify this law was a result of the increased use of the laws against attempted sodomy and unnatural assault in the courts. Not only did these laws allow men to bring their social betters into court on their word alone, but the accusation impugned the character of the accused in a way particularly egregious to men invested in current notions of respectability. This consequence partially explains why the penalties for making a false accusation were so much more severe than those for unnatural assault itself. Close examination of the revision of the laws related to sex between men indicates the ways in which class antagonisms and differing definitions of masculinity shaped the reform process.

The interconnected themes of class antagonism and transformations in systems of state control are explored further in chapter 4, which focuses on the early years of the Metropolitan Police. Contrasting the policing of the 1820s to that of the 1830s and 1840s, this chapter argues that many aspects of the public policing of sex between men were established in West End neighborhoods well before 1829. The most important changes after 1829 consisted of the increased frequency of arrests, the new uniformity of the police presence throughout the city, and the self-policing this inspired. This chapter also focuses on the difficult position of the common officer in policing sex between men, which reflected the problems of working-class men in general when invoking these laws against propertied men. The precarious line these officers walked became most evident in 1830, when, on their own initiative, a small group of constables went into Hyde Park to entrap men who were soliciting sex from other men. The controversy that erupted when these officers began to bring middle- and upper-class men to court on unnatural-assault charges is examined as a microcosm of the clash between competing notions of class, morality, and masculinity that was sparked by the institutionalization of a police force of working-class constables.

Chapter 5 focuses on newspapers in the early nineteenth century, comparing the ways that different publications chose to cover unnatural-assault stories from the 1820s through the 1860s, when such coverage was at its height. Although it also brings to light some major events and "scandals" centering on sex between men that have not been discussed in the secondary literature, this chapter focuses on the brief reports of sex between men that appeared in the court sections of some papers. The *Times,* the *Weekly Dispatch,* and the *Morning Post* are analyzed as the leading middle-, working-, and upper-class newspapers of their day, respectively; together they published nearly one thousand reports over a fifty-year period. This analysis reveals that the liberal daily press was responsible for the greatest number of stories concerning sex between men. The chapter ends with an examination of newspaper readership among different segments of the population and argues that the majority of men in mid-nineteenth-century London were most likely aware of what was reported in "that part of the paper." This and other evidence suggests the need to reassess assumptions about how and to what degree sex between men was discussed within the public sphere.

The third and final part of the book assesses the impact of the changes discussed in part 2, beginning in chapter 6 with the identification of patterns in the new systems regulating sex between men. Certain types of cases, such as those involving only working-class men, were regularly underreported in the liberal newspapers, just as sexual acts between men occurring in certain geographic locations, like the West End, were more likely to lead to arrests. Contrary to what might be expected, it was not the male cross-dresser, the debauched aristocrat, or the man already repeatedly engaging in sexual acts with other men who was the primary target of the new systems of regulation. The state and the newspapers instead most often drew attention to casual sexual encounters in public space between men of differing class backgrounds who could otherwise present themselves as respectable. In such encounters, the focus of the reporting was the sexuality of the respectable middle-class man.

The concluding chapter takes the idea that the sexual desire of respectable middle-class men was the most problematic for society and attempts to understand the medical theorization of same-sex desire in light of this fundamental point. British physicians shared the common cultural view that sex between men was incompatible with moral behavior, and this view has led to sharp contrasts being drawn between these physicians and Continental theorists such as Richard von Krafft-Ebing, who developed and popularized a theory allowing for same-sex desire to be inborn in an individual rather than acquired over time through immoral behavior. Greater awareness of how class structured understandings of sex between men in Britain, though, reveals that Krafft-Ebing's work represented less of a break with the ideals of character and respectability in Britain than has sometimes been assumed. Ironically, the first important attempt to explain sex between men by a British physician, Havelock Ellis (working in conjunction with John Addington Symonds), represented a more significant rupture with past British understandings. This innovation of Ellis and Symonds was as much related to the shifting intellectual climate of their time as it was to the evolution of sexology as a scientific discipline.

The conclusion reinforces the book's argument that shifts in the conceptualization of the self and in perceptions of experience can be understood only in the context of the culture within which they are generated. We can better understand the cultural significance of male same-sex desire at any given time by looking at the society in which it is expressed. Such an inquiry may have broader implications than simply providing a better understanding of sexual acts between men. For a generation, scholars have been formulating useful cultural insights over the increased attention to homosexuality at the end of the nineteenth century and its relationship to the generally perceived decline of bourgeois values. Similar cultural insights may come from a better understanding of the characteristically different but also prominent discussion of sex between men that accompanied the ascendancy of middle-class men into social and economic power in the first half of the nineteenth century.

PART ONE

Understandings

CHAPTER I

Families
and Sex between Men

The anonymity of urban space has long been viewed as important to the history of sex between men in modern European history, but such anonymity was always limited.[1] Moments of standing alone in a park at night, in front of a picture-shop window, or in a particular kind of public house in anticipation of a sexual encounter with another man were stolen from lives that were lived within family and community networks. Although there was a continuous homosexual subculture from the eighteenth through the late nineteenth century, the vast majority of the evidence for sex between men preserved for the first half of the nineteenth century does not relate to it but rather to a much broader group of men whose sexual acts with other men, rather than being separated from the rest of their lives, were relegated to the "twilight moments" within them.[2] For the majority of the existing evidence, the context is the family rather than the molly house.

The family was a site where the transgression represented by sex between men was assessed and where the consequences of those acts were decided. Many situations that eventually became court cases had first been debated and assessed within families, and family interventions long preceded increased state interest in this behavior. Families invariably condemned sexual acts between men when they were made public, and in all recorded cases they also worked privately to separate and sanction men known to be engaging in such acts; but family reactions also varied widely. By understanding patterns in the regulation of sex between men within the family, and how those patterns differed according to class, we can form a clearer picture of how society understood these acts. Although sex between men was almost always treated as a crisis when the families discovered it, its designation as "the worst of crimes" seems accurate only for a minority of the families examined and for a minority of individuals within those families.

Family connections and networks of mutual economic support were essential to individual survival and social status at all levels of British society, especially for the urban working class, whose existence was dependent on continuous wage labor. In an age of rapid economic change and severe limits on labor organizations, a family's economic situation could deteriorate rapidly for reasons beyond its control. Although workers clubbed together in friendly societies and other self-financed insurance programs to insulate their families from shocks in a laissez-faire economy, the most pervasive survival strategy was to employ the labor of wives and children.

Although this use of family economic resources was often a necessity, it undermined the authority of the father as the head of the urban working-class household. It also reduced fathers' already-circumscribed ability to control the marriage choices of their children. The ability to pass on artisan skills and tools, or to arrange for the employment of a son based on a father's position within the community, were both diminished in the urban capitalist economy. In rural communities, various forces had worked to regulate the marriage of the young, to ensure that any new household would be economically viable and lessen the risk that the children would become a burden on the parish.[3] These forms of community supervision of marriage, based in part on the imperatives of a rural subsistence economy with limited geographic mobility, were not replicated in urban centers.

Middle-class individuals were also highly dependent on family for securing their economic position, but here the mechanisms at work tended to increase the authority of middle-class fathers. At the start of the nineteenth century, middle-class men often did not monopolize either the capital or the labor that went into the building of their family enterprises: they relied on their wives to manage smaller businesses and oversee accounts and employees. They also depended on the capital resources and family alliances that women brought with them into a marriage. As the century progressed, however, the size and scale of businesses increased, marginalizing women's participation and increasing the control of the father over the economic life of the family.[4] Likewise, a father's power over his children increased as a son's training in the family business or education for a profession became more dependent on the financial support of the father. Daughters were even more tied to the economic fortunes and good favor of their fathers, dependent as they were on dowries and having no other option for supporting themselves that would allow them to maintain middle-class status.

For the upper-class family, continuity was the overriding characteristic of their experience of the economic changes and urbanization in this period. Although the fear of social revolution was palpable in certain years, only in the 1880s did the broader economic and technological changes that altered the fortunes of so many others in society finally begin to affect the upper classes, primarily through the importation of cheap foreign grain. The expanding economy and empire offered opportunities for younger sons in the military and in the financial sectors, but otherwise it did not greatly affect the relationships within the upper-class family. With social position linked so closely to family connections, most individuals carefully guarded their status within the family.[5] Upper-class individuals were among the few with the wealth necessary to live independently of the labor and support of a family, but almost no one seems to have made such a choice. Even within the anonymous city, therefore, almost no one lived without family connections for an extended period, and few were ever alone for long.

Even among the massive influx of new immigrants to the city, experiences were mediated through the family. For the whole of the period under study, the birth rate in London was lower than the death rate, so that London's steady increase in size over these years was sustained through migration from the countryside. Many working-class migrants practiced forms of serial migration, obtaining housing, social contacts, and information on employment from relatives and friends who had already moved to the city. In this way, cities like London "became studded with little districts, sharing common rural origins . . . perhaps spread over two or three streets, as a system of mutual affection, sociability, and support."[6] Professions such as domestic service and policing, unpopular with long-term city dwellers, eased the transition from rural to urban life, as they explicitly recruited employees from the countryside. For many otherwise unconnected rural migrants, these forms of paternalistic employment provided networks of support.

Likewise, prostitutes in central London, once thought to epitomize the isolation of the urban individual divorced from family networks, retained their ties to working-class families and communities to a much greater degree than previously assumed. They did so by separating their work both temporally and spatially from their family lives. The number of prostitutes in the West End of London was never higher than in the nineteenth century, yet many of these women lived elsewhere, mainly in the working-class communities south of the Thames. After engaging in prostitution for a number of years, often as a part of a calculated strategy to avoid more onerous employment in an economy that offered few desirable options to young women, these individuals often became wives and mothers. Scholars such as Judith Walkowitz have shown that the sentimentalized literary depictions of fallen women (replete with remorse, social ostracism, and tragic early death) cannot be taken as a guide to social experience in the early nineteenth century.[7] For prostitutes as for new urban migrants, family ties have been shown to be more persistent and durable than previously assumed.

The effects of urbanization and economic change were also tempered by the persistence of many earlier forms of employment. In the first half of the nineteenth century, the single largest occupational category in London by far was domestic service, which was structured by social relationships that carried over from the eighteenth century. In many trades and professions, especially those catering to the luxury trades of the capital, the small workshop, the live-in apprentice, and the patriarchal relationship between employers and employees remained strong. As Raphael Samuel has argued, the persistence of labor-intensive building techniques extended long into the Industrial Revolution. Although the Crystal Palace was intended as a symbol of the new modern age and built at the midpoint of the century, it was realized largely with labor-intensive techniques such as hand-puddled iron beams and hand-blown glass window panels.[8]

If such a spectacular argument for the modern world as the Crystal Palace was made in 1851, it was in part because only three years before, it seemed as if the lower orders might finally engage in a full-scale revolt against that modern industrial world, which up to that point seemed far more detrimental than beneficial to them. The disputed five million signatures on the Chartist petition of 1848, and the threatened march of tens of thousands of workers on Westminster in that year to demand political inclusion, challenged the viability of the current political structure in Britain and of the laissez-faire relationships that were eroding the previous social forms. That no revolution actually occurred should not diminish our appreciation of the political tensions of those years. There was nothing inevitable about the triumph of the new economy in the first half of the nineteenth century and the new forms of social organization that came with it; many, even in the middle class, argued against its worst aspects.

The protected space of the family was consistently invoked as a bulwark against the abuses and excesses of the modern world. The middle-class home, as celebrated in the late eighteenth-century poetry of William Cowper and embraced by the Evangelical middle class, was seen as a refuge from the complexities and immoralities of the modern world. The home preserved the religious and moral values that were under threat elsewhere in society. A properly constituted family, sanctioned by the state and the church through marriage, and secured by the income earned through diligent work in the world, could insulate itself from outside intrusions.

The concept of the home was less private and less inviolate for the working class, but working-class families aggressively resisted attempts by outside authorities to impose regulation on them. Lacking the financial resources that would have allowed more social functions to occur within the home, they placed a higher value on community, with celebrations such as Christmas and Easter being community rather than private family rituals. Yet the working class also invested in rituals of the home, such as the creation of the parlor, when resources allowed.[9] The workhouses were seen as egregious in part because they broke up families, an action justified by the state on the grounds that when individuals abrogated the responsibility of supporting themselves, they lost the right to a private family life as well.

The right of a family to protect its members from the intrusions of the law was also enshrined for the upper classes. The most prestigious families in the realm were entitled to special treatment before the law. Their debts were treated differently from those of others, and their other transgressions before the law might be heard before special juries, drawn only from men of similar status. All levels of society, therefore, in some respects manifested the idea that belonging to a functioning family accorded the individual a degree of protection from the intrusions of the state. The ideal of English liberty was strong: that ideal included the conviction that the power of the state should be limited, and that a wide range of behavior, especially within families, was outside its purview. This was an era long before the extension of state regulation into the sphere of the functioning family, such as in the Education Act of 1870, which sent inspectors into working-class homes. In the first half of the nineteenth century the state was only just beginning to regulate even the level of violence in society that fell short of grievous bodily injury. Involving the state in physical assaults within the family was rare, and most domestic abuse within a marriage was not recognized as criminal. Many of the physical disputes and moral transgressions that happened within families stayed within them and were settled within them.

Because so little attention has been given to the families of the men who engaged in sex between men, it is worthwhile to work through a number of examples. Doing so not only shows the variation between reactions of families of different classes but also illustrates the divisions and conflicts that arose over how to respond once sex between men was brought to light. Sometimes fathers and sons were united in their responses; at other times their reactions were starkly different. At many points wives, mothers, or sisters took the lead in resolving these crises, which seemed to undermine masculine status and power.

These differing responses both within and between families of different class backgrounds can be seen in the series of letters left by the Franklin and Geldart families, written in the months before and after the state ended the relationship between their sons. Thomas Franklin was a railway inspector, and, like many fathers of the time, he attempted to ensure that his seventeen-year-old son Henry would be placed "in an honorable way of getting a living."[10] Thomas had great difficulty in finding a position for his son, though, and could ultimately do no better than obligating him to serve aboard a merchant ship for five years. Henry Franklin was apparently very dissatisfied with this arrangement, and within a short time he had deserted his ship, sold his clothing, and taken to living on the streets in London. Friends of the family reported this outcome to Henry's parents, who had recently moved to Scotland. The father especially felt that it would be best "to leave him a little time in adversity to see if it would bring him to a sense of duty."[11] It came as something of a shock to the parents when they heard again from London friends that their son was seen to be very well dressed and enjoying a comfortable life. This sudden improvement in Henry's circumstances "created serious suspicion" in the parents, and Henry's mother set off for London to discover what exactly was going on.

The fact that their son seemed to be living beyond his means made his parents "fear evil has befell him, and he has become badly associated." Although they may have worried that he had fallen in with a band of thieves or other rough individuals, the mother's fears were not allayed when, after some effort, she found Henry, and he told her that it was "a gentleman [who] had taken compassion on him." She told her son that "all this looked suspicious, [and] she would not be satisfied until she had seen this gentleman." When the two actually came face to face, the mother's attitude toward the man, Joseph Geldart, mingled cordiality and suspicion. She asked him for his full name, occupation, and address, saying that "if a gentleman, [he] will give me credit for my duty as a caring mother, it carries with it a great suspicion."[12]

Before she left town, Mrs. Franklin arranged a job for her son with "a respectable house of business," and found him lodgings to her liking as well.[13] Unknown to Henry, she also arranged for more London friends "to be the guardian" of her son and to report on his actions to her and her husband. The closest the Franklins came to explaining why they did not remove their son from London entirely was their admission that they "could not afford with a large family and limited income to keep him in idleness at home."[14] Economic realities had to come before suspicions of immorality; the parents hoped that the constraints that Mrs. Franklin placed on her son would suffice to isolate him from improper behavior.

Ultimately the barriers proved insufficient. Henry continued to spend time with the older gentleman and became careless at his job, to the point of dismissal. Henry's "guardians" reported back to his parents that he had stayed out all night with Geldart and that the relationship between the two men was indeed sexual, as the parents had feared.[15] Shortly thereafter, it was discovered that Henry had embezzled twenty-one pounds from the shop where he worked, and the police began to pursue him on charges of committing unnatural acts. Henry managed to elude capture long enough to arrive in the Scottish town where his parents lived. It is unclear what sort of protection Henry might have felt they could provide him, but none was forthcoming. Thomas Franklin refused to see his son, stating that "I have so often forgiven his disobedience to us his parents, but in this his last act, which is a severe stab to me, I will not screen him from justice."[16] Henry fled the town and was apprehended a short time later, at which point he confessed his criminal and sexual acts to the police.

Yet even after such an emotional conflict between father and son, Thomas did not shut Henry out of his life or leave him entirely to the mercies of the legal system. He wrote to the Home Office asking that his son be tried for the theft alone rather than the unnatural crime. He did not want to ascribe any of the responsibility for the sexual relationship to his son, and instead wrote to ask the home secretary to punish and make an example of Joseph Geldart, "to protect society from such monsters." Thomas wrote, "I verily believe [Henry] would have been active and attentive to his masters, and a comfort to us again his parents had he not been bent by this *wicked man* and made a victim to his base purpose."[17] Although there was little more he could do, Thomas traveled to London to witness his son's police-court hearing and wrote at least one further letter to the Home Office to plead for the mitigation of charges.

For the Franklins, controlling Henry was more important than hiding his relationship with another man, and they considered enlisting the help of friends preferable to any form of appeal to the state. They suspected the sexual nature of Henry's relationship with Geldart before recruiting London friends to help keep an eye on the two men.[18] Their decision sharply differs from the recorded concerns of Geldart's family. In contrast to the Franklins, this family appears to have been wealthy and well connected. Their letters express very different concerns about how unnatural-assault charges might affect the family's future.

In his first letter to Home Secretary Earl Grey, written on 8 July 1850, Thomas Geldart declared that he was "somewhat emboldened" to write "from being well-known as the Secretary of the town Missionary Society by the Dow[ager]. Lady Grey."[19] After dropping this hint of a personal connection, he went on to say that he wrote not so for the sake of his imprisoned brother but instead for his father, who was on his deathbed. He stated that the entire family must be assembled to pay their last respects. It was somewhat ironic to request Joseph's release for this reason, because in the same letter Thomas describes his brother's actions as a cause of great distress for their father and a significant factor in the rapid decline of his health. But neither the crisis within the Geldart family nor the connection between them and the Greys was enough to sway the home secretary, and the request for an early release was denied.[20]

Any appearance of genuine emotion in Thomas Geldart's first letter quickly gave way to practical concerns in the second. After relating to Earl Grey that his father had just died, he again made a plea for his brother's release, this time wholly for the benefit of the family's reputation. Thomas wrote: "No tongue can tell the anguish of my spirit at the prospect of the public exposure of the pain that must be endured by many most respectable and innocent parties on the occasion of the funeral, should [my brother] not be permitted to be present."[21] The Geldart family had been spared the shame of Joseph's arrest and trial more than ten months before because his name had appeared in the papers only as "Joseph Smith."[22] The Geldarts felt that Joseph's absence from the funeral would have raised difficult questions among their friends and family, but they were nevertheless forced to face them, as the Home Office once again denied the request for release.

This example and others like it provide evidence of divergent concerns based on income and social class. While apprehensive about their son's morals, the Franklins had to consider their family's economic position as well. They could not afford to remove their son from temptation despite their fears for him, and at least part of their hope for their son's reform was based on their need for him to be of some economic use to them in later life. The Geldarts, by contrast, based their appeal in the first instance on sentimental and familial emotion, and in the second instance on the need to maintain appearances within their social network. That the Geldarts and the Franklins were typical of their respective economic classes in these concerns is suggested by other examples in the court records.[23]

No acrimonious exchanges between the Franklins and the Geldarts occurred, presumably because the families existed in separate social and economic worlds and could ignore one another. The Franklins referred to Joseph Geldart in their letters only briefly, as a corrupting, older, "wicked man" who bore the responsibility for what occurred, while the Geldarts made no mention of Henry or the other Franklins at all. Yet cases in which a man was accused of taking advantage of someone younger and poorer were often those that generated the strongest confrontations between families, especially when the families had a long-standing relationship. These cases show just how powerful the charge of sex between men could be in disrupting usual patterns of class deference and gender hierarchy between and within families.

Such results were evident when John Richard Seymour was accused of engaging in unnatural acts with Charles Macklin. The significance of this case is indicated by the fact that in addition to the newspaper coverage it received, it was also one of the five trials selected for inclusion in the *Annual Register* of 1828. Along with providing a historical summary, Parliamentary summary, and upper-class obituaries, every year's issue of the *Annual Register* summarized a handful of significant court cases. In the *Annual Register* account, John Richard Seymour was described as "a gentleman of rank, fortune, and education," who, in spite of these social advantages, had been taken to court and ultimately convicted of unnatural acts on the word of only his servants.[24]

Because at that time all upper- and middle-class households had at least one servant, the role of the servants in this case was of concern to all men of even modest property.[25]

The courtroom testimony revealed that once the household staff of six began to suspect an affair between the master of the house and the young servant Charles Macklin, they organized themselves to spy on the two men. Phoebe Hopkins, the lady's maid and head of the female servants, took the lead in the early stages of the investigation. She testified that "it was agreed between the servants to watch the parties. . . . I saw Hanna Watts (a nursery maid) kneeling on the steps, and looking under the door. She spoke to me, and I went to the door, and looked under. I saw Macklin leaning on the bed, and Mr. Seymour behind him."[26] Hopkins went on to describe the sexual acts they observed between the two men, of which the *Annual Register* noted only that "the witness here described, in the most explicit terms, what cannot be repeated."[27] The secret observations went on for several days, and several other servants took turns looking under the door to increase the number of witnesses. It was only after most of the household staff had witnessed sexual acts that Hopkins took the matter to Henry Boucher, the butler and head servant of the house. At the same time, Hopkins and three of the other female servants went to Mrs. Seymour and confronted her with the story of her husband's behavior.

Although Phoebe Hopkins was well aware of the option of taking her charges to the courts, she and the rest of the household staff chose first to confront the Seymours. The family's initial reactions were similar to those seen when sexual impropriety was discovered between a male family member and a female servant. The young Macklin was fired on the day after Mrs. Seymour was told of the affair, and the rest of the staff seem to have accepted this dismissal without dispute.[28] Mr. Seymour also attempted to intimidate the female servants into dropping the matter, curtly telling one of the women that "as for you, Bailey, you saw nothing."[29] Hopkins recounted that on the night after she told Mrs. Seymour of the affair, "the servants were all in the kitchen at dinner-time; the dinner was served up as usual, but I believe that no one ate anything." When the servants spoke of the matter together later, they expressed concern that they all remain united, or else "Hopkins . . . and the rest of the servants would be imprisoned as long as [they] lived" for putting forward a false accusation.[30] In spite of this potential risk, the servants felt compelled to go through with confronting the Seymours, because, in Hopkins's own words, "we could not think of staying in his family after what had happened."[31]

Yet they did stay on in Seymour's service, and for more than eight months after the initial incident they did so without making use of the courts. Instead they exercised a power of their own, based on their unresolved grievance against Seymour. The vicar of Crowood related that John Seymour had told him that "for the last twelve-months he had neither been able to change a shirt, or make water, or do anything whatever without being watched by these servants."[32] They stayed in his household, but they also felt empowered to police him. Over time, the allegations began to leak out, leading Seymour to move his family and household staff from Crowood to Worthington in an attempt to escape the rumors. The move was short-lived, though, and he returned to the town a few weeks later to face down the speculations.

It was in this period of growing community suspicion that Seymour tricked Hopkins into signing a refutation of her charges on a sheet of paper that she had not read. He then had this document printed up as an advertisement in the local Reading newspaper. Hopkins was furious at this deception, and although the facts of the incident remain somewhat unclear, it seems to have been pivotal in the decision of the staff to take the matter to court in March 1828. There Hopkins denied that her story had ever changed, and she recounted some of the other schemes and subterfuges that John Seymour had used over the months to undermine the story and the unity of the servants. Not only did the newspaper advertisement make her and her fellow servants look like liars or extortionists, but it also took the dispute out of the household and into the community. A negotiated settlement within the household would no longer suffice, because if the advertisement were not publicly refuted it would be the servants and not John Seymour who would most likely be subject to community suspicion. Seymour's attempt to avoid resolving the situation on the servants' terms by appealing to the community seems to have pushed the servants to take the risk of going to court.

The fact that the servants ultimately prevailed in the case was greatly aided by the strong evidence of John Seymour's guilt and his contradictory statements about the events in question. Seymour's defense shifted between accusations of a conspiracy among the servants and claims that what they had seen actually had an innocent interpretation. With his stories both inconsistent and implausible, he had difficulty gaining support even among the other propertied men of the town. At several points before the servants went to court, prominent local men were prepared to support him in taking legal action against them, but Seymour's own reluctance to start this process undermined their belief in his story.[33] If other similar cases can be taken as a guide, it is likely that had Seymour been able to marshal the support of the local men of his class and gone to court first, he would have been exonerated.[34]

Exactly what Phoebe Hopkins and the other servants felt to be the proper punishment for sex between men remains unclear. The personal welfare of Charles Macklin was not their primary concern. After his dismissal he was sent back to his parents' farm, where he resided for at least the next year. Rather than providing for him as an individual, or seeing that either he or Seymour received the proper state-sanctioned punishment for unnatural acts, the servants' primary concern seemed to be that the order of the household be restored and some form of restitution made. Although their demands were not specifically recorded, they were apparently ready to wait. They were also, it seems, willing to remain in the household once the demands were met. This acquiescence was in part due to their dependence on a good letter of character from Seymour if they were to seek other jobs, and he attempted to use this lever against at least one of the women. Most likely it was because the household was at something of an impasse that Seymour took the gamble of publishing the newspaper advertisement. Tied together by mutual obligation, mutual dependence, and mutual threats in an increasingly tense situation, the servants ultimately resorted to the state's authority to rectify a situation that they seemed unable to either forget or resolve.

Macklin's feelings toward Seymour were not directly recorded. He apparently did not seek help in stopping the repeated sexual acts with Seymour, although this omission should not be taken as evidence of conscious complicity in "unnatural crime." Others of Macklin's age, class, and rural background are recorded as expressing a lack of awareness that sex between men was wrong, or even that it was named. Young men in similar circumstances but with more knowledge of the world took more control over their situations. John Yoread was a fifteen-year-old servant who worked for the proprietor of the Anatomical Museum at 280 Regent Street, whose employer, from "the first day I went there . . . took liberties with me and felt my legs, which I didn't like." Yoread, in turn attempted to extort money from his employer for his silence, stating that he would accept "not less than 100*l*." as "he knew a boy in Birmingham who had got 200*l*. or 300*l*. from a gentleman that way."[35] Knowledge of the seriousness of sex between men, let alone the extortion that might be possible because of it, seemed foreign to Macklin, though. Whether out of ignorance, affection, or simple deference to the older and socially superior Seymour, Macklin took no action of his own but left the matter in the hands of the other servants.

Although wealth was a great advantage in such trials, the critical factors were the way character was defined and the great weight that assessments of character carried when decisions were made regarding whose testimony to believe. Men of all classes were judged by the same yardstick of character, which involved criteria such as standing in the community, respectability of occupation, and responsibility to family. Seymour lost his case in part because his actions among his own social peers, long after the alleged incident with Macklin, seemed to call his integrity into question. Other men of good standing in the upper and middle classes who had not so compromised themselves could often prevail in a contest between accuser and accused.

In perhaps no other case does the privileging of the word of a middle-class man over that of a working-class man seem more pronounced than when Patrick Dawley and his two sons were twice made the victims of John Webber. In the early fall of 1842, Patrick Dawley, a "dealer in cakes," was locking his outer door after 1:00 A.M. when John Webber came up to him and asked where he might get lodging for the night.[36] After being told that no places would be open at that late hour, Webber asked if he might be able to stay with him until morning. Although Patrick had never met Webber before, he "looked at him, and seeing he was most respectably dressed, said 'You don't mean to say, Sir, that a gentleman like you would sleep in the beds with the poor people down here?'" Webber responded by telling Patrick, "I shall be under a great compliment or obligation to you, if you will allow me to sit in a chair until morning." Patrick replied: "It is a pity that a gentlemanly man like you should be without a lodging, so you may come in and sit till morning." The two men talked together for some time in the kitchen, "and the more they talked the more [the] witness [Patrick Dawley] liked the prisoner [John Webber]."[37] When Patrick was ready to go to bed himself, he told Webber that if he liked, he could sleep in the bed in the kitchen, where his two sons were currently asleep. Patrick first attempted to wake one of his sons and send him upstairs to sleep with his sisters, so that there would be more room for Webber, but Webber told him not to bother the younger boy. Patrick left his guest and his sons in the kitchen and went to bed, but within the hour he was awakened by the shouts of his elder son, James.

It was the younger son, the thirteen-year-old Thomas, who explained to the police court that "on the night of Sunday last, about 2 o'clock, while asleep with his elder brother in the kitchen of the house, he was awoke by the conduct of the prisoner, who was then also in bed. He immediately called out, and endeavored to awake his brother, but the prisoner prevented him. The witness then proceeded to enter into the details of the prisoner's conduct, and said that . . . his brother woke and found what the prisoner had been doing."[38] It was at this point that James called out to his father, while holding down Webber to prevent his escape.

Once Patrick was downstairs, his first inclination was to tell his elder son to "turn [Webber] out of doors instantly." James, however, resisted his father's request, telling him, "No; he shan't go till I have got a policeman." The two argued for some time, with Webber's offers first of ten pounds and then of any amount to let him go not seeming to affect the argument one way or the other.[39] Other fathers, such as one Matthias Cundal, were willing to go directly to the police when a son came seeking advice regarding an incident of sex between men.[40] It may have been Patrick's complicity in the event that motivated his reluctance to call the police, or it may have been that he was more aware than his son of the dangers inherent in prosecuting men of higher social status, even in instances when guilt seemed clear. James eventually prevailed, and a policeman was called.

When the case came before the first magistrate, most of the details were published, and the sympathies of the court reporter seemed clearly on the side of the Dawleys. This report included a mention of the crowds that gathered to hear the case, as well as a reference to the two medical examinations that the thirteen-year-old Thomas underwent to confirm the crime.[41] The criminal-trial coverage, by contrast, did not recount how Webber came into contact with the Dawleys or even mention that the assault occurred in the Dawleys' home. This short second report instead devoted most of its space to the defense's claim that there were "great discrepancies which appeared in [the Dawleys'] evidence, not only on the present occasion, but also before the magistrate." This claim was made in spite of the fact that the police court coverage stated that James Dawley "was cross-examined by Mr. Wontner at great length, but without at all shaking his testimony."[42] Webber's defense was that the three men's stories were contradictory and that the whole incident was simply a conspiracy to extort money. He was found not guilty, after which Patrick Dawley and his sons became liable on charges of threatening to accuse of an infamous crime.[43]

Undoubtedly many men in London did use the accusation of unnatural assault to extort money from other men, and it is problematic to second-guess a particular court decision based on the limited information that remains, but this case represents an improbable scenario for unnatural-assault extortion. The Dawleys had been in their own home and extended a courtesy to a stranger at the request of that stranger. That this was the preliminary step to extortion seems highly unlikely. This case does, however, reflect the tendency evident in multiple examples, and discussed in detail in the final two chapters, for middle- and upper-class men to be believed, and for courtroom and other officials to assume that sexual desire for other men, or the willingness to invoke it for mercenary reasons, resided almost exclusively in those of lower character, from the lower classes, who were less in control of their base desires.[44]

The Dawleys would have been better off had Patrick prevailed in the argument and simply turned Webber out of the house. Other examples suggest that fathers and sons usually were not so divided in their response to such threats. A working-class father who believed his son to have been sexually assaulted by another man often accompanied his son to confront the attacker, usually seeking restitution for the injury done to the family. Middle-class fathers and sons sometimes recruited one another as witnesses at such meetings. Middle-class men in these situations also presented themselves to their family members as victims of extortion attempts by lower-class men. Both middle- and working-class men who could plausibly present themselves as victims rather than instigators of such incidents often seemed willing to seek the help of a father or a son.

For an upper-class man facing a public accusation, the reputation and character of his father were powerful defenses. In two high-profile cases involving upper-class men from the period, it was the father who marshaled the friends of the family to speak in defense of the accused son's character, and the good character of the family was also invoked to refute the accusations against the son. In one case it seemed that the father truly believed in the son's innocence, whereas in the other the strain between the father and son was evident to court reporters. Presenting a united front against working-class accusers generally enabled upper-class fathers and sons to weather the crisis with their reputations intact, provided that the sons were never involved in another such incident.

This pattern can be illustrated through a comparison of the obituaries of the two members of Parliament arrested on indecent-assault charges in 1833. Both William John Bankes and Charles Baring Wall, through the help of their fathers, were able to employ the best barristers of the day for their defense. They also drew on their family networks to obtain impeccable character references, and their trials found them innocent of the charges.

Wall, who was never involved in another such public incident, went on to have an impressive career in Parliament. Although he had served as a member of Parliament only sporadically from 1819, 1832 marked the beginning of a string of election victories. In 1835, 1837, and 1841 he was returned as a member for Guildford, and in 1847 and 1852 he was elected to represent Salisbury. He was the director of the British Institution for a number of years, "and his aid was usually sought in Committees of the House of Commons on matters relative to art. . . . Among his immediate friends and dependents he was much esteemed for his kindness of disposition and unaffected simplicity of manners."[45]

Examples like Wall's counter the many courtroom speeches suggesting that a man could be ruined for life by even being associated with a case involving sex between men. His election to Parliament after 1832 can be understood, at least in part, as a ratification of his character by voters of the middle and upper classes. Wall asserted that he was innocent of the charges: he was the victim of a lower-class policeman who had accosted him at night in an attempt to obtain money. Wall's defense asked "what were likely to be the habits of a man capable of committing the act imputed" and then called attention to Wall's past character to indicate that such behavior was unthinkable for him.[46] The jury did not even allow the presiding judge to sum up the evidence before declaring Wall innocent, and it was said by a juryman that Wall left the courtroom with his character "entirely spotless." His later success seems to have borne out that assessment, and Wall was never again publicly associated with sex between men.[47]

William Bankes, however, was less careful, and ended his days in disgrace and exile. Bankes had also been found innocent in 1833, but the newspaper coverage of his unseemly statements at the time of his arrest and of the cold distance at which his father held him throughout the proceedings meant that he was considerably more compromised by the process than Wall had been. The obituary for Bankes in the

Annual Register of 1855 is unusually short: for the years after 1833, the only fact mentioned is his failure to retain his parliamentary seat for Dorset.[48] Although his parliamentary career ended after his trial, he did not leave London. It was when he was again brought before a London magistrate in September 1841 for "indecently exposing himself with a soldier of the Foot Guards in the Green Park" that he "forfeited his recognizance, disappeared from society, and has not been heard of since."[49] His father, William Bankes Sr., had been able to muster many of the most prominent men of the day to speak for his son's character at the first trial, but the son must have felt no such effort would be made for him a second time.

Another upper-class man who lost the protections of his class only after multiple public associations with sex between men was George Dawson Lowndes. Both his parents had died when he was a young boy, but they had left him a personal fortune of between fifteen and twenty thousand pounds, and "a small patrimonial estate amply sufficient for his station as a gentleman."[50] Whether because of his lack of parental supervision or some other combination of factors, he had been in the police courts numerous times on unnatural-assault charges in the space of a few years.[51] It was his repeated assaults on a sixteen-year-old bookseller's assistant that led to his criminal trial in February 1841.

Lowndes had significant advantages going into his 1841 trial, but he squandered them with reckless behavior. His wealth allowed him to retain two highly experienced attorneys to argue his case, and one of their first actions was to request a change of venue. As an upper-class man, Lowndes was entitled to have his case moved from the Central Criminal Court to the Court of the Queen's Bench. This change meant that the case would be heard before a jury of individuals of high social rank, and nearly all the men put on trial at this venue for unnatural assault charges between 1820 and 1871 were acquitted.[52] Yet on the day of the trial, he all but threw away these advantages by arguing the case himself. Being wholly inexperienced, he made a poor job of it. Among his mistakes was citing the previous unnatural-assault charges against him, from the Bow Street and Marlborough Street police courts, as evidence of his innocence and susceptibility to false charges.[53] His arrogant manner in the courtroom also seems to have greatly irritated Lord Chief Justice Thomas Denman and did nothing to sway the jury. Lowndes was sentenced to twelve months' imprisonment at Coldbath Fields for his acts.

A few weeks of imprisonment appear to have made Lowndes more contrite but did not diminish his desire for special treatment. He wrote several letters to the Home Office in the first months of his incarceration, asking if his sentence could be replaced by a fine to the Crown "or some charity."[54] Even at this point his letters seem to show disbelief at his incarceration and a certainty that the situation could be rectified when the proper personal connection had been established. His fear, he said, was that his friends and relations would not bother to distinguish between his rightful or wrongful imprisonment if he was not released soon. The marginal notes of the home secretary and undersecretary in his letters to them indicate that they had little sympathy for a young man whom they considered dissolute and out of control, and no special considerations were given to him.[55]

Despite Lowndes's expressed worries over his friends' and relations' opinions, no family member or long-time friend wrote letters or spoke on his behalf, either before or after his trial. Witnesses from Lowndes's social class were more likely to be believed when they were pitted against those from the lower classes, but with no respectable individuals of any class to speak for his character, no one except Lowndes himself could dispute the word of the shop boy who had accused him. By contrast, the shop boy in this particular case, as well as other young men whom Lowndes had previously accosted, did have family members and friends to testify on their behalf. Under such circumstances and in light of his previous actions, Lowndes's wealth alone, bereft of the social and familial connections that usually went with it, was insufficient to shift the outcome of his criminal case in his favor.[56]

Lowndes's behavior led to his abandonment by his family, and yet not all upper-class men, even those whose guilt was strongly assumed, faced such ostracism. An extremely favorable obituary in the *Annual Register* commemorated Richard Heber, whose sexual desires for younger men had received substantial publicity less than a decade before his death. Heber's assumed sexual relationship with a young man was the central issue in a 1826 libel case brought by the young man's father against the editor of the *John Bull* (see chapter 5). The obituary printed at the time of Heber's death in 1833 acknowledged this incident in a reasonably frank manner: "In 1826 he [Heber] resigned his seat [in Parliament]. He had quitted England in 1825, and he prolonged his stay on the continent for several years. . . . In the year 1831, he returned to England, but not into the society which he had left; for rumors had been in circulation degrading to his moral character. With the exception of his visits to the auction-rooms and booksellers' shops, he lived entirely secluded among his books at Pimlico or Hodnet."[57]

Heber was neither the defendant nor the plaintiff in the libel trial, yet during the proceedings the editor of the *John Bull* had done much to establish the existence of a sexual relationship between him and a younger man.[58] After staying abroad for four years, he was able to return to his home in the London district of Pimlico and resume his free if isolated life. The obituary mentions the books Heber wrote, the catalogues he compiled, and his extensive library of rare books. It notes the kindness that he had always shown to his younger brother and the steps Heber took to ensure that the brother received a good education. There is every reason to believe that its writer knew of Heber's earlier sexual relationship with the younger man and assumed that readers did also, yet that knowledge did not stop him from presenting a positive assessment of Heber's life.

The 1844 obituary for the Rev. Percy Jocelyn, second son of the Earl of Roden, also demonstrates the continued involvement of a family in the life of a man who had become involved in one of the most scandalous incidents involving sex between men in the first half of the nineteenth century. Twenty years before his death Jocelyn had held the title of bishop of Clogher, and under that title he was brought before a magistrate for an unnatural crime.[59] Released on bail, Jocelyn disappeared and was not heard of publicly until his death.[60] The obituary indicated that Jocelyn had lived a simple and pious life of exile in a small Scottish town, where "the post occasionally brought him letters, sealed with coronets." Some of his books and articles of furniture had been sent to him, although with the family name "obliterated" so as to protect the family's reputation and preserve his exile. Jocelyn's career was destroyed, and he paid for that mistake for the rest of his life; yet even in his disgrace, family letters and artifacts were shared with him, and the story of his pious penance, demonstrating the availability of grace even to those who had so transgressed, was eventually reproduced in numerous publications throughout the nation.[61]

The siblings of John Joyce were more divided in their attitude toward a disgraced relative. Joyce, from a wealthy family, had been involved in a well-publicized case involving sex between men and related extortions. Stories had been printed in the *Times* giving his name, and the circumstances surrounding his arrest made his guilt appear extremely likely. He was convicted and transported to Gibraltar. His sister, Johanna Carrington, wrote many letters over several years to the Home Office, arguing for her brother's release from transportation into her care.[62] The ten-year mark was the conventional point at which men sentenced to transportation for life were released on a ticket of leave, and Johanna, anxious to see her brother again, began writing to the Home Office to inquire into the prospects for his release. Her letters stated that her brother was "no common ruffian, but was educated with care and brought up in luxury by a good father whom he lost very young." Knowing the Home Office concerns in these matters, she also stressed that "he will not; like many ticket of leave men, be thrown on the wide world without the means of sustenance as I can offer him that."[63]

Eventually, Carrington began to suspect that someone in the family was working against her efforts, and she began to mention this issue in her letters. She wrote to Earl Grey that she had "wondered whether any influence of a Wealthy Brother—who has reasons for keeping the convict where he is—could have operated against his release."[64] Not wishing to harm her own case by an improper insinuation, she quickly added, "I trust the cause of justice or mercy could not be so tampered with."

The actions of another family member were unnecessary to ensure her brother's continued detention, however, as the men of the Home Office had extremely strong feelings against John Joyce based on the trial itself. Undersecretary Waddington, assistant to the home secretary, scrawled on the outside cover of one petition letter that release "was quite out of the question. It was one of the worst cases ever known."[65] Waddington seemed to be referring to the fact that Joyce had befriended a group of working-class extortionists and aided them in the exploitation of a member of his own class. This breach of class solidarity in combination with sexual acts between men seems to have turned the men of Joyce's own social class strongly against him (see chapters 6 and 7). Joyce's transgression against class as well as "nature" struck a particularly sensitive nerve. Something of his fate is indicated by the last letter in the Home Office file on him, written by Joyce himself after thirteen years of transportation. Perhaps suspecting that there were no plans to release him, he requested to be sent to Western Australia, where at least he would have the chance to build something of a life for himself.

In spite of his conviction and more than ten years of exile and imprisonment for what men at the Home Office apparently considered to be one of the most egregious transgressions related to sex between men, Johanna remained devoted to her brother: she was willing not only to accept him back into her life but also to provide financial support. Given the publicity at the time of the trial as well as the length of his sentence, her community and her family most likely knew the nature of Joyce's acts. Her willingness to face criticism from these sources is implied in her offer to take her brother in.

Like other women of the middle and upper classes, Carrington defended her brother in a way at least partially in keeping with the conventions of her gender and class. She wrote letters to the Home Office after the trial, rather than appear in court herself to testify to her brother's character. Women, especially those of upper- and middle-class backgrounds, were more active in private and familial negotiations over sex between men than in public forums. Following this pattern, the middle-class Anne Seymour dealt privately with the man who blackmailed her husband on three occasions, but it was her husband who brought in the constables who made the final arrest.[66]

The middle-class Mary Legg was also extremely resourceful when dealing with the men who blackmailed her uncle before the case became public. Legg began to suspect that something was the matter when her uncle's increasingly anxious behavior began to coincide with the disappearance of large sums of money from the household. She began to watch and listen in on him, and by degrees "she obtained some clue to the mystery . . . [until] she intruded herself upon the meetings" where her uncle met with his blackmailers and "demanded an explanation." At first one of the men involved "said it was not a subject for the interference of a woman" and indicated that it involved allegations of her uncle's sexual desire for other men. Although Henry Tiddeman "saw tears in Mrs. Legg's eyes" when he confronted her about the sexual advance that her uncle had made on him, she did not shrink from the confrontation with the four men.[67] Mrs. Legg "took part in the negotiations from this time, and made an appointment to meet them all at the shop on Tuesday night, when they fell into a trap."[68] As her sixty-year-old uncle had grown ill from the stress of the extortion and was confined to his bed, Mary dealt with the repeated visits of the four men and their most recent demands for fifty pounds. At their final meeting, she told the extortionists to "walk into the parlour, gentlemen," and then induced them to recount enough of their extortion activities to allow the hidden constables to pounce from behind the curtains and make the arrest.[69]

Other women whose male relatives were threatened also stepped in to defend them. Although many parents attempted to deny that their children were actually guilty of the acts they were charged with, Margaret Nugent held more strongly than most that her son Edward had been made the victim of a workplace plot to discredit him.[70] Edward was the primary source of support for the family, but at his most recent job he had had a serious dispute with the foreman he worked under. The foreman wanted to replace Edward with a personal friend, but as soon as he did so, the head contractor of the job removed the friend and reinstated Edward. According to Margaret, tensions mounted between the two men to the point at which "the wicked ganger having sworn falsely against my son" made allegations that led to Edward's imprisonment for two years for unnatural assault.[71]

When Margaret Nugent wrote the letters to the Home Office on behalf of her son, thus taking on a task that might be seen as belonging to the head of the household, it was not because her husband was deceased or absent. It is clear from the letters that she and her husband were still married and living together, but that since at least the time of Edward's arrest she had assumed the responsibilities of the head of the household. After arguing for her son's innocence in her first letter, she began to relate the plight of her family. Most deeply affected, she wrote, was "his father and my husband William Nugent [who] is gone mad and is insane since he has heard what is become of his son."[72] Margaret was left to provide for herself, her husband, and nine other children, most of whom were too young to earn significant wages.

Such representations of the failure of will or health of fathers (more than mothers or other relatives) were common in these cases. Edward Park, "a gentlemanly-looking young man," invoked the health of his father on his second arrest for making a sexual advance on another man. He reportedly implored to the arresting officer "Oh! Pray don't; have mercy on me; it nearly broke my father's heart when a charge was made against me on a former occasion. I am sure it will be the death of him now."[73] The Rev. John Greaves pleaded with the court to let him serve his sentence for attempted unnatural assault in the jail of a county other than his own, so as not to hasten the death of his aged father, who lived nearby.[74] It was often the father's emotional stability that was reported to be most disturbed when a man was convicted or accused of a crime of this type. It was the father who required nursing by the rest of the family, and it was the father's failing health that was invoked in requests for mercy or pardons. In such times of crisis, it was up to women like Margaret Nugent to take on the responsibilities that were abandoned by their husbands; Margaret continued to look after Edward's interests as well as those of the rest of her family.[75] Margaret's fourth letter to the Home Office helped to obtain Edward's early release from Durham jail.[76]

A working-class woman was much more likely to intervene on behalf of a family member she believed to be innocent than one she believed to be guilty. One of the few such examples of the latter situation, though, is Mary Ann Campbell, who began writing to the home secretary beginning on 24 August 1849. Campbell asked Earl Grey if he could "be pleased to cause a further inquiry into the distressing matter" that had led to her husband, John Campbell, being placed under a sentence of transportation for life.[77] Although Mary Ann Campbell was one of the individuals best placed to know the events of that "distressing matter," she made no effort to explain its specific details. She chose instead to dwell on the hardship of her current situation: after the arrest, she was left to care for three children under nine years of age and was pregnant with a fourth. Almost as an afterthought, at the end of the letter she noted that two of her older sons by a previous marriage had led respectable lives and served in the military in India.

Mary Ann Campbell's reluctance to dwell on the details of her husband's case can perhaps be understood in light of the fact that the man her husband was accused of assaulting was Henry Campbell, Mary Ann's fifteen-year-old son by her previous marriage.[78] Mary's letter was unusual for a petition to the Home Office in that it did not attempt to speak to the good character of the accused or try to deny the charge. She simply asked for "further inquiry into the distressing matter," as though she could not accept the situation as it was, but could not articulate a preferred outcome, either.

John Campbell was less evasive in his own letter, written just over six months after his conviction but before his actual transportation. He denied that he had made any advance toward his stepson and repeatedly railed against the fact that he was imprisoned on the evidence of "a publican's pot boy."[79] Campbell argued that "nature required" him and his stepson to stop on Bexley Heath at about 11 o'clock one morning, and it was their making water that the pot boy had actually witnessed. He cited as evidence of his innocence the fact that a medical examination of his stepson, carried out within an hour after their apprehension, did not conclusively prove anal intercourse.[80] Campbell also cited his two long marriages and a twenty-year history of steady and sober work as proof of his innocence and good character. There was nothing in these arguments that moved Undersecretary

Waddington to recommend a review of the case, though, and the Home Office did not intervene.

Mary Ann's troubles only increased in the months after the denial of the petitions for her husband. She and her young children spent at least some time in the St. Martin's Workhouse during the following year, and her economic situation remained dire despite the return of one of her older sons from Bengal. In her letters to the Home Office of the following year, the emphasis on economic over emotional concerns becomes increasingly pronounced. John had since been transported to Bermuda, but she asked the Home Office that he "be sent to some other of the penal settlements where he could have some means of earning something towards the maintenance of his wife and family."[81] The next letter, dated only four months later, further detailed her plight after the death of two of her children, one of whom had been working and was able to bring in a bit of extra money. She closed her letter by writing that she was in an unsustainable circumstance, and that only "God and the Home Department" had the power to save her.[82]

Although Mary Ann's situation remained desperate for the first years of John's sentence, he managed to improve his lot after his ship set sail for Bermuda. English prison sentences, wherever they were served, typically entailed labor. For many transported convicts, this meant unskilled labor on a prison hulk or in the colonies themselves, but those with special skills were able to put them to use. John's good conduct and ability as a tailor soon earned him such a position on his ship. John wrote Mary Ann with this news, and she in turn informed the Home Office that "he made several suits for the authorities on his voyage out, for which they were highly pleased with him. . . . He has already received a commutation of sentence to six years on account of excellent conduct."[83]

Mary Ann's last letter to the Home Office, five years after the conviction of her husband, is the most revealing of them all. For the first time she admits that her husband "in a fit of drunkenness committed an unnatural crime" upon her son.[84] She had likely known the truth of the matter from the start. Perhaps this was why, in this letter, she asked to be allowed to go to Bermuda herself. Her husband, she said, had been promoted to "Master Tailor" on the hulk ship *Midway* on which he was serving his sentence, and he was now earning enough money to support her and her remaining children. If he were granted a ticket of leave within the colony, she would be able to stay with him and resume their family life.[85] Whatever anger Mary Ann Campbell felt toward her husband over what he had done to her son was overcome by her belief that living with him would provide the best future for her family.

The private decisions of Mary Ann Campbell, as well as the other examples given above, contrast with the typical public depictions of communities, families, and the women within them reacting to men who had sex with other men. The most commonly invoked example from this period relates to the 1810 raid on the White Swan, a molly house on Vere Street in London, where more than two dozen men were arrested and six convicted of having sex with other men. Newspaper and pamphlet accounts told of the convicted men being transported in an open cart to the pillory where they would serve a portion of their sentence. The route, it was said, was lined with thousands of individuals, who hurled insults and missiles at the convicted men. In front of the pillory where the convicted men were to be placed, "upwards of 50 women were permitted to stand in the ring," where they "assailed them incessantly with mud, dead cats, rotten eggs, potatoes, and buckets filled with blood, offal, and dung."[86] The participation of women, and the invective they directed at the convicted men, was also reported at the execution of Captain Henry Nicholls, who had been involved not only in sexually assaulting young men but also in murdering at least one of them. It was recorded that among the large crowd that gathered, "a number of females also presented themselves, and by their shouts manifested their abhorrence of the criminal."[87]

At other times, the punishment that working-class communities directed at men accused of sodomy exceeded that of the state. In 1817 the Rev. John Church was released after his detention on sodomy charges, but it was reported that local residents surrounded his London home that evening, burning him in effigy and throwing stones at his windows.[88] A crowd of more than one hundred women and men banged pots and generated other forms of "rough music" in front of his house throughout the night. Primarily because of this community pressure, Church, his wife, and their children were forced to leave London. It was also reported that Percy Jocelyn's home in Ireland was burned by an angry mob after he was arrested for unnaturally assaulting a soldier in London in 1822.[89] After John Sugden, William Jones, George Hamon, and George Fennell were convicted of a conspiracy to commit sodomy after a molly-house raid, the *Times* reported that "the moment they left the Court, in custody of the gaolers, the reception they met with from the populace was such as they cannot easily forget, or even recover, for some time to come."[90] The report of another unnatural-assault case in the *Weekly Dispatch* ended by noting that "it was with the greatest difficulty that a strong body of officers, in conveying the miscreants back to prison, could protect them, so strong was the indignation of the populace."[91] Finally, in 1810, nearly the whole of the coverage of George Rowell's arrest for "detestable acts" was devoted to describing how "the Irishman" with whom he was locked up was angered at being detained with a man accused of having sex with men. The Irishman was in jail at the request of his wife for beating her, and he threatened to do the same to Rowell if he so much as spoke to him. It was also reported that the wife "appeared with angry countenance, and demanded [her husband's] liberation, as she would sooner be bate by him every hour, than that he or his family should be disgraced by being shut up with such a fellow."[92]

If in most histories working-class women and working-class communities are shown expressing anger toward men who had sex with men, upper- and middle-class women are usually represented as unaware of or shielded from knowledge of such acts. Women of high social status avoided the courtroom itself, and those who did appear at trials involving sex between men were reported to do so with reluctance. Robert Allpress, a footman, was in desperate need of a testimonial to his character from his employer when he became involved in a case of unnatural assault, but because both his employer and all the "other inmates of the house" were women, Allpress had to do without a character witness, as "he could not bring them forward in such a case."[93] Although Henry Walter's aunt immediately went for a constable on seeing another young man sexually assault her nephew, she testified only "reluctantly" in the public courtroom when compelled to do so.[94] In cases involving sex between men, female spectators were also sometimes cleared from the courtroom before testimony began.[95] After George Cull was sexually assaulted on Marylebone Lane, he avoided asking another man passing by for help. "I should have mentioned what had happened to me if the gentleman whom I saw in Marylebone-lane had been by himself," he later said, but "he had a lady with him, and I thought it too delicate a matter to speak of to him while he was in her company."[96]

When confronted directly with evidence of this behavior, middle- and upper-class women were frequently represented as extremely unsympathetic. Frederick Buller, a retired colonial judge, tried to appeal to Mrs. Jane Humphrey's sense of family in order to dissuade her from giving evidence against him related to his sexual assault on a young man in her parlor. Buller implored "Pray, my dear madam, consider before you make a charge . . . perhaps you have a family of your own. If you make this charge you will ruin me and my family too." To this Jane Humphreys curtly said: "You should have thought of this before you came into my house."[97]

The evidence of forgiveness within families does not call into question the idea that disapproval and condemnation were overwhelmingly the most common reactions toward men discovered to be engaging in sex with other men. Even if forgiveness might come in time within a family, and even if individuals still remained in a man's life for reasons other than economic dependence, discovery of their actions still elicited shock and anger. The evidence does, however, provide some correctives to the conclusions drawn from the public statements of middle- and upper-class men, whose opinions are often taken as representative of those of the population as a whole. Although it is relatively easy to find a middle- or upper-class man profess in a courtroom, a newspaper report, or other published sources that sex between men is an "unspeakable crime," the "worst of crimes," and that to imply that a man was guilty of sex with another man was "worse even, than a charge of murder," this intensity of language is not easily found within the family.[98]

This contrast between public and private views is related to what John Tosh and other scholars of masculinity in nineteenth-century Britain have revealed about the relationship between character, reputation, and the ideological system that supported the political and economic power of middle- and upper-class men.[99] The qualities of these elite Englishmen were regularly contrasted with those of working-class men, of women, and of members of other races and ethnicities: the deficiencies supposedly found in the latter groups were used to help justify their exclusion from power. Although middle- and upper-class men defined respectability differently, both defined it by exclusionary criteria, making it difficult to achieve without the economic resources available to their social class. Working-class men also had a code of masculine honor that condemned sex between men, but being accused of it did not undercut their social power in the same way as it did for middle- and upper-class men. As George Mosse, Sean Brady, and others have argued, same-sex desire was seen as so antithetical to the qualities that defined good character among both middle- and upper-class Englishmen that it was unimaginable in a man of good standing in these groups.[100] The accusation of sex between men was so serious because it was an affront to a man's character and his honor. No middle- or upper-class man considered that men who worked for wages possessed these attributes in the same way that they did themselves. Denouncing a crime against reputation and honor as the worst possible is a prerogative of the powerful, and only those with political and economic power that depended on their honor had much to lose when that honor was called into question.

Assessments of the social transgression represented by sex between men in the first half of the nineteenth century have largely been shaped by the views of upper- and middle-class men from that period. If today we recognize the self-interested nature of arguments for aristocratic government and laissez-faire economics made by these groups, we have been more willing to take their pronouncements on sex between men as representative of the views of the society as a whole. In part this generalization has occurred because so few personal papers or memoirs record information on this topic. Individuals of all social classes seem to have been reluctant to discuss the topic, let alone preserve records of what was spoken or written. But because people were forced to publicly voice their views on this behavior in the courtrooms, with hundreds of records surviving for cases occurring between the 1820s and the 1860s, it is possible to gain insight into that institution so vital to the control of the sexuality of its members: the family.

The family provided an alternative forum to the courtroom, where individuals assessed the transgression represented by sex between men and imposed punishments and sanctions deemed necessary to resolve the crisis caused within the family. It continued to exercise these powers throughout this period, even as social and legal changes (discussed in greater detail in chapters 3–5) impinged on its prerogatives. Surely many more such incidents were discovered, adjudicated, and settled solely within the forum of the family than ever came before the courts. Although some of the punishments decided within families were no doubt harsher than those family punishments described above, more often the transgression seems to have been accommodated. Families faced trade-offs: forgiving sex between men might be preferable to allowing children to suffer privation for want of the financial support of a father. It might be preferable to face the social stigma for taking a disgraced relative back in than to allow him to languish in permanent exile. The threat of sex between men might be more tolerable than the prospect of keeping a son idle at home, where he would become an economic drain on the family. None of these alternative views of sex between men is more "accurate" than the more familiar views of upper- and middle-class men: each is just as particular to individual circumstances as the views of those elite men. These examples suggest, though, that the pattern of designating sex between men as "the worst of crimes" was characteristic of a particular segment of British society. If we are to understand what such a designation means, we need to examine the groups that propagated and supported this idea.

CHAPTER 2

Class, Masculinity, and Spaces

Circumstances played a large role in how men understood their sexual activities with other men. The class backgrounds of the participants, the relative ages of the individuals involved, and the spaces in which those sexual acts occurred were all important. How men felt about their male sexual partners differed if the other man was met in a public school, known as a family friend, or encountered in Hyde Park at night. Sexual pickups in front of shop windows, lingering in certain sections of city parks, and suggestive stares in and around public urinals were recurring themes from the early eighteenth century to the early twentieth century, as was the existence of certain public houses and commercial spaces where "mollies" or "pooffs" congregated.[1] These relationships were also shaped by the exercise of power, resulting in more or less overt forms of influence, coercion, and violence. Many of these aspects of sexuality between men during this period have been identified by other scholars, but they have not been differentiated according to class and geographic location.

One model for differentiating patterns of behavior and motivation between groups of men, grounded in the concerns of the early nineteenth century, is provided by Anna Clark's analysis of the diaries of Anne Lister. Lister's diaries are one of the few detailed autobiographical narratives from the early nineteenth century whose author specifically identifies and describes in detail her same-sex desire. In analyzing the diaries, Clark isolates three main areas to understand how an individual might have constructed an identity that positively incorporated same-sex desires: the desires that originate within the individual, the material conditions that structure an individual's options, and the available cultural texts through which that person can interpret experience.[2] Lister's narratives provide excellent evidence of all three factors, but the usefulness of Clark's approach is not limited to such fortuitous circumstances. Even when the internal desires of individuals are less well documented, it is possible to gain considerable insights from categorizing evidence of material resources and available cultural texts. I draw on this approach to demonstrate the forms of sex between men most typically associated with the working, middle, and upper classes, respectively. The resulting analysis demonstrates that the state was involved most heavily in situations where those acts had the greatest political consequences.

As Clark demonstrates in the case of Anne Lister, positive representations of same-sex desire in the ancient Greek and Roman texts carried great cultural authority among the upper classes. An upper-class young man's education in the early nineteenth century would have incorporated such texts by Virgil, Lucretius, Horace, Tibullus, Martial, Tacitus, Suetonius, and Petronius.[3] From the military prowess of the Sacred Band of Thebes to the example of the Roman emperor Hadrian and his beloved Antinous, the ancient world provided a counterpoint to the condemnation of sex between men in the Christian tradition.[4]

Upper-class men also had knowledge of the contemporary Mediterranean world, where some cultures allowed more open expressions of sexual desire between men than was allowed in Britain. Michael Rocke has demonstrated that patterns of age-structured sexual relations between older and younger men associated with ancient Greece and Rome persisted on a wide scale into the early modern period.[5] The work of Graham Robb and George Mosse indicates that into the eighteenth and nineteenth centuries, Mediterranean cultures continued to make allowances for certain forms of sexual contact between men. This aspect of Italian society was sometimes encountered or sought out when upper-class British men undertook a grand tour of Europe as the culmination of their education. According to at least one visitor to Naples, "Love between men is so frequent that one never expects even the boldest demands to be refused."[6]

Upper-class men looking to ancient literature or to the contemporary Mediterranean found cultural texts and practices that demonstrated that such acts did not have to damage a man's masculine status or reputation. Within the ancient world, sexual acts between men were not effeminizing, provided that a man was not seen to be submitting to the desires of another man. He asserted his own desires primarily by pursuing younger men and by always playing the penetrative role. Within this model of masculinity, only some men can achieve full masculine, or *vir,* status, and their success is based on their economic, social, and sexual domination of others.[7] Evidence of a similar pattern of male sexuality and masculine status, based on the domination of a partner rather than on the sex of that partner, has been discussed for early modern England by Alan Bray and for eighteenth-century England by Randolph Trumbach, and it is within this tradition that the acts of same-sex desire exhibited by early-nineteenth-century upper-class figures, including Lord Byron, seem best explained.[8] Although often eclipsed by the passions Byron felt for women, the homoerotic allusions in his writings and his sexual interest in younger men both conform to this pattern.[9]

Upper-class British culture also demonstrated a tolerance for extra-marital sexuality, so long as the indiscretions did not lead to a public scandal. This tolerance applied to the sexual affairs of men and, to a lesser degree, women in the eighteenth century, although the allowance for women's sexual indiscretions diminished as the century progressed. In their sexual affairs with other men, individuals such as George Dawson Lowndes seem to have been breaking the rules of decorum as much as the laws, and Lowndes consequently faced a great deal more ostracism than other men of his own class, like Richard Heber (see chapter 1), whose behavior became more discreet after the initial exposure of his affair with a younger man, thus allowing him to recoup a significant portion of his reputation by the time of his death.

As John Tosh observes, reputation was a pillar of an upper-class man's masculine status. With their incomes secured by ownership of property, upper-class men did not regard hard work as a status marker. The upper-class focus on reputation placed the emphasis on sociability. This view derived in part from the need to temper the martial values of the upper class in order to avert internal conflicts like those that had erupted in the seventeenth century. Sociability among men was cemented in multiple ways, including drinking, hunting, gambling, demonstrations of sexual prowess, and a willingness to aggressively defend one's honor.[10] The focus on reputation thus had direct political consequences, fostering conviviality among the English upper class that secured their hold on political power.[11]

The strength of the upper-class identity, and the power that it had to shape the perception of upper-class men's actions into the late nineteenth century, can be seen in the work of Morris Kaplan. Through his careful analysis of the public statements associated with the 1889 Cleveland Street Scandal, Kaplan shows that even when charges of sex between men were involved, the overriding public concern was their abuse of class position rather than disapproval of sodomitical acts. Kaplan's analysis of the rhetoric associated with W. T. Stead's campaigns in relation to both the 1885 "Maiden Tribute of Modern Babylon" stories and the Cleveland Street Scandal shows that the dominant theme in both instances was the abuse of upper-class privilege as it related to sexuality. Whether the victims were working-class girls or young men in the employ of the Post Office, the criticism by radicals like Stead, as well as by feminist and working-class allies, was directed at an upper class that made its own rules and was allowed to evade the laws that constrained people of lower classes.[12]

If radical, feminist, and working-class critiques of upper-class masculinity became strongest in the late nineteenth century, it was in the late eighteenth and early nineteenth centuries that middle-class men put forward their most sustained challenge to the norms of upper-class masculine behavior. As Linda Colley notes, even though the French Revolution did not topple the English upper class, the privileged were nevertheless affected by the pressures of a generation of warfare.[13] In order to safeguard their social position, the British upper ranks, led by the example of men such as William Pitt the Younger, responded to middle-class criticism of an idle aristocracy and worked to reform the government system of sinecures and other elements of "Old Corruption"; but they did so only to improve their own governing ethic, not to replace it. Upper-class men continued to argue for aristocratic leadership on the basis that the men of the middle class, insecure in their new personal wealth, could not be trusted to govern in the interests of the society as a whole. In both their distinct political values and their assertive rejection of the middle-class values of hard work and restraint, upper-class men remained distinctly different from their middle-class rivals long after the two groups began to share political power in 1832.

Middle-class men were also confident in and assertive of their distinct form of masculinity. In response to upper-class arguments for the merit of economic independence, middle-class men countered that it was precisely because they were self-made that they were fitted to participate in running the state. Aristocratic leisure could too easily become destructive self-indulgence, and the upper-class models of patron and client could easily turn a man into a sycophant. From Thomas Carlyle's famous critique of the 1830s dandy in *Sartor Resartus* to the popular celebration of distinctly middle-class masculine values in the 1850s in Dinah Craik's *John Halifax, Gentleman,* middle-class men prided themselves on their independence, and their criteria for success and respectability were very different from those of the upper class.[14]

As Leonore Davidoff and Catherine Hall have demonstrated, middle-class identity also depended on religion and domesticity, virtues that were mutually reinforcing. Stricter adherence to religious principles gave the middle class a positive means by which to define itself against a hedonistic upper class and an improvident lower class.[15] In consequence, the middle class placed a greater emphasis on marital fidelity and took a far more skeptical attitude toward the pursuit of pleasure. Education was also focused on practical pursuits rather than ancient literature and other forms of high culture. For all these reasons, the cultural texts and practices available to upper-class men, the ones that with work and care a man might fashion into a limited justification of the sexual pursuit of other men, were largely absent from middle-class male identity. Although it might make allowances for the indiscretions of youth, no elements of middle-class masculine identity in the early nineteenth century could be refashioned or realigned to justify sexual desire for other men (see chapter 6).

The rigidity of the middle-class masculine code stemmed in part from its rejection of the upper-class ideal of reputation as the central pillar of masculinity and its alternative emphasis on character. Middle-class men were uneasy with the degree to which reputation rested on the opinion of others. Following the pattern of Evangelical religion, they believed, in John Tosh's words, that "instead of being guided by the opinion of others, the serious Christian was urged to listen only to the inward monitor of conscience, and to appear to the world as he really was."[16] Such a distinction has implications for the ways a man might interpret and justify his actions to himself, including sexual acts with another man. Discretion could enable an upper-class man to avoid reproach from his peers and retain his reputation, but it was of much less value to a middle-class man in preserving a sense of his own character: for him, the most important judge of a particular action was his own conscience.

Although upper-class and middle-class masculinity were distinctly different in these ways, they were not mutually exclusive. Many of the early prominent leaders of the Evangelical movement were members of the upper class; marriages between the daughters of the upper middle class and the younger sons of the upper ranks were common; and younger sons of the upper class had long gone into business and the professions, where they mixed with middle-class men. These contacts led to the erosion of certain contrasting characteristics, although it never entirely erased them. As the nineteenth century progressed and the middle class shared political as well as economic power with the upper class, it became necessary for at least some middle-class men to enter into some of the upper-class forms of sociability.

The main sites for incorporating young men from both the middle and upper classes into the upper ranks of society were the public schools. In the first decades of the nineteenth century, there were only nine public schools in Britain, all of which were dominated by the upper class. As in the eighteenth century, the public schools existed primarily to teach the sons of the elite how to function in the world of men. The emphasis was placed not on deference to authority, as the masters were well below their pupils in social rank, but rather on the boys' establishing relationships and reputations among their peers. The links and sociability forged in these locations carried over into men's adult lives in politics and society, as well as into some areas of commerce associated with the upper classes, including long-distance trade, banking and finance. Even though, according to Roy Porter, many families "mistrusted the public school . . . with its diet of birch, boorishness, buggery and the bottle," the schools were considered a critical element in the forging of upper-class masculine culture.[17]

The assimilation of middle-class sons into the public schools altered those institutions. Between 1830 and 1860 more than thirty new public schools were established, and reforms in the curriculum and the culture of the schools reflected a stronger focus on academics, testing, religion, and team sports. Appointed as headmaster at Rugby in 1828, Thomas Arnold instituted such reforms; he also strengthened the system of peer supervision. Arnold's widely copied model improved the academic seriousness of these institutions, although at their core they remained fundamentally rooted in upper-class values.[18]

Unfortunately for the administrators, reforms in the public schools could not end their association with homosexual acts, at least at the level of innuendo, supposition, and after-the-fact memoirs. Men like Benjamin Disraeli, Thomas Carlyle, and John Addington Symonds wrote of both the intimate and the brutal contact between young men that took place in these schools, but such behavior was almost never discussed in the newspapers. A wealthy Briton living in Paris in the mid-nineteenth century wrote of allegations that had spread in the newspapers twenty years before concerning the unnatural propensities of the boys at Harrow, but the fact that he had to reach so far back indicates the rarity of such reports.[19] Many seemed willing to hint privately that vice at the public schools was rampant, and yet the sexual acts alluded to were rarely recounted explicitly. Understanding why this was so highlights how age, class, and space could alter the distinctions between acceptable and unacceptable acts.

Compared to other schools for boys in the period, in fact, the public schools were less frequently associated with homosexual acts. English education for boys outside the public-school system in the early nineteenth century was a hodge-podge of small day schools and boarding schools, many run by a single master and catering to a small group of pupils. It was these institutions whose masters appeared most frequently before the courts and in the newspapers in connection with the sexual abuse of pupils. John Spencer, a "tall, respectable-looking man, grayhaired, and about 60" was charged with "infamous conduct" with several of his pupils at his school in Hackney.[20] A few years later, Neville Plumer was charged with assaulting four of his students at his school at 14 Charles Street.[21] Twenty years earlier, the *Times* had printed a story about the alleged sexual assaults of Edward Caston on pupils under his care.[22] John Wall's "abominable conduct" toward the boys in his school was said to have been so persistent "that it became the general subject of conversation amongst boys from other schools."[23] Thomas Anderbon, a forty-five-year-old schoolmaster, described as "of superior education" in the *Weekly Dispatch,* was indicted for having committed an indecent assault upon one of his pupils on more than one occasion.[24] These and many similar incidents were crimes of opportunity, in which older men took advantage of their positions of authority to abuse those younger and more vulnerable.

One of the few public-school cases reported in the press also involved the abuse of boys by an older individual, but not a schoolmaster. In 1842 Patrick Leigh Strachan, about thirty-eight years old, "of gentlemanly appearance, and who has since been discovered to be a man of considerable property," was known to have gone to Harrow and Sandhurst College on at least three occasions and persuaded young men to accompany him back to his chambers in London, at which point "he proceeded to conduct himself in such a manner as to leave the criminality of his intentions beyond a doubt." Based on the courtroom testimony, the authorities had "been making inquiries at other large establishments of a similar description, and there was every reason to believe that the prisoner had formed a deep-laid system of attack upon the youth of many of the public schools in the country."[25] Strachan had access to the boys at public schools because he himself had attended one, and he used his background as a pretext for his interest in these upper-class young men. His method on one occasion, it was said, was to "introduce himself into a respectable family [and make] arrangements for the youth to remain with him a few days in London, previous to going home." The magistrate in the case observed "that at present he believed the extent of the prisoner's proceedings had not been ascertained, but it was to be hoped that what had already occurred would operate as a sufficient warning to parents not to allow their children to make such visits for the future."[26]

Strachan's sexual acts with public-school students were publicized because he was essentially a predator from outside the school system, taking advantage of the trust that families extended to a member of their own class. The public disclosure of his activities was seen as a warning to other parents. Situations involving individuals within a school were more likely to be dealt with internally, as when William Johnson Cory, a master at Eton, was dismissed because of his romantic relationships with a small circle of his students.

This incident highlights the way in which allegations of sex between men wholly internal to the public schools often remained shrouded in ambiguity, even in the better-documented cases. In this instance, letters that seem highly suggestive of sexual desire between men survive. The language the correspondents use with each other, the jealousies that developed, and the male companions they took later in life all point to homoerotic desires.[27] Yet it is impossible to say conclusively even whether allegations of sex between men were the cause of Cory's dismissal from Eton, because the school did not make public or keep a record of its reasons, and the individuals involved never explicitly identified any sexual act between men in their copious correspondence. Instead they point to an environment of privilege and privacy, where disputes were settled among gentlemen without resorting to the law.[28]

The ability of those in elite schools to resolve these matters discreetly among themselves can be better understood by looking at one instance in the mid-nineteenth century when this practice broke down. The events of 1850 involved both the Royal Military Academy at Woolwich, founded in the eighteenth century to train commissioned officers for the Royal Artillery and the Royal Engineers, and at the Carshalton Academy, started only in the mid-1840s as a preparatory academy for potential Woolwich students. The incident began when "three boys, who had recently been draughted in a lot of 10 from Carshalton to fill up vacancies at Woolwich, were accused by their new schoolfellows of grossly immoral practices."[29] The parents of the boys were informed, private hearings at the school were held, and the three were expelled. The incident did not end there, though, because "in the course of the investigation it unexpectedly transpired that the practices in question were more or less prevalent amongst the pupils of Carshalton Academy, whence the culprits had recently come."[30] These revelations sparked an extended investigation, "conducted by officers of the highest rank in the most cautious and secret manner," that resulted in thirty pupils, mostly from Carshalton Academy, being sent home or withdrawing from the schools.

Roughly two-thirds of the parents of the accused boys complied with requests that they remove their boys rather than have them expelled. The remaining parents objected that they did not have the chance to confront their sons' accusers, with one angry father, described as an officer of thirty years' service, writing that "a secret committee has sat with closed doors and has examined 33 children in a way calculated to criminate [sic] themselves without any possibility of their knowing what charges are brought against them, or who were their accusers!"[31] It was the objections of these parents, and their decision to make statements to the newspapers about the incident, that brought it to public notice; otherwise, it would almost certainly have been contained within the elite community of the schools.

Defenders of the schools' approach argued that secrecy was maintained precisely for the protection of the accused boys. "Had a public investigation taken place . . . every one of their schoolfellows would have been cognizant of their disgrace . . . and the stigma thus affixed upon them would have clung to them in after life."[32] Because the matter was dealt with in secret, "their names are known to but a few, and would have been known to still fewer, had it not been for the injudicious contumacy of the parents of the 10 boys." This correspondent to the *Times* also held out the hope that because these offenders were "mere children," and because their names were not publicly revealed, "there is surely no reason why, having been thus promptly removed from the scene and from amongst the witnesses of their shame and their disgrace, they should not, in another career or amongst other associates, become in due time virtuous and estimable members of society."[33]

But others responded that the secretive nature of the proceedings was not necessarily for the boys' protection and did not necessarily serve their interests. If the behavior among the boys was really so wide-spread, it was suggested, then the administrators had been negligent in their oversight; and if it was not, then the administration had over-reacted, using the protection of secrecy to err on the side of extensive dismissals, and in the process inflicting a severe punishment on boys who were perhaps guilty of only the slightest infractions. A different letter to the *Times* speculated that "the authorities of Woolwich are . . . building up for themselves a reputation for vigilance and discipline out of the mutilated characters of these sacrificed children."[34]

Another line of accusations was directed not simply at the adminis-trations of Woolwich and Carshalton but at the way boys were super-vised in such institutions in general. One writer pointed out that in both schools, older boys shouldered the responsibility of supervising the younger ones. The *Times* indicated that it had heard from other credible sources that part of the problem lay within Woolwich Academy itself, where "tyranny of the most oppressive kind, and all the more resistless from being systematized into a part of the institution, is said to prevail."[35] But Woolwich, and the system of peer supervision, also had its defenders. In the midst of the controversy, Sir Eardley Wilmot defended the practices at Woolwich, claiming "that the guiding prin-ciple of the whole system is reciprocal confidence between officers and pupils; that appeal is expressly made to the instincts of honour on the part of the cadets; that the fact of their being gentlemen is never lost sight of."[36] As gentlemen, the boys in the school were expected to be able to govern themselves, and even scandals like this were not enough to undermine support for this central aspect of elite education.

In this instance and in many others, men within the privileged classes treated sex differently when it occurred exclusively among men of similar backgrounds. These men had long-standing ways of settling disputes among themselves without involving the police or the courts, and rarely did any of them feel so aggrieved as to appeal to a more public forum, as the parents of some of the Carshalton students did.

It is difficult to know exactly what occurred at Woolwich and Car-shalton. No police reports exist. Many of the sources describing similar cases refer only to "brutal" or "beastly" acts, without actually defining these terms.[37] Some slightly more specific evidence of what happened comes from a statement printed in the *Weekly Dispatch,* which indicated a hope that "youths guilty of such offences, before they even know the opprobrium or the criminality to which belongs to them, may grow up to be manly citizens."[38] But outside the protected space of the public schools, behaviors as benign as "spooning" beside another boy in bed or mutual masturbation could be grounds for criminal charges of indecent assault or attempted sodomy. Similar ambiguity surrounds the practices related to hero-worship of older boys, and the romantic or excessive language in their conversations or letters, all of which might occur between two pupils away from home for the first time, forming new kinds of intense attachments with others.

If few rigorous efforts were made to prevent or stamp out sexual contact between youths, this was in part due to the idea that some early sexual experimentation was acceptable. Nineteenth-century medical literature argued that sexual acts between males were worrisome only after the teen years. As late as the 1880s, Richard von Krafft-Ebing argued that homosexual acts before puberty were not significant; it was those occurring afterward that were dangerous to a man's development.[39] Havelock Ellis, almost two decades later, also observed that many in his own day still held that undifferentiated sexual feelings were normal in boys in the first years of puberty.[40] Lesley Hall's examination of the purity literature of the late nineteenth century also finds no fear in Britain that "adolescent homoerotic experimentation" would lead to permanent sexual inversion.[41] Undifferentiated sexual urges were thought to be more common in the less mature as well as the less civilized. Masturbation was the more serious threat to the young, because as a solitary activity it was more difficult to observe and detect, and thus it was more likely to encourage the habit of vice and sexual excess.

As the reforms at Rugby spread to other institutions, the public schools cemented their high standing among both the middle and upper classes. They were places where men could find their own position among their peers, and they fostered a fierce loyalty in those who passed through them. The public schools were, therefore, to borrow a phrase from James Scott, off the stage of the performance of power in society. For their pupils, the public schools offered a break from the power relations enacted in the regular face-to-face communications between the "lower ranks" and their "social betters." They were in preparation for the future politics of Britain, not fodder for the current version of it.[42] The privacy of these spaces was protected by the same code of behavior that assured elite men that their behavior in the clubs of the West End would not be used against them.[43]

The political power of sexual issues made public had been demonstrated in the first decades of the nineteenth century, when the morality of George IV sparked the enormous popular protests associated with the 1820 Queen Caroline Affair. The sexual impropriety of the governing elite evident in this and earlier events, such as the Mary Anne Clarke Affair of 1809, were seized on by middle- and working-class radicals and others as examples of the abuses of "Old Corruption" and further evidence of the need for political reform.[44] Attitudes toward sexuality also played an implicit political role in parliamentary reform, when, for the first time in generations, the line was being redrawn between those who deserved to be citizens, with the right to participate in parliamentary politics, and those who would remain subjects. It was not at all clear where that line would fall in the years before 1832, and, as Dror Wahrman, Leonore Davidoff and Catherine Hall, and Anna Clark have argued, the rhetoric of morality was central to the justifications of upper-, middle-, and working-class men for their respective visions of the political future.[45]

While the middle class questioned the morality of the upper classes in order to bolster their own access to the vote, they also denigrated the morality of the lower classes in order to justify the continued exclusion of them from the franchise. The improvidence of working-class masculinity was characterized as one of the causes of poverty. Working-class male pub culture was denigrated as demonstrating a lack of thrift and self-control, and working-class tolerance of sexual relations with a prospective spouse before marriage was not recognized as any less promiscuous than casual forms of extramarital sexuality.[46] The physicality and violence of working-class masculinity were interpreted as pointless brutality. These and many other issues were framed by middle-class men in a way that justified denying working-class men the right to greater political participation.

This criticism of working-class men's masculinity was part of the ideological armor that allowed the middle class to push forward with an economic program which, by eighteenth-century standards, was itself of questionable morality.[47] By shifting the focus of morality away from the economic obligations between the higher ranks and lower orders and instead upholding personal and family conduct as the measure of the moral, the middle class was able to seize the rhetorical high ground even as its actions seemed to lead to widespread impoverishment through a laissez-faire implementation of wage labor and the factory system. The stakes were raised in this contest of moralities with sweeping changes to the system of poor relief in 1834. This abolition was justified not only in terms of economics, as part of an effort to free up underutilized labor, but also as a moral reform that would encourage self-reliance among the poor and break the degrading habit of dependence.[48] Yet this was not how the New Poor Law was seen by the working class, for whom the previous system of relief might have sustained a family through a temporary factory closing or a slump in the business cycle. In the name of fostering moral and responsible behavior, the newly reformed Parliament removed what many in the working class considered a central pillar of social justice in Britain, and one that a large percentage of working-class families had drawn on. It was a brutal clash of competing definitions of morality that had ramifications for decades to come.

Because it was the form of morality on which they themselves chose to be judged, accusations of sexual impropriety by middle-class men became a powerful weapon for the working class. Anna Clark has shown that within working-class popular culture, the threat of sexual violence for working-class girls, especially household servants or factory employees, was most often represented as coming from middle-class men. This belief persisted even though legal records demonstrate that the majority of sexual violence inflicted on poorer women was perpetrated by men of their own class.[49] Representations of middle-class sexual impropriety were powerful because they could reverse the power dynamic between the classes, allowing working-class men to present themselves as the defenders of women against rapacious and uncontrolled outsiders. Such representations later had resonance in arguments for the family wage in working-class politics. In arguing that they should be paid enough to keep their wives at home and protected from the dangers of the workplace, working-class men turned the arguments of the middle class, centered on the sacredness of the family, to their own ends.[50]

As for men of other classes, full masculine status for working-class men came with the establishment of a household and the fathering of children, although the achievement of this ideal was constrained by economic circumstances.[51] Working-class households depended on the wages of all family members of working age. To dampen the shocks of periodic economic dislocations, members of the working class spread their financial risks across wider networks of family and community, and through formal organizations such as friendly societies and trade unions. Working-class masculinity thus placed a greater emphasis on a man's status and social standing, and thus in some respects it had a greater affinity with upper-class masculine values than with the more religiously inflected concept of character that defined middle-class masculinity.[52] Although some within the working class were committed to rigorous versions of Christianity, such as Methodism, the economic imperatives of these men's lives played a greater role in shaping their definition of masculinity, which continued to value physical strength, masculine dominance, and community obligations, even when economic conditions forced compromises of these ideals.

These conditions did not make working-class men more inclined to sexual acts with other men, or any less likely to denigrate such acts publicly, but they did shape judgments about the severity of such transgressions and the circumstances under which they were felt more or less onerous than other options in a given situation. Evidence from the period suggests that understandings of masculine dominance might allow for sex with another man, provided that other man was rendered subordinate by being younger or rendered effeminate by the performance of more submissive acts. The work of Matt Houlbrook has shown that in early twentieth-century London, age-structured systems of organizing sexual relations between men were still found within the working class. Men retained their masculine status after such encounters even if the working-class "lads" they partnered with were well into their twenties.[53] This assessment coincides with the remarks of nineteenth-century observers who found "less repugnance" to homosexuality among the lower orders of British society.[54] In the case of soldiers and working-class extortionists, masculine status among peers could be sustained even with an association to sex between men, provided it was for financial gain, and it was the partner of the working-class man who was effeminized by the act. Although there were clearly many working-class men who would not and did not condone such associations, and who would not have seen themselves reflected in the actions of soldiers or extortionists, working-class masculinity, like upper-class masculinity, might allow sexual acts between men to be justified, either to an individual himself or to a small community of trusted men, in a way that middle-class masculinity did not. If cultural texts from the ancient world allowed for at least a potential alternative understanding of sex between men for some upper-class men, as discussed earlier, the economic resources and imperatives of working-class men provided the context for a similar potential proximity for at least some of these men as well.

These differing ways of configuring masculine status among the different classes are important for understanding the changing nature of the regulation of sex between men in early nineteenth-century London. In the 1820s, new methods of policing and publicizing sex between men came into force, including the establishment of London's first professional police force and a rise in the circulation of newspapers. Although wealth could be used to carve out spaces of comfort, privilege, and relative privacy, the urban environment of London was not a protected or safe space for anyone. In the city, men and women from all backgrounds and classes mixed, and none of those interactions could be entirely controlled. The geography of London was not offstage in British politics, but rather center stage.

The sexual encounters between men in London that were most often uncovered, disrupted, and discussed involved two men of different classes. Certain broad spatial patterns are also evident. Locations such as parks, urinals, and public houses, noted in eighteenth-century accounts as locations where sex between men occurred, continued to be prominent. Police-court records indicate that the West End neighborhoods served by the Marylebone and Marlborough Street police courts accounted for the greatest number of arrests (see chapter 6). But there is also a great deal of evidence that sex between men was not just confined to the entertainment districts of the West End or locations like the molly houses. Sex between men occurred in a wide variety of locations around the city, and men who strongly identified with their feelings of same-sex desire were only one part of the story.

True, many associated London with opportunities for sexual encounters between men. When trying to convince a police constable to commit sexual acts with him one evening on the street, Thomas Hosier reportedly described "the crime as one of common occurrence in both London and France."[55] In 1843 the presiding judge at the Central Criminal Court sentenced two men for indecently assaulting each other "after alluding to the painful increase of such offences" in recent years.[56] Several months earlier a magistrate at the Marylebone police court also commented that "it was a melancholy thing that cases of so shocking a description should be of such frequent occurrence."[57] At the end of a case centering on an indecent assault between men standing in front of a shop window, the presiding magistrate lamented that "he believed assaults of that kind were of common occurrence in the city of London, and that the police would say the same thing."[58]

The types of sexual encounters referred to in these cases were those that occurred in public space, those which one of the involved parties chose to make public via the legal system, and those observed by a third party. It was often difficult to find privacy. Sex between men could not be regularly engaged in even in the home without a substantial risk of detection. Working-class homes were crowded, and in middle-class homes individuals were constantly under the eyes of servants and family members. Although quiet sexual contact might occur between men sleeping in the same bed in a working-class home, and quick encounters might take place in opportune moments in a middle-class house, such behavior was difficult to sustain.[59] Moreover, although families might make grudging accommodations for a family member caught engaging in such acts, they would not permit sexual relationships between men to continue once discovered.

Even men who lived alone took a great risk when bringing another man home. One man who took that risk was John M'Dougal, a twenty-year-old clerk in the War Office, who picked up a younger man, Thomas Dolamore, in the Strand around nine o'clock on a Monday night and took him back to his nearby rooms at 6 Warwick Court, Charing Cross.[60] But M'Dougal's sexual advance was not welcomed. The younger man left M'Dougal's house in anger, quickly returned with a constable, and gave him in charge.

Frederick Randall's problem, by contrast, was that the young man that he brought home would not leave. Randall had first met the twenty-year-old John Joyce at the Lyceum Theatre, and subsequently the two men met at the Half Moon public house and on the London Bridge Wharf. Randall took Joyce up to his rooms, ostensibly to show him the "fine view" he had from the window, but while there Randall gave Joyce alcohol and started a suggestive conversation that included showing him "indecent prints" and "French letters," or condoms. The evening did not go as Randall had planned, though: Randall took the risk of leaving the young man alone in his rooms and went out to get a constable, allegedly telling the policeman whom he eventually found "not to take [Joyce] into custody if he could get him out of the house without."[61]

Even without such problems, men still risked observation by neighbors or others. One man living in Soho brought men to his lodging house on Macclesfield Street, but the visitors raised the suspicions of a fellow lodger, who bored a hole through the wall between their rooms and observed what was occurring inside.[62] The Rev. John Doyle took more precautions before bringing Private Samuel Roberts back to his lodging house. The two men had met in a public house near Portman Square and walked back to Doyle's nearby rooms. When they reached George Street, Doyle "left the soldier and went forward a short distance, opened the door of the house No. 27 with a key, and shut it gently. The soldier walked backward and forward in front of the house for a few minutes, when Doyle opened the door, and beckoned with his hand to the soldier, who then entered, and the door was gently closed."[63] Back at the public house where they had met, however, a constable had noticed the two men "walking side by side conversing together, and having frequently seen Doyle in company with private soldiers, . . . he began to form conjectures, from the disparity of their apparent condition, that such a communication could not tend to any good purpose."[64]

George Sharp, a butler to Lord Ward, was among the most inventive and the most brazen in his efforts to bring other men to his lodgings for sex. One evening in 1850 he approached a constable in Park Lane and told him to come back to the house of his employer, as he had a man there that he wanted to give into custody to the officer. When the constable arrived at Dudley House, Sharp led him "into a small room and asked him what he would have to drink." After giving him some brandy, Sharp "began talking in a loose way, and showed him an indecent picture." The constable later said that he suspected that something was placed in the drink, as he "felt giddy, and as if he was going to sleep" before being pushed onto a sofa by Sharp. Some time later he was "roused by the prisoner's conduct (which is unfit to be described)."[65]

For these reasons, other spaces, where men could shield their identities, were often employed for sexual encounters. One frequent choice was the park, with Hyde Park being the most often mentioned as a site of sexual acts between men. In one typical case, a footman and a "fashionably dressed person," probably employed in a high capacity in a mercantile house in the city, were found there together by a constable in the evening. The constable saw the two men behind a tree, and, "suspecting what they were doing, he went behind another tree and watched them."[66] In another incident, Thomas Wilson, "a respectably dressed middle-aged person," and John Clark were seen committing "filthy and disgusting practices in the north wood, Kensington Gardens, one afternoon."[67] On the eastern side of the park, the police observed a gentleman, Edward Camps, approaching young men as they bathed in the Serpentine in Hyde Park, making "remarks that [are] unfit to repeat . . . and . . . proceeding to further indecencies."[68] Regent's Park also had its share of incidents, as when Richard Bird and William Morgan hoped to avoid detection by meeting there at two o'clock in the morning but were caught by constables and charged with having attempted to commit an unnatural offense.[69] Mark Miller and Henry Usher, "two gentlemanly looking young men," were accused of engaging in a sexual act with each other in Regent's Park on a Sunday afternoon as they were lying on the grass, although they protested that they were only reading.[70]

Men chose to meet in the parks for many of the same reasons that heterosexual couples did. Servants, apprentices, and other dependent members of a household unable to bring a partner home often chose to meet in the park for both companionship and sex. Such meetings might be part of ongoing relationships, lasting for months or even years, perhaps even anticipating marriage; or they might be anonymous, sometimes commercial, transactions. Yet, as these examples show, the quiet corners that might conceal a couple could just as easily allow an observer to hide behind a tree or to sneak up on them. Parks provided an anonymous meeting place, but not necessarily a private or safe one.

If some men brought their sexual partners to the park, others went there to find one. George Marsh, "a person of respectable appearance," struck up a conversation with a soldier in Hyde Park around nine o'clock in the evening, and after only a few minutes Marsh "caught hold of him in an indecent way" and attempted to entice him into a sexual act.[71] In another incident, a "gentlemanly man" who admitted to being "in public office" was loitering around the Duke of York's Column in the park around midnight before making an indecent assault on a soldier who was on guard duty there.[72] Private Robert Precious, of the Coldstream Guards, was likewise approached by Edward Peckham late one night in St. James's Park. Peckham, after asking a few leading questions about when the young soldier would be off duty, "approached him in an indecent manner, and made disgusting proposals to him." Private Precious remembered Peckham's making a similar approach to him three months before, when he had been on duty in a different part of St. James's Park.[73]

In the majority of reported cases, when one man in a park rejected a sexual approach by another, it was the man of higher rank who attempted to instigate a liaison with a working-class man or soldier. The assumption seemed to be that a sexual advance, often accompanied by an offer of money, would be accepted by a man of lower rank found in the park alone at night. Soldiers especially seemed prone to this type of advance, but other working-class men were approached in a similar way. It also seems evident that many lower-class men and soldiers used these assumptions as a way to extort or steal money from higher-class men. Although it is not possible to know what percentage of anonymous pick-ups in the park involved men of different classes, it was encounters involving social inequality that were most likely to lead to an accusation of indecent assault or attempted extortion.

Sexual encounters between men in urinals and other public conveniences around the city followed a somewhat different pattern. It was only in the second half of the nineteenth century that municipal authorities began the systematic construction of urinals around London. The municipal urinals, with their multiple adjoining bays and often clear lines of sight for observing the approach of other men, proved especially conducive to sexual encounters.[74] Yet public conveniences had been associated with sexual liaisons in earlier decades as well. James Asperne, a "fashionably dressed" man said to be of some position in society, was seen loitering in the outdoor convenience at the Elephant and Castle public house around nine o'clock in the evening. Asperne was seen to "peep out of the place, as if to see if he was observed . . . came out, and walked away about 300 yards, but returned almost directly afterwards." This happened, the witness said, at least half a dozen times, during which it was seen that "a young man" and two others also went into the convenience while Asperne was there. A policeman also confirmed that he "had known [Asperne] for some time previously to have been pursuing similar practices."[75]

More common than reports of behavior like Asperne's around a urinal, however, were the claims and counterclaims made by two men over such incidents. Jonathan Tyler said he was sexually assaulted in a watering place in Church Lane, Whitechapel, by a man who followed him there.[76] A gentleman who entered a public urinal just off Regent Street at two o'clock in the morning made a suggestive statement to an entering constable and grabbed his hand.[77] Another man said that Andrew Cunningham "behaved in a most disgusting manner to him while in a urinal in Little Bridge-street," after which he followed the man "up Ludgate-hill, through St. Paul's churchyard and Cheapside, into Gutter-lane" in an effort to find a constable and place a charge against Cunningham.[78] Although urinals close to parks and theaters and in the West End are mentioned most often in the records, urinals in other parts of the city were also sites for such encounters.

Urinals, like the parks, provided a modicum of privacy; they were also sex-segregated spaces. A suggestive look might be all that was required to determine whether another man was interested, and the regular traffic of men through such places provided multiple chances to approach other men. Although some of the encounters that occurred there seemed opportunistic, others were carefully planned. Thomas Eames did not think anything unusual was occurring when he entered the urinal near the Drury Lane Theater around six o'clock one evening. Four other men were in the convenience, which had a total of eight compartments. While in one of the compartments, Eames heard another man say, "I have just left work," and on looking up, he saw that one of the men had moved into the compartment beside him. This man then said to Eames, "You can give me what you like, but I sometimes get 5s." When Eames showed no interest in the offer, the other man "buttoned himself up and left."[79]

Public houses and coffee shops, even those not fitting the model of a molly house, could also serve as meeting places with a modicum of privacy—though not always enough. Robert Whitehead was a middle-aged surgeon who lived on Westminster Road, but he regularly met Edward Nushouse, a younger mechanic, in a coffee shop in Southwark. Over time, the couple became conspicuous enough to be suspected by the owner of the shop, who tipped off a policeman. The policeman later witnessed the two men engaging in "the capital offence" in a room rented for the night.[80] Charles James Kilpin, a student at Oxford, had met Joseph Edwards, a soldier in the Light Dragoons, twice before for drinks. On the third occasion, Kilpin asked for a private room at Hampshire Hog public house, and as the two men sat together in the otherwise empty parlor, Kilpin made his advance on Edwards.[81] James Simpson "had by artifice introduced himself into the bed-room of the waiter of the Man in the Moon public house" and committed an unnatural assault on him.[82] Augustus Cordner, a poet, was caught "in an indecent position" in a water closet with Robert Godbold, a cab driver, at the Grapes public house on Albemarle Street, Clerkenwell. When another patron of the place, a Mr. Barker, suspected men might be having sex in the outside water closet, he rounded up two or three other men before they "broke the door open, and found the prisoner and the other man inside."[83]

None of these public houses or coffee houses bore the familiar signs of a molly house: no "painted and powdered" men were described, and the other men present, especially at the Grapes public house, did not seem to have chosen the location because of any reputation it had for being conducive to sexual liaisons between men. Although there is evidence into the nineteenth century for the existence of commercial spaces where "men in ringlets" were visible patrons, after 1830, ordinary public houses and coffee houses were much more common in newspaper accounts of sex between men than were segregated spaces like the molly houses. As in the parks, men not only took sexual partners into public houses but also instigated sexual encounters in such spaces with men they had only just met. David Patching was a twenty-three-year-old police officer in plain clothes investigating a burglary with another officer in the Hackney Road. In the afternoon they went into the Queen Eleanor public house, "where they began to drink gin and beer to a considerable extent." Later the thirty-two-year-old, "gentlemanly-looking" Charles Richards came into the public house and treated the two men to more drinks. They stayed until the early hours of the morning. Patching offered to walk with Richards, "to see him safe home," and the two went off together. The other constable, however, was suspicious, and followed them "to the rear of some unfinished houses, where, according to his evidence, he found the defendants in such a position as could leave very little doubt . . . as to the guilty nature of their intentions."[84] The Queen and Prince Albert public house, Knightsbridge, was where an upper-class young man named Rogers met some "rough common soldiers," and by the end of their drinking session Rogers accused them of stealing his watch, and they accused him of attempting an unnatural assault on them.[85] Alfred Burrows, an unemployed chemist and druggist, said that he was sexually assaulted in the Owen Glyndwr public house, on the road where he lived, but no one believed his story. Burrows stated that he was sitting in the taproom when Private James Bissett of the Scotch Fusilier Guards "committed the assault." Burrows said he then "retired to the watercloset, and was followed [by Private Bissett] who, here attempted to repeat the assault."[86]

Sexual advances such as these complicate narratives that posit sexual encounters between men as occurring primarily in a narrow section of the city or in select locations. In another unlikely location, William

Jones, "a gentleman of fortune," was charged with indecently assaulting three separate young men in the space of thirty minutes in the Guildhall as they watched the polling that was then being conducted.[87] Charles Leivikie claimed another man made a similar assault on him in a crowd in front of a booth at Bartholomew Fair.[88] John Pinson, described as "a gentleman of independent property," indecently assaulted a fellow guest, a young medical student, in the house of a mutual acquaintance as the assembled party was listening to a singer.[89] Thomas Smith, a waiter at the Railway Hotel, Nine Elms, was indecently assaulted while at work by the older and wealthier Charles Aylmer.[90] George Low, an office boy in the service of the London and North-Western Railway Company at the Camden Town station, was also indecently assaulted at his place of work by an older and wealthier man.[91]

As the courts and the newspapers began to record and report more cases involving attempted sex between men in the early and mid-nineteenth century, it became clear just how diverse and how public were the locations where those advances occurred. None of the public spaces described above had any strong associations with sexual acts between men, and none were especially dark or secluded. Mundane and respectable public and commercial spaces could become sites for sexual advances between men, and many such spaces were appropriated for these purposes.

One typical space was outside a shop window. One such encounter occurred when a draper by the name of Colls was standing in front of a shop window around three o'clock in the afternoon in the Strand. When another man came up beside him, Colls "immediately felt a slight pressure" on his body from the other man, but at first, he said, he was willing to consider it accidental. "Directly afterwards, however, he found the [other man] placing his hand indecently upon his (witness) person."[92] In another incident, Benjamin Smith had stopped to look at something in an optician's window near the Bank of England when another man, who had already been standing there, "looked at [him] and then up and down the street, and then touched [him] in an indecent manner three or four times."[93] Michael Tasburgh, a man in his seventies, had stopped to look at a craftsman making billiard balls in a shop window in Hemming's Row when he felt another man "pressed very much against me." At first Tasburgh felt the man was just trying to get a better look at the craftsman through the small crowd that had gathered, but Tasburgh later recounted that "in a moment or two afterwards I perceived that he was pressing his private parts against my hand."[94] A young man by the last name of Roper had stopped to look in a picture-shop window in Cheapside when John Pacey "came up and stood by my side, and took my hand and put it to the front of his person, in an indecent manner." Roper said he moved away from Pacey after the first touch, but "he again came up to me and took my hand and put it to the flap of his breeches."[95]

Some shop owners knew of these practices and endeavored to stop them. Mr. Fores kept a store at the corner of Sackville Street, in Piccadilly, and he described one man as someone "he had often observed through his window, at which there is generally collected a crowd of persons." The man would "make his way gradually through them, until he got close to some youth (Mr. Fores here described the most scandalous practices . . .)." The owner had gone to two magistrates to see if the man could be arrested and removed, "but they gave it as their opinion that Mr. Fores's evidence would not go far enough." Fores was reduced to attempting to try to remove the man on his own. He "often endeavored to make the prisoner aware that he knew what he was at, and if possible, to shame him away from the place, by holding up to his face a print of the Bishop of Clogher." Instead of leaving the scene, however, the man "often stood and looked at [the print of the bishop] with the utmost unconcern."[96] Such shaming seems to have had little effect, as Fores went on to say that he had seen this particular man engage in this type of behavior before his shop window for more than sixteen years.

Some men who approached others in public space did so while walking down the street. James Cannon, employed at the Army and Navy Club as a fishmonger, was walking down the street one evening when he heard another man "make a noise (imitating kissing), and he followed me down St. James Street, and kept on making the noise, and he used his hand in an indecent manner." Cannon turned down another street, but the other man, "described as a gentleman, came just before me and repeated the noise and made a beckoning gesture to me with his head." Cannon later told a constable "that there was one of those nice fellows about, and that he had been treating me like a girl."[97] Edward Park was likewise less than subtle when approaching a man for sex. Meeting another man on Weymouth Street at five o'clock in the morning, Park suggested they walk together for a few blocks toward the mews, at which point Park "pushed him against the wall, exposed his person, and otherwise acted improperly."[98] James Williams, "a well-dressed man," tried a similar approach on the seventeen-year-old Henry Welch, and "assaulted him in a most indecent manner." When the sexual advance was not reciprocated, Williams tried to hurry away, but Welch "pursued him through a number of back streets and gardens, for a distance, he thought of about two miles, without once meeting a constable."[99] William Maiden, described as "a well-dressed man of about thirty-five years of age" and the proprietor of a photographic establishment, approached a young man named Challenger on Bloomsbury Street before sexually assaulting him. Another young man, William Fisher, said that Maiden "had assaulted him in precisely the same way about nine months previously, and . . . several of his acquaintances had pointed [Maiden] out to him as having treated them in a similar manner."[100]

Many advances on the street happened in broad daylight. Thomas Wright, "a lad about seventeen years of age" and a servant to a member of Parliament, was walking down the street at two o'clock in the afternoon after leaving the house of the Duke of Newcastle in Portman Square. Wright noticed the Rev. Dr. Morris Johnson, an older man of about seventy years "who attracted his attention by smiling at him, and following him about." The older man caught up with Wright, "offered him a shilling, and behaved indecently." The older man then went down an adjacent alley "and acted very indecently. On his return he again offered the shilling, and conducted himself as at first."[101] Another young man, Henry Maling, was walking down the street on a Monday afternoon near his own house when another man singled him out for a sexual advance. Maling, only sixteen years old, said that he noticed James Thomas "looking hard in his face" before Thomas came up to him, asked him if he wanted a pint of beer, and then somewhat briskly told the lad to "come along." They first had a pint in one public house, and Thomas then wanted them to move to another, "where there's a parlour" for greater privacy. The two settled into the parlor of the Beehive public house; Thomas ordered and paid for two glasses of stout, and then "committed . . . an indecent assault" on the younger Maling.[102]

These examples show that acts related to sex between men occurred in spaces not necessarily distinct from others in the city and involved men who did not look noticeably different from other men. Advances could be opportunistic as well as planned. This is not to say that some of the more furtive encounters were not carried out by men who might have strongly identified with sexual desires for other men. James Cannon's identification of the man who followed him as "one of those nice fellows" indicates his belief that there were specific types of men drawn to other men for sex and that they could be identified by appearance. Anderson Massey must have had a similar set of assumptions and stereotypes in mind when he called Henry Harrison "a pretty sort of gentleman" after Harrison had made a sexual advance on him in a public urinal.[103] Testifying at an unnatural-assault trial for a man he knew, a Mr. Sherwood told the court that "I do not think this bail is sufficient; the fellow is well known about town for his propensities."[104] Similarly, another man was sure that the shop owner that he and his friend had just spoken to strongly desired sex with men, telling his friend that "if that is not an old *puff*, my name is not Jack Sullivan, for you can see sodomy printed on his face."[105]

The men whose sexual desire for other men seemed most manifest in their actions, appearance, and self-perceptions were the men who cross-dressed. They were comparatively few: such men are mentioned in approximately 4 percent of all the stories in the *Times* involving men having sex with men and in a slightly higher percentage of stories in the *Weekly Dispatch* and the *Morning Post*. In one such case, "a young man, whose exterior denoted respectability of position," was out at night around twelve o'clock dressed in women's clothes, "walking with a gentleman . . . and they entered a public-house." The cross-dressed man "got into conversation with some loose women there, and after staying some time came out with his friend, who then left him. The [cross-dressed man] then spoke to and clung to several gentlemen passing along."[106] The man did not seem to be making any efforts to limit his visibility, and it was evident to observers that those in the public house knew he was a man in women's clothes. This individual's public cross-dressing was not limited to the entertainment districts of the West End but occurred north of the City on the Hackney Road.

This cross-dressed man did not seem to experience any harassment, but his dress did make it harder for him to blend into the crowd if it became desirable or necessary to do so. Although police did not generally arrest cross-dressers simply for their appearance, as successful prosecutions usually required additional evidence of wrongdoing, there were instances in which men might not want to be conspicuous. Other signals, easier to remove at will, seem to have been used by men such as William Tarbuck, a twenty-three-year-old who had been seen loitering around Hyde Park at night for at least two months by one constable.[107] According to two accounts, he acted the part of an aggressive extortionist in conventional masculine dress, following his victim for blocks after an alleged incident, demanding money, and threatening to go to the police. And yet that evening he also had "a small packet of rouge in his pocket such as people rub their cheeks with."[108] Rouge, as Jeffrey Weeks first observed decades ago, was one of the conventions of dress of the nineteenth-century mollies, and its presence in his pocket indicated that Tarbuck might have used more than one approach toward men in the park at night.[109]

Perhaps most interesting about the male cross-dressers is the fact that they were able to create spaces in which they were free to express themselves. One such example came to public attention in 1854, when the police received information that there was a "frequent congregation of certain persons for immoral practices" at the Druids' Hall, in Turnagain Lane. It was said that men met there in the "unlicensed dancing-room, for the purpose of exciting others to commit an unnatural offense," and two constables who arrived there in uniform at two o'clock in the morning "saw a great many persons dancing there," two of whom especially "rendered themselves very conspicuous by their disgusting and filthy conduct." It was determined that a number of those "who were present in female attire were of the male sex."[110] One of the cross-dressed men, whom a constable said he had seen there frequently before, was "behaving with two men as if he were a common prostitute."

Cross-dressed men had been making use of the Druids' Hall for some time. Another man claimed he had been taken there seven weeks earlier by an individual whom he later understood to be a cross-dressed man. Another police officer said he had been on duty around the Druids' Hall for the past eighteen months, and he had seen "several of these balls, and [men] frequently attended them dressed in female attire."[111] The officer also said that "on such occasions [he] had noticed disgusting conduct on the part of other men towards the prisoners while in their company" but had been told by his sergeant "not to interfere unless [he] saw such conduct take place in the public street." Moves had not been made against the men in the Druids' Hall itself, the officer said, because it was "very difficult to catch them in the act, as they have men placed at every outlet to keep a lookout."[112]

These parties at the Druids' Hall closely resembled the one given by Amos Westrop Gibbings at Haxell's Hotel, the Strand, fifteen years later, and famously attended by the young, middle-class cross-dressers Ernest Boulton and Frederick William Park. Each event was referred to as a *bal masqué*, each required tickets for admission, and at each,

cross-dressing was a central part of the festivities. As with the later
Boulton and Park trial, the landlady of one of the cross-dressed men
involved in the 1854 case stated that she knew that her tenant "had
a sort of mania for masquerades, and [she] had seen him dressed for
every one he had attended since they had known him."[113] Yet unlike
the Boulton and Park case, which remained in the news for more than
a year, stories of the cross-dressing that had occurred in and around
the Druids' Hall over the previous eighteen months disappeared after
only a couple of weeks in the newspapers. The elements that made the
Boulton and Park case so sensational, including the central involvement of Arthur Pelham Clinton, the son of a peer and a member
of Parliament in his own right, were missing from this earlier case.
Nevertheless, festivities at the Druids' Hall demonstrate that the more
famous party attended by Boulton and Park was preceded by similar
events at which, if precautions were taken, cross-dressing men and
those who admired them could drink, dance, and enjoy themselves
without interference.[114]

Unless someone attending these parties made an accusation against
another man, they remained private spaces. The police had limited
power to disrupt them; also lacking were the vice societies like those
of the eighteenth century, which might have targeted such spaces. As a
result, little is known about these types of parties. The court and newspaper records for the early to mid-nineteenth century do not reveal all
the locations where male same-sex desire was manifest but only those
marked by tension or confrontation, and no such tensions seem to have
been generated behind the closed doors of the Druids' Hall.

In the geography of sex between men in London in this period, the
weight of the surviving evidence speaks not to separate and segregated
spaces, such as the Druids' Hall, but rather to the ways in which it
was part of the everyday life of the city. Such liaisons happened in a
much broader range of locations than has been assumed, and those
propositioned for sex were not only men who felt same-sex desire. One
such unwelcome proposition began when Arthur Hume Plunkett, "a
young man of good family," tried his luck with a police constable on
arriving home by cab to Gloucester Place at two o'clock in the morning. Plunkett was drunk when he struck up a conversation with a local
constable, offering him three pounds and then five to accompany him
to a dark place off his beat, and at the same time told the constable
that he "wanted as much persuading as a girl of 16."[115] The constable
had only disdain for Plunkett's offer, as did the upper-class men who

listened uncomfortably to the details of his unseemly behavior in the courtroom. In the following day's issue of the *Times* and the *Weekly Dispatch,* the working-class constable embodied respectable masculinity, while the upper-class man was held up to ridicule and shame. In many instances, such indiscretions had only slight consequences for the systems of hierarchy and deference that structured social relations between the classes, but at other times they could serve as a catalyst for challenging even the widest social divisions.

One of the starkest examples of how allegations of sex between men could lead to a profound breakdown of social hierarchy in London occurred between Edward Davis Protheroe, member of Parliament for Halifax, and James Newbery, a valet. The seriousness of the case was highlighted by the opening statement for the prosecution, which observed that the case involved a servant prosecuting his gentleman employer, and that the issues involved "struck at the very root of society."[116] How the two men initially met is unclear, but, according to Newbery, Protheroe had promised him that if he left his current employer, Protheroe "would do something" for him. Protheroe subsequently hired Newbery as a temporary valet while he was in London for the season, leaving his regular valet at his country estate. Conflict between Newbery and Protheroe arose not so much because Protheroe dismissed Newbery six weeks later, but because in the subsequent months Protheroe had not made provisions to help Newbery secure his next position. Newbery claimed that Protheroe had promised to secure him a job with one of Protheroe's friends but had not done so, and also apparently delayed more than seven months in providing Newbery a suitable letter of character. While he was waiting for the job offer and the letter, Newbery sent Protheroe several short notes requesting loans of between one and two pounds, all of which were ignored.

Normally, the twenty-four-year-old Newbery would have had little recourse against a man like Protheroe, as he was almost as far below Protheroe on the social scale as it was possible to be. Yet rather than simply go away or call on Protheroe at his home, Newbery began to call on him at the Travellers' Club, the oldest of the gentlemen's clubs in Pall Mall, and leave angry letters. In one, Newbery wrote: "Sir, I feel very much disappointed in not having the place with Sir George Hamilton, after having promised me; I should have thought, after what has passed between me and you, you would have got me the place. I shall go to the club, or clubs, which you belong to, and tell them what you are, which I can prove; I shall likewise let your father and mother know what you are, and likewise the public, if you do not do something for me I shall acquaint a lawyer of it."[117]

Only the day before, Protheroe had attempted to placate Newbery at a face-to-face meeting, after finally supplying him with an extremely positive letter of character. He shortly thereafter also wrote another letter to Newbery attempting to paper over their differences, indicating that he did not really believe the threatening letters came from Newbery and that a positive letter of character had now been written.[118] Newbery, however, carried on, writing letters to other club members, visiting the club, and making direct and indirect accusations that Protheroe had engaged in unnatural acts.[119] Although Newbery was ultimately the loser in the resulting court case (he was convicted and sentenced to transportation), his ability to challenge such a prominent figure, and for a time to reverse the power dynamic between them, indicated the power of a charge of unnatural assault to disrupt class relations.[120] One such case might have little in the way of lasting consequences, but the hundreds of cases that occurred every decade in London, and the dozens that were subsequently reported in the newspapers, might over time have made more of an impact.

The traditional pattern of deference, mutual obligation, and personal loyalty between the upper and lower orders should have been strongest in relationships like that between Newbery and Protheroe, and yet here it broke down. Newbery knew how to press his advantage and how to seek redress. Newbery's desire to avenge himself against the man who had broken his word, as well as his desire to stave off financial disaster, apparently overrode any qualms he may have had about publicly admitting to sexual acts with another man. Because his sexual relationship with Protheroe could be explained as financially motivated, it might have been considered acceptable among his own peer group. The upper-class Protheroe seems to have taken the initiative in pursuing the younger and socially inferior Newbery and could have justified his actions to himself as permitted by the codes of upper-class masculinity. Thus each man could have perhaps rationalized his involvement in a sexual relationship, at least so long as those acts remained private.

Yet these men were operating in a society where such incidents were not guaranteed to remain private. In the first decades of the nineteenth century, the laws related to sex between men, the means by which those laws were enforced, and the methods by which such acts were reported were all revised. These changes brought greater public attention to sex between men than had existed in the eighteenth century;

it also focused on different types of sexual acts and participants than in earlier decades. This shift altered the consequences of such acts in London, where they most often occurred and where they had the greatest potential political consequences. In its policing of sex between men, the state was not specifically upholding morality but rather supporting the system of social and property relations that sustained the society, as the judges in the Protheroe case said and well understood.

PART TWO

Early Nineteenth-Century Changes

CHAPTER 3

Law and Reform
in the 1820s

The most significant British law reforms of the nineteenth century happened in the 1820s and 1830s. These reforms were begun by the Tories before the Great Reform Act of 1832, completed under the Whigs in the years after 1832, and imposed on a majority that had no hand in shaping them. They set a new pattern for imposing order by the use of criminal law, shifting away from the use of rare but brutal displays of state power on the body of the convict and toward a system where less severe punishments were implemented with much greater frequency and consistency. This shift required the creation of a more pervasive and bureaucratic system of law enforcement and the inclusion of more types of behavior within the scope of the law. It built on elements inherited from the eighteenth century but adapted them for the conditions of the nineteenth. This broad modernization of the British law had significant implications for the regulation of sex between men and highlights the ways in which different forms of law enforcement brought different behaviors under public scrutiny and judgment. It also reveals the priorities of upper-class men, as they adjusted the laws, especially in the 1820s, to make the regulation of sex between men conform to their ideas of morality and reputation.

Many of the features of the eighteenth-century system of British law were justified by reference to "English liberty." The freedom of Englishmen was secured, it was argued, by limiting the direct control of the state over mechanisms for law enforcement. Magistrates at the parish level were gentry of sufficient income to support themselves independently as they carried out their unpaid official duties. All those who enforced the law, from the sheriff to the watchmen, were also unpaid property holders, and prosecutions were privately initiated and financed.[1] The minimal institutions that existed for detention, including prisons, gaols, and houses of correction, were expected to be self-supporting and existed only for holding misdemeanor offenders or those awaiting execution or transportation.

To make up for this scanty enforcement apparatus, punishments were based on the principle of maximum severity, relying on the specter of execution as the primary deterrent to crime. Executions were attended by large crowds, and descriptions of them were printed in pamphlets and in other news sources, where the moral lessons to be drawn were supposedly rendered in high relief. For lesser offenses, the pillory was used, allowing popular anger to be vented on the publicly displayed criminal. The popular elements at both executions and the pillory most often served the purposes of the state, although the reactions of the crowd could not be controlled, especially when the conviction was controversial. The ability of the crowd to turn against the spectacle of punishment was also seen as a potential check on the abuse of state power; this limitation, along with the minimal tools for incarceration, law enforcement, and prosecutions granted to the central government, was seen as a way to safeguard the benefits gained by the gentry at the time of the Glorious Revolution.[2]

The eighteenth-century punishment of sodomites followed the general patterns of law enforcement. Prosecutions were private, rare, and thus often sensational. The best-known eighteenth-century raids on molly houses received a great deal of publicity precisely because this was the intent of those who carried them out. Hiring their own constables to infiltrate molly houses, the Society for the Reformation of Manners paid for the prosecution of such cases from their founding in 1690 to their first disbanding in 1738. In 1707, 1709, 1726, and 1763, the society was responsible for the arrests of groups of men ranging in size from four to fifty.[3] Those who financed these and other moves against homosexual behavior did so in part through their desire to publicly shame the government into greater action against the molly houses and other visible elements of the homosexual subculture of eighteenth-century London and to call for the strengthening of English manhood and English morality against such internal threats.[4] When deciding which cases to pursue, prosecutors chose the most sensational material to present to the public. In an era when punishments were severe, juries were reluctant to convict defendants in any but the most egregious cases. In one of the most famous incidents, the society sent in agents into Mother Clap's Molly House, where they slowly gained the trust of the patrons over time and were eventually allowed into the private rooms. The bacchanal scenes of sex between men they observed were later described in court. Such tactics ensured that the sodomites presented to the public for prosecution seemed far removed from the experience of average, respectable Englishmen, and clear moral contrasts could be drawn.

Sometimes these tactics backfired. The use of spies, even for entrapping men engaging in immoral behavior, was deeply unpopular. The society was roundly criticized for this and other tactics, especially after 1726, when public anger was raised, during a prosecution of more than forty men, over the methods used by the society's special constables. The inability of the society to sustain the private subscriptions that financed its prosecutions led to the collapse of this sort of inquisitorial activity, and the number of court cases related to sex between men dropped precipitously. In the twenty-one years between 1730 and 1751, only twenty-two cases with any connection to sodomy were heard in the Old Bailey in London; between 1749 and 1790, only two men were executed for sodomy in all of England.[5] The English hostility to any form of domestic spying persisted, hanging over the Metropolitan Police in its first years of operation. The handful of covert police operations to entrap men seeking sex with men attracted enough public condemnation to end such practices at an early stage.

Because the surviving evidence, preserved through law-enforcement records, seemed to highlight the separateness of men who had sex with men, scholars of eighteenth-century England have emphasized the development of a distinct homosexual subculture in London. By contrast, the pattern of law enforcement in the early nineteenth century produced a much greater volume of evidence relating to men having sex with men. Because of the lack of an inquisitorial or investigative police force, and because the early Metropolitan Police needed to avoid offending the public any more than its very presence already did, most of the evidence preserved related not to raids on private facilities but to the disruption of more casual sexual acts. These occurred in more accessible public spaces and between men who seem for the most part to have been unconnected to any subculture but were well connected to family and community networks.

This distinction is not cut and dried: we still gain glimpses into what seems like a homosexual subculture in the early nineteenth-century material, and the eighteenth-century records contain many reported instances of the arrest and prosecution of seemingly unexceptional men in unexceptional locales. Therefore, actual sexual practices do not seem to have changed abruptly in the early nineteenth century; rather, the change was to the primary method by which sex between men was publicly represented. There is a shift from the public image of the sodomite of the eighteenth century, who was used as a foil for defining normative masculinity, to the image of the more average man that dominates the public representations of sex between men in the early to mid-nineteenth century.[6] The Vere Street molly-house raid of 1810 was the last instantiation of the eighteenth-century pattern: as new law-enforcement approaches took hold, beginning around 1822, such events were supplanted in the public record by smaller stories of more ordinary men.

Legal reform became necessary because of the pressures that developed as British society became more urban, more capitalist, and more invested in enforcing a market-based notion of property rights. The number of crimes carrying the death penalty steadily increased during the eighteenth century, from 50 in 1688 to 225 by 1815.[7] Much physical violence still went unpunished: the principal aim of criminal law was the preservation of private property. By 1820, stealing fish from a pond or gathering wood on what had once been common land could cost an individual his life. Juries, however, were often reluctant to impose the ultimate penalty for small infractions against property rights, and "pious perjury" became just one of the methods used to avoid sentencing an individual to death for stealing. In such instances, juries would find an individual guilty of the theft, but then value the worth of the articles stolen to be just under the threshold that would trigger the death penalty. In one famous case from the period, a jury valued twenty-three guineas stolen from a house to be worth only thirty-nine shillings, just under the forty-shilling threshold.[8]

Ideally, the prerogative of mercy was intended to rest not with the juries but rather with the upper-class judges, who since 1718 had had the ability to commute a sentence of death to a sentence of transportation.[9] It was argued that the judge's exercise of mercy through this application of "secondary punishments" instilled deference and respect for both the law and the social order. From the 1770s on, the percentage of those pardoned began to increase, so that by the 1810s on average

85 percent of men and women sentenced to death had their executions reprieved in this way.[10] To those opposed to the system, this pattern made just punishment seem more a matter of chance than the rational outcome of a functional system. Reformers also highlighted the arbitrariness of the pillory. Because the actual pain and injury inflicted on a pilloried offender depended on the size and mood of the crowd of the day, this form of punishment did not represent a rational, measured, or consistent application of the law.

There were many potential avenues of reform. Efforts in the Enlightenment tradition to think systematically about the criminal law began on the Continent with Montesquieu's 1748 *De l'esprit des lois,* and continued, more comprehensively, with Cesare Beccaria's 1764 *Dei delitti e delle pene.* Montesquieu's work represented the first attempt to categorize criminal acts according to their severity and to create a corresponding scale of punishments. Beccaria further theorized methods to rationalize criminal law and, like Montesquieu, denounced the principle of maximum severity in assigning punishments.[11] Aside from the cruel and arbitrary abuse of power that these penalties often represented, Beccaria argued, they were also ineffective deterrents to crime because of the reluctance of many to prosecute or convict when the sentence would be death. The writings of Montesquieu and Beccaria were especially influential in discrediting the excessive use of the death penalty on the Continent, and they were the inspiration for law reforms that substantially reduced the number of capital crimes in Sweden, Prussia, Austria, and Russia before 1789.[12]

Until the 1820s, however, England's legal system was not influenced by these trends. The laws passed in Parliament were hardly influenced either by the Continental writings that circulated in England or by indigenous works on reform, such as William Eden's 1771 *Principles of the Penal Law.* This situation led some reformers in Parliament, such as Sir Samuel Romilly, to declare that the current exercise of justice was closer to a lottery than a rational system, and that the prestige of the law was damaged by such a disjuncture between the sentences handed down and those implemented. Romilly was among the first to seriously advocate for reform, although his twenty-year effort resulted in the repeal of only three minor capital statutes before his death in 1819.[13]

The British reluctance to curtail the use of the death penalty was tied up with the gentry's jealous hold over the local dispensation of justice, as the minimal infrastructure in the areas of both policing and incarceration would need to be changed before such changes could be implemented. At the start of his career as home secretary, Robert Peel tried to create a new police force, only to have the idea defeated in Parliament. A committee set up by Peel to study the prospect of a national system of policing presented its report in March 1822 to the House of Commons, which unambiguously rejected the idea. The committee report argued that any gain in public order would be outweighed by the loss of "that perfect freedom of action and exemption from interference" that Englishmen had enjoyed and grown to expect.[14]

Some innovations in incarceration were also attempted, with nearly as little success. The first national penitentiary, Millbank, was approved by the Tory government in 1810 and constructed on a site only a short distance from the Houses of Parliament. In size and scale, Millbank was unlike any other prison ever constructed in Britain: it was capable of holding more than one thousand prisoners and based in part on the panopticon design of Jeremy Bentham. Yet from the start the new prison was plagued with problems. Its design still allowed for the communal holding of prisoners, and consequently it suffered a series of riots. In 1818, order was restored only by the armed intervention of the Bow Street Runners, and in 1826–27, rioting prisoners demanded to be transferred to the remaining prison hulks rather than remain in Millbank. Poorly built on marshy land, the prison was closed temporarily in 1823 to stem outbreaks of scurvy and contagious diarrhea. The inability to control the prisoners was exacerbated by the difficulty of finding qualified and competent staff, contributing to the assessment that Millbank's approach to holding large numbers of prisoners was an "unmitigated disaster."[15] By the early 1840s, Parliament decreed that the facility should be used only as a departure point for convicts sentenced to transportation.[16]

Not until the construction of Pentonville in 1842 did a national prison fully incorporate the liberal vision of transforming the individual through incarceration.[17] Many of the individuals who argued for this new approach in England were Evangelicals and utilitarians. Evangelicals supported such plans in part because of their belief that spiritual salvation could result from ordering the physical environment of an individual; utilitarians and other rationalist reformers felt that the individual was born morally neutral and therefore would be susceptible to reform through proper training. In Pentonville, institutional space was designed so that prisoners were kept at regimented work routines in total isolation from one another. For the inmates, this and other versions of the "separate system" were among the most hated forms of punishment, and the length of isolation was progressively lessened to reduce the number of inmates who were driven mad.[18] Although the houses of correction earlier in the century also enforced a regimented work routine, those efforts were minor and piecemeal when compared to the fully implemented "separate" or "silent" systems that dominated incarceration in the second half of the nineteenth century. The willingness to create such total institutions, and the optimistic belief in the ability to remake the individual that inspired and sustained them, though, were foreign to the upper-class men controlling the British government in the 1820s, and this skepticism was one reason for the failure of earlier experiments such as Millbank.

The success of such new institutions was not a prerequisite, however, for the systemization of the criminal code that occurred in the 1820s, which had to do only with condition and organization of the written law itself. The form in which the law was written was considered to be an impediment to its effective implementation. Criminal statutes were not consolidated into a single body of legislation; often they were buried in legislation primarily concerned with other matters. The boundaries between statute law, common law, and legal behavior were unclear. Many defended this state of affairs. The inclination of the prime minister, Lord Liverpool, had long been to support traditional arrangements and institutions and to resist the calls for even incremental reform. In this view he was aligned with Tory intellectuals such as Edmund Burke, who argued that challenges to the individual elements of the law weakened the authority of the whole edifice.

Despite Liverpool's opposition to reform, he headed an administration that had the political strength to carry it out. Liverpool was the longest-serving prime minister of the nineteenth century. The era of liberal Toryism, from 1822 to 1828, saw resistance to change in some key policy areas diminish as the economy recovered from the dislocations that followed the Napoleonic wars.[19] The ascendancy of able ministers, including George Canning at the Foreign Office, William Huskisson at the Board of Trade, and Robert Peel at the Home Office, also contributed to these shifts in policy. Although Peel failed to institute a police force in 1822, he continued his efforts to reform the legal code, building on the recommendations of the earlier 1819 Parliamentary select committee on legal reform.[20] March 1824 saw the creation in the House of Commons of a new committee charged with consolidating and amending English criminal law, as "there had hitherto been no regular system for the reduction of those statutes into any order or methodical form, [and] they had at present attained to a considerable bulk, and were in a state of the greatest possible confusion."[21]

The most radical reformers hoped that this reform would also encompass the system of punishments itself, but Peel aimed to diffuse this radical pressure by having the government push through a more modest reform. Under Peel's program, the miscellaneous statutes relating to a given crime, such as forgery, larceny, or assault, were grouped together in the new consolidated criminal law. The death penalty was preserved for most of crimes, but its use was regulated and rationalized. The Whig administration elected after the 1832 Reform Act kept Peel's consolidated law code but reduced the use of the death penalty, so that by the end of the 1830s the number of capital crimes had been reduced by more than 90 percent.[22] The regular use of execution or lifelong transportation as punishments for minor offenses was curtailed by the end of the 1830s, and the following years saw a new emphasis on rehabilitation as a goal of incarceration.

Peel presented the broad outlines of the committee's proposed changes to the criminal law in a speech to the House of Commons in March 1826 and subsequently introduced the four separate bills that embodied them. The Larceny (England) Act and another bill relating to malicious injuries to property were introduced and passed in 1827. The Offences against the Person Act was made law in 1828, and the act consolidating the laws on forgery was passed in 1830. These four acts comprised the substance of some three hundred previous statutes, which constituted more than four-fifths of the English criminal law. Although two of the new acts—the 1827 Larceny (England) Act and the 1828 Offences against the Person Act—addressed sexual acts between men, such provisions were only a very small portion of the overall legislation.

Although the acts were largely consolidations without amendments, as their proponents intended, some alterations were made in the law regulating sex between men. One of these changes became evident during Robert Reekspear's trial on sodomy charges in 1832. The case against Reekspear was brought by a fourteen-year-old boy who accused the older man of forcing him to engage in sexual acts against his will. In summing up the case for the jury, the presiding judge, Justice Gaselee, "left it to the jury to say whether there had been penetration, stating that, if so, the crime was complete."[23] But there was some controversy within the courtroom as to whether penetration alone was sufficient to convict with the death penalty, because under the Elizabethan sodomy statute, which had been the law for well over two hundred years, both penetration and emission were required. In the face of challenges to this effect in the courtroom, Justice Gaselee began to doubt his own reasoning enough to stay the execution until his advice to the jury could be reviewed.[24] The reviewing panel, led by the lord chief justice, upheld the death sentence for penetration alone, but the dissent of two justices on the panel denied a unanimous decision on what should have been a basic point of law.

The confusion among the judges stemmed from a provision in the 1828 Offences against the Person Act. The 1828 act repealed the Elizabethan sodomy statute and replaced it with one of very similar wording but which no longer stipulated that proof of emission was necessary for a sodomy conviction. This alteration made the charge of sodomy easier to prove, as at least one writer of the day observed with dismay.[25] It also distanced the sodomy law from its original association with the ecclesiastical concern with the physical waste of semen and other nonprocreative sexual acts; the statute was now more closely allied with the moral objection held by most upper-class men to sexual acts and sexual desires between men.[26] Despite the significant implications of the change, no objections were raised in Parliament when the act was passed. Changes to the law regarding sex between men were often passed in Parliament without debate, and as a part of legislation that was primarily concerned with other matters.

Although some legal officials had earlier questioned whether emission was a necessary element of the crime of sodomy, that standard had been followed as long as it had been a part of the law. In 1811 John Parker, a sailor, was convicted at court-martial of sodomy even though there was no evidence of *injectio seminis*. The judges in his case felt their decision to convict was justified, "as they make no distinction between the moral and legal guilt of a person tried for this offence, and feeling also the necessity of making some severe examples to check a crime which . . . is thought to gain ground in the naval part of the community."[27] On reviewing the case, however, the attorney general and solicitor general rejected this reasoning. In their joint statement on the legality of the decision, they observed that "the court martial did not proceed on the belief that what the law requires was proved but they chose to set up a law of their own in direct opposition to the opinion of the Judge Advocate on the question of the law."[28] The overturning of Parker's conviction underscores the fact that the government upheld the requirements of the law even when they were felt to be archaic.

Although removal of the emission requirement significantly broadened the legal definition of sodomy, it was not the most significant change in the regulation of sexual acts between men. That distinction belongs to provisions within the 1827 Larceny (England) Act. Within that act, sodomy was subsumed under a broader definition of "infamous crime," which became the most common legal term for a spectrum of acts related to sexual desire between men. The "infamous crime" clause of the 1827 act began with the language of the Elizabethan and future 1828 sodomy legislation but then went far beyond it. It read:

> IX. And, for defining what shall be an infamous Crime, within the Meaning of this Act, be it enacted, That the abominable Crime of Buggery, committed either with Mankind or with Beast, and every Assault with Intent to commit the said abominable Crime, and every attempt or Endeavor to commit the said abominable crime, and every Solicitation, Persuasion, Promise, or Threat offered or made to any Person, whereby to move or induce such Person to commit or Permit the said abominable Crime, shall be deemed to be an infamous Crime within the Meaning of this Act.

This terminology marked a major reconceptualization of the offense. Similar phrasing had been used in 1825 legislation pertaining to threats of extortion, but now, as a consequence of the consolidation process, it became a general definition that was inserted and invoked in a range of subsequent legislation.[29] Not only was the act of sodomy criminalized, but so too were attempts at, solicitation of, persuasion to, and even promises of sodomy. The law now prohibited not only a whole new spectrum of acts but also potentially even the language that might suggest such acts.[30]

This legislation marked a significant break with earlier statute law, but it does not seem to have greatly affected the common-law practice of prosecuting cases of attempted sodomy and unnatural assault. The trial testimony that survives from these cases does not indicate a significant change in the circumstances that led to prosecutions after the late 1820s, and prosecutions were already increasing in number. In the criminal courts of London and Middlesex, the number of attempted sodomy cases averaged fewer than two per year for the whole of the eighteenth century, and in the first decade of the nineteenth century, still, on average, fewer than five attempted sodomy cases per year reached the criminal courts of London.[31] By the 1810s this figure had risen to an average of eleven, with twenty-nine per year in all the criminal courts of England and Wales. In the 1820s it rose again to fifteen cases per year in the London criminal courts and thirty-six for England and

Wales. For the 1830s, the numbers were thirty for London and sixty-three for England and Wales. Conviction rates for attempted sodomy remained above 50 percent in London until the end of the 1820s, and the sentence, which had ranged from as long as four years to as little as three months and three days, stabilized at either six months or one year, depending on the circumstances, in the 1820s.[32]

By the mid-1830s the average sentence for attempted sodomy had increased to two years, partly as the result of legislation affecting misdemeanor sentences in general. The Hard Labour Act of 1822 specified a magistrate's options in mandating forced labor as a part of a misdemeanor sentence, and the Offences against the Person Act of 1828 stipulated two years' imprisonment, with or without hard labor, as the maximum sentence for a long list of enumerated misdemeanors, including "assault with intent to commit felony." A two-year sentence with or without hard labor eventually became the standard penalty for unnatural-assault cases, although it took some years before the average sentence in these cases approached these new maximums.

Through such changes, statute law incorporated aspects of established common-law practice. This is a common pattern within British law and is evident also in Henry Labouchère's famous amendment to the Criminal Law Amendment Act of 1885.[33] Among the innovations associated with the 1885 amendment was the definition of admissible witnesses. The designation "in public or in private" was a reference to the fact that under English law, a private act was one not witnessed by an uninvolved individual. The phrase was meant to ensure that these acts could still be prosecuted even without an uninvolved witness.[34] But even this change was only another case of statute law catching up with common-law practice. Individuals involved in sexual acts between men had regularly given evidence against their partners in various circumstances, and these "private" acts led to conviction just as frequently as the "public" acts witnessed by an uninvolved third party.[35] The 1885 amendment also reflected previous practice in that it was part of a larger piece of legislation and was not debated separately on its own merits.[36]

Long before the Labouchère Amendment, then, the attempted-sodomy charge, carrying roughly a two-year sentence, was easily the most common rubric under which acts of sex between men were brought before the London criminal courts. Between 1811 and 1860, there were 864 trials for attempted sodomy held in the London criminal courts, compared with only 116 cases of sodomy.[37] One reason for this disparity was that the proof needed for an attempted-sodomy charge was easily acquired or invented. Henry Webb, for example, spent two nights in a Bow Street holding cell after Thomas Addy pulled him toward an officer in Covent Garden and said, "I give this gentleman in charge for an indecent assault."[38] No further evidence was needed to hold a man on such charges.

The court and newspaper records consistently show that it was easy for one man to press charges against another after only a brief encounter in public space. Joseph Scott told the court that he was simply asking directions from George Webb when he approached him in Hyde Park around 12:30 A.M. on a Saturday night. Webb's version of the story provoked Scott to yell at his accuser in the courtroom, "I did not stop you in the park and ask you * * * and undo your flap."[39] William White faced numerous questions as to why he followed a soldier off the lit path in Hyde Park after the soldier had "laid his hands on * * * outside my trowsers [sic]."[40] In neither case was there more than each man's word and previous reputation to support his version of events. But little more was needed to initiate a prosecution.

Criminal cases typically involved wealthier individuals prosecuting those lower down the social scale, in part because for the whole of the nineteenth century, four out of five indictable committals were for non-violent offenses against property.[41] By contrast, the surviving documentation shows that a high percentage of unnatural-assault cases involved men of modest means, including soldiers, laborers, apprentices, and tradesmen, prosecuting those higher on the social scale. Attempted sodomy seems unique in English criminal law for the high percentage of cases that involve working-class men bringing charges against upper- and middle-class men.

Yet the same period also witnessed the rapid evolution of a related area of the law that decidedly favored wealthier men: the laws concerning the threat to accuse another man of an infamous crime. Although not formally applied nearly as often as they were invoked as a courtroom defense, they did restore an advantage to men of property. They provided a means by which wealthier men could convict those who accused them of attempted unnatural assault or sodomy and also protect themselves from prosecution on the original charge.

These extortion laws generally carried more severe penalties than those for sodomy or attempted sodomy. Although sodomy still formally carried the death penalty, and in practice was punished with a ten-year sentence after the mid-1830s, the two-year sentence for attempted sodomy was more often applied. At the same time, however, the sentence for threatening to accuse another man of an infamous crime was reset at seven to ten years' transportation. This difference seems to indicate that to the upper-class men who still controlled the legal system, the slander to a man's reputation caused by the accusation of sex between men was considered a graver crime than a homosexual advance.

As with the attempted-sodomy charge, extortion cases centering on the threat to accuse another man of unnatural acts predate the legislative changes of the 1820s and 1830s.[42] Anthony Simpson's comparative study of rape and sodomy convictions has shown that extortion based on such threats occurred in eighteenth-century London as well. Simpson's work not only describes individual and opportunistic extortions but also examines the evidence for the existence of organized groups who extorted money from men in this way. Simpson finds that many victims paid off their accusers rather than face the publicity of a prosecution, so that "police could rarely combat this sort of activity, and the extortionist could operate with every expectation of success."[43] The most regularly used legal tool to combat these extortions in the eighteenth century was a 1707 judicial decision that made it possible to consider such threats as misdemeanors. In a 1779 case covered in the *Annual Register,* Lord Mansfield observed that this was a "specious mode of robbery of late grown very common. . . . God only knows what numberless robberies of this kind would have been perpetrated by these detestable wretches on timorous minds" if he and his fellow judges had not upheld the principle that robbing a man using the threat of accusing him of "an 'unnatural crime' was equivalent to an actual violence."[44]

A judicial decision in 1805 eliminated this tool for fighting such extortions, making it necessary to employ less effective legal remedies. The next best way to prosecute extortionists was through the 1722 Black Act, which had provisions that made demanding money by threat in an anonymous letter a form of robbery. Even after the expansion of the threatening-letters provisions in 1754 and 1757, though, they applied only in a very limited range of cases, as most extortion threats were spoken rather than written.[45] Thus, during the first decades of the nineteenth century, as the number of prosecutions for sodomy and attempted sodomy was steadily increasing, the law was becoming less conducive to the instigation of countercharges of extortion.

It was in this context that the laws relating to the sending of threatening letters received their most substantial revision and for the first time became relevant to spoken as well as written threats to accuse of an infamous crime. An 1823 act removed the requirement that such letters be anonymous, but much more important, it also "defined a wide range of extortion demands made in person, and now considered these a species of attempted robbery."[46] The 1823 act repealed and replaced provisions of the eighteenth-century legislation that governed assaults with intent to commit robbery and expanded the definition of such assailants to include those who "maliciously threaten to accuse another person of any Crime punishable by Law with Death, Transportation or Pillory, or of any infamous crime, with a View or Intent to extort or gain Money."[47] The sentence for such acts was reduced from death to transportation for life, or no less than seven years.[48]

In an early case tried under these new provisions of the law, one newspaper report observed that this case was "deserving particular attention . . . being the first instance of a prosecution under the late statute (4 George IV)."[49] One indication of the importance of these changes is the fact that a court case stemming from them was covered in the *Annual Register* of 1825. Between 1820 and 1833, four separate cases centering on sex between men appeared in issues of the *Annual Register*, dealing with either recent changes in the law or the trial of a famous individual under those laws. After 1833 no trial centering on acts of sex between men appeared in the *Annual Register* until 1871.[50]

The 1825 trial of Charles Holder and David Gardener centered on their attempt to extort money from the Rev. Edmund Cartwright by threatening to accuse him of an infamous crime.[51] The report in the *Annual Register* seems to offer an object lesson in how to use the laws against extortion to subvert an impending charge of attempted sodomy. The *Annual Register* report did not dwell on the evidence presented by Holder and Gardener but instead showed how Cartwright was able to discredit them. After consulting with his lawyer, Cartwright arranged for Holder and Gardener to meet him at his house, with constables concealed in the next room to overhear the conversation. Cartwright persuaded the men to admit their attempted extortion by asking a series of leading questions. The *Annual Register* reported the conversation as follows:

> "What could induce you to write such a letter, which you must know to be untrue?" said Cartwright. Gardener said "It is all true; I was close by where you were, and I heard and saw every thing. After you were gone, I

went up to Holder, who was crying like a child, and he then told me what
had passed." Cartwright repeated that the charge wasn't true, and then
asked how much the two men wanted for their silence. Gardener said that
"the same thing lately happened to another gentleman, whom he, witness,
knew very well, and was a rich man, and he gave him £50."[52]

After this, the constables came out from their hiding place and arrested
Gardener and Holder. Cartwright had not only successfully established
a counterclaim against his accusers but also virtually ensured his own
acquittal on an unnatural-assault charge. By proving, with witnesses,
that Gardener and Holder were extortionists, Cartwright destroyed
their credibility as witnesses against him. When Cartwright's attorney
tried to offer further evidence of his client's innocence, "the learned
judge said that such evidence was quite unnecessary, the utter false-
hood of the charge having already been demonstrated." The *Annual
Register* summary ended by stating "the jury immediately found the
prisoners guilty," with Gardener and Holder sentenced by Mr. Baron
Graham to transportation for life.[53]

The new law clearly improved the chances for men of property to
face down an extortionist, and it may have been inspired by events
of very personal significance to the men who drafted the legislation.
The year before the passage of the new law, one of the most prominent members of Britain's political class faced just such an extortion
attempt. Lord Castlereagh was the British foreign secretary from 1812
to 1822 and the architect of British policy at the Congress of Vienna.
In August 1822, Castlereagh confessed to George IV that he was being
blackmailed over the accusation that he had committed sexual acts
with another man, and less than two weeks later, he cut his own throat
at his country estate.[54] If Castlereagh's suicide influenced Peel's decision to amend the law shortly thereafter, or Parliament's decision to
pass the changes, this was not recorded in the relevant parliamentary
debates, and yet the timing may not be coincidental.

The influence of these changes on courtroom contests involving sex
between men was profound. Discussion of the validity of the initial
claim of attempted sodomy was always complicated and often compromised in the courtroom when a man countered it with an accusation of extortion, even if no formal charge was made to this effect.
The younger and poorer men to whom those with greater wealth often
turned for sex were particularly susceptible to the offer of a week's
or even a year's wages in return for silence, and the burden of proof
was often placed on them in the courtroom to demonstrate that they

had not asked for or accepted money. Disproving such allegations was critical for a working-class man, because evidence that he had accepted payment for his silence left him open to prosecution, even if he had been the object of an unwanted sexual advance.[55]

The outcome of a courtroom contest that pitted one man's word against another's often hinged on who had gone to the police first, but this situation in itself favored the propertied. Working-class resentment of police forces in their neighborhoods made it unlikely that men would turn to either the watch or the Metropolitan Police, especially in the early stages of a dispute. They were much more likely to follow older patterns of conflict resolution in their communities, which often involved seeking face-to-face redress. What might seem to a working-class man a negotiated exchange to resolve a dispute could be interpreted in court as an act that would condemn him to transportation for a decade and rob him of the power to prosecute the man who had initially made a sexual advance against him.

In addition to the changes described above, it was also in the 1820s that the definition of *infamous crime* was both expanded and more strongly identified with the regulation of sexual acts between men. Before 1825 only felonies were infamous crimes, sodomy among them. The primary purpose of the 1825 Threatening Letters Act was to revise the meaning of the term *infamous crime* as it had been used in the 1823 legislation discussed above.[56] It decreed that "not only every Crime now by Law deemed infamous by reason of the Person convicted thereof being thereby rendered incompetent to give Evidence, but also that each of the several Offences hereinafter mentioned shall be deemed and taken to be an infamous Crime." The only crimes mentioned after that point, though, were "every Assault with Intent to commit any Rape, or the abominable Crimes of Sodomy or Buggery." Thus attempted sodomy and attempted rape, both misdemeanors, were now legally classified as infamous crimes.[57] This step toward making *infamous crime* a designation for acts of sexual assault between men was taken further when the 1827 Larceny (England) Act, discussed and quoted above, incorporated a definition of infamous crime that centered exclusively on sexual acts between men.

The impetus for the Threatening Letters Act of 1825 came directly from a controversial court case of the year before that ultimately had to be decided before the review panel of London judges. The case centered on a letter that Thomas Hickman sent to his landlord, John Fabling, in the midst of a dispute between the two men. It read:

Sir,—You have taken possession of all my property and disposed of it in a way very disgraceful to man or manhood, and you have ruined an industrious man and an innocent family to serve your friend Tom Hoar, and make yourself look great; but you should have recollected who you had got to contend with, and what I can bring against you, and though it was years ago, I can indict you for it. You well know you have several times made overtures to me, of which I can indict you for sodomy, you have done all you can to bring disgrace and ruin on my family, and I can bring more disgrace on you than you have in your power to bring on me. . . . Yours, &c. Thomas Hickman.[58]

Hickman had been convicted for sending Fabling a letter threatening to accuse him of an infamous crime, but the panel of London judges reluctantly overturned the decision. Though sympathetic to Fabling, they noted that Hickman had charged him only with making overtures to commit sodomy. Such an overture might constitute attempted sodomy as it was regularly defined in the courtroom under common law, but attempted sodomy was not an infamous crime under the 1823 act. It was precisely this sort of exception that the 1825 Threatening Letters Act was meant to eliminate, and the points of law in question were discussed by the lord chief justice and Robert Peel shortly after the Hickman case.

The 1825 act was one of the few bills passed in the nineteenth century that exclusively addressed acts related to sex between men, rather than dealing with such issues in sections of much larger bills. There was no parliamentary debate over its passage, though, as Peel brought it before Parliament along with another criminal-law bill and requested that the two be debated at the same time. Peel introduced the threatening-letters bill first, stating that under the current law, sending a letter threatening to charge a person with sodomy was a felony, because sodomy itself was a felony. Yet because attempted sodomy was only a misdemeanor, sending a letter threatening to charge someone with attempted sodomy was also only a misdemeanor. Peel was reported to have said: "Now, without entering into any detail on the subject, it was enough to say that, in a moral point of view, the attempt and the offense were alike infamous, and the danger from a charge of either was to be equally apprehended."[59] This logic could have been applied much more widely, to include letters dealing with accusations of crimes such as attempted murder or attempted arson, but it was not. According to the records, Peel did not say anything further on the matter, and the subsequent discussion focused on another bill introduced at the same time.[60]

The 1825 legislation made attempted sodomy an infamous crime for the first time, and it was also the first occasion on which attempted sodomy was explicitly defined. In what seems a direct response to the circumstances of the Hickman case, the 1825 act included not only attempted sodomy and attempted rape within the definition of infamous crime, but also "every Attempt . . . every Solicitation, Persuasion, Promise, Threat or Menace" of rape or sodomy. Hickman's letter, after all, had described Fabling only as having made overtures, not as actually having attempted a physical act. Thus the more exacting and expansive definition of attempted sodomy later incorporated into the 1827 Larceny (England) Act seems to have had its roots in this case.

After 1825 any communication in which a man contemplated accepting payment in return for his silence about a sexual advance from another man had the potential to make him a felon. Such counter-charges were not often prosecuted, but cases based on them generally succeeded when they went to trial. It was not until 1838 that the annual returns of Criminal Offences began to separate cases of extortion for threatening to accuse of an infamous crime from other categories of extortion, but these statistics tell a revealing story. Between 1838 and 1860, only thirty-three cases of threatening to accuse of an infamous crime were heard before the London criminal courts, but of those cases 84 percent ended in conviction, with three-quarters of the defendants receiving sentences of ten years or more. For all of England and Wales between 1838 and 1870, there were ninety-seven such cases, with 73 percent ending in convictions carrying equally severe sentences. This contrasts significantly with a conviction rate of only 42 percent for attempted sodomy and 28 percent for sodomy cases in London between 1838 and 1858. Even though the number of cases of threatening to accuse of an infamous crime represented less than 3 percent of the total number of criminal trials for sodomy and attempted sodomy for England and Wales between 1838 and 1870, they nevertheless provided wealthier men with a highly effective tool for avoiding unnatural-assault convictions.[61] In one of the several threatening-to-accuse cases that occurred in 1825, "the Judge, in summing up, remarked upon the increase of crimes of this nature since the passing of the act of the 4th Geo. IV."[62]

Although statistics like these are helpful in discerning patterns in the regulation of sex between men, they have many limitations. They describe the process of constructing a new framework of state control more accurately than they represent changes in the behavior they purported to track. The availability of regular and relatively consistent statistics on crime and punishment in England and Wales, beginning in 1805, is itself a result of the Home Office's efforts to gather information needed to counter a perceived crime wave. For most categories of crime, including those involving sexual acts between men, national statistics do show a rising number of cases in the early 1800s, but it is unlikely that these numbers represent any real increase in sexual behavior between men.

One thing that does seem certain is that the recorded cases represent only a small portion of the relevant behavior. In the absence of regular public prosecutions, these cases began with the decisions by individuals to make use of the courts in instances where they would not previously have done so, and this was a learned response. Even when an individual chose to pursue legal redress, a substantial percentage of such prosecutions failed when the police, the magistrate, or the grand jury decided there was insufficient evidence on which to proceed. Prosecutions lapsed or never began if an individual could not pay the legal costs, even after legislation was passed in the early nineteenth century providing for the reimbursement of some of the plaintiff's costs. Between 1810 and 1870, 24 percent of all sodomy and 33 percent of all attempted-sodomy cases faltered between the time they were first heard before a magistrate and their scheduled appearance before the criminal courts, either because a grand jury rejected the case on its merits or the prosecutor failed to proceed.[63]

No such exact figures exist for the abandonment of other potential prosecutions at different points in the process, although scattered evidence indicates that many incidents that could have resulted in criminal trials for unnatural assault were instead disposed of summarily before the police courts. Examples include the release in 1830 of James Byrne, a clerk in the audit office of India House, with only a five-pound fine. Byrne had been arrested by a police officer on charges of unnatural assault, but the magistrate of the Grosvenor Square police court chose to impose only the penalty for common assault.[64] James Caldwell, a Presbyterian minister, was fined only five pounds by a police-court magistrate, although he was accused of indecently assaulting several men one Monday night.[65] At least ten men arrested in the spring of 1830 by police on charges of unnatural assault had their cases disposed of summarily as common assault before magistrates, and they were therefore not recorded in that year's official statistics of sexual crimes between men.[66] However, examples like this can indicate only that such outcomes were possible; they tell us little about the frequency with which charges were reduced and summary decisions made.[67]

The impact of the Vagrancy Acts is equally difficult to discern. These acts greatly increased the power of the London watch and later the Metropolitan Police to detain individuals deemed suspicious. The offense of loitering with intent to commit a felony had been introduced in 1783 with reference to private property and was extended in 1802 to streets and public places. The 1822 Vagrancy Act empowered police to arrest prostitutes and other individuals whom they considered to be wandering about and unable to give a satisfactory account of themselves, with such individuals classified as "idle and disorderly persons," subject to imprisonment for up to one month of hard labor.[68] This earlier legislation was consolidated and enhanced in the 1824, 1834, and 1844 Vagrancy Acts. Scholars such as Anna Clark cite the later two modifications as being largely responsible for making any woman on the street subject to arrest by the police for "suspicious loitering."[69]

Although the Vagrancy Acts certainly suppressed various forms of urban street life in early nineteenth-century Britain, it is not clear that they were used in the regulation of sexually suggestive behavior between men in public spaces. Police compelled suspicious men to move along from the parks, picture-shop windows, urinals, and other public sites, but such coercion rarely resulted in written records. We know that James Simpson's arrest under the Vagrancy Acts was related to sexual advances between men only because he ran afoul of the law at a later date on more serious charges, at which time the details of his earlier three-month sentence for being "a rogue and a vagabond" were publicly recounted.[70] Because arrests made under the Vagrancy Acts were subject at most to summary judgments, the London cases based on them never moved beyond the various police courts, and in general, newspaper accounts of police-court activities gave almost no attention to the violations of the Vagrancy Acts.

Lack of newspaper coverage is a serious handicap to understanding the impact of these laws, as newspapers provide the best surviving documentation for proceedings in police courts. The few official records of cases before the police courts in the first half of the nineteenth century, such as a register kept by the Home Office of selected daily cases from 1830 to 1839, list only a small fraction of cases. Convictions under the vagrancy laws were listed as just that, with no additional details given on the nature of the infraction.[71] Before the 1855 Criminal Justice Act required the depositions from summary convictions to be preserved, records were destroyed, and regular daily summaries of proceedings at individual police courts did not begin until 1877. Although newspapers are not entirely reliable guides to events in these courtrooms, they are often the only sources.

Even with all of these gaps in the records, for both the police courts and other levels of the justice system, the written records generated by legal reforms in the 1820s provide insights into the reshaping of the state's role in the regulation of sex between men. The evidence from the 1820s adds weight to the assumption that the upper-class men who framed the laws avoided talking about this behavior publicly, and it also indicates that these men were especially concerned about how public disclosure of sex between men would affect a man's reputation, setting the penalty for making accusations of such practices much higher than that for "unnatural assault" itself. These laws were not revised for the rest of the nineteenth century, even after the enfranchisement of middle-class men in 1832 and working-class men in 1867 and 1884. It was therefore in the period when upper-class men still fully controlled Parliament that the state's regulation of sex between men took shape. These changes were not informed by a liberal vision—there was no hope of reforming the sodomite in Pentonville as one might remake the petty thief—but rather by the perspective of liberal Toryism, incorporating the British upper-class masculine concern for the importance of reputation.

In making these changes, the British upper class was once again going against the Continental trend in legal reform. By the first years of the nineteenth century, laws against sodomy had been eliminated in France and in many regions of Western Europe through the Code Napoléon.[72] These changes were made quietly, by simply omitting the previous penalty for sodomy from the new collections of statutes, rather than by defending those sexual acts outright. Although liberal legal theory led many to the conclusion that the state had no authority to regulate private, consensual sexual acts between adults, the public defense of such a conclusion was beyond the pale of liberal politics for most of the nineteenth century.[73] In practice, French and Dutch "pederasts" were subject to an elastic interpretation of laws against "public indecency" that still exposed them to a great deal of police scrutiny and prosecution, but their situation was better than that of similar men in states where sodomy itself remained illegal, such as Prussia.[74] Thus there were models in Europe for legalizing sex between men while still maintaining social and moral sanctions against such practices. In

England, however, the upper class held more closely to its own traditions as it modified the laws in the 1820s.

Once modified, however, these laws were available for the use of all. Eighteenth-century English law was justified in part by the idea that it applied to everyone. The occasional trial of an upper-class individual on charges of murder or forgery was held up as evidence of this evenhandedness, even as in practice the system was undoubtedly skewed to favor the propertied.[75] As long as the courts were little used by most of society, the full implications of this apparent egalitarianism as it related to sex between men were of little consequence. But this changed as policing and the courts began to be used to a much greater degree to discipline urban society, and as newspapers became the preeminent means of shaming the convicted after the 1817 abolition of the pillory. The potential leveling effects of this area of the law, where most men started with a greater equality in the property of their reputations and their bodies, were pronounced, yet the change did not constitute a utopian moment for any group involved. No man who defined himself as respectable from any class background wished to be associated with charges of sodomy, attempted sodomy, or threatening to accuse of an infamous crime. Any man attempting to bring an unnatural-assault prosecution was involved in a dangerous game in which he could quickly go from the accuser to the accused.[76] Wealthier individuals were able to exercise a great deal of leverage on the system. Yet the relatively new ability of a man of any background to defend his reputation, and perhaps send another man to prison for up to two years, was real. The two-year sentence for attempted sodomy was not new in the 1820s, but for many men this was when using it first became a real possibility.

CHAPTER 4

Public Men

The Metropolitan Police

Police Sergeant David Cooper was fairly well known around the Uxbridge region of Middlesex in 1838. During his rounds one evening, he came across a local married householder by the name of Pearce in his stable with a prostitute. Although Sergeant Cooper apparently did not feel that any infraction had occurred, Pearce was of a different mind. He did not acknowledge Sergeant Cooper's right to enter his stable, even while on patrol, and he confronted Cooper several days later, saying, "D——n you, what business did you have in my stable the other night?" Unsatisfied with Cooper's response, he shouted, "You b——y police, we will get you out of this town; we will make this town too hot for you; we will do your business."[1] A fight then broke out on the street between the two men that attracted a growing crowd, until finally Cooper and another policeman who had joined him managed to subdue Pearce and another equally violent man and take them to the police station. Cooper's wife met them inside the station, and the three then attempted to force Pearce and the other man into the strongroom.

The prisoners were able to break free after Pearce's companion drew a knife concealed in his clothing. The fight then spilled out into the police-station courtyard, where it was witnessed by a crowd of more than two hundred gathered outside the gates. The crowd, which later broke through the gates, was unanimous in its support of the prisoners, with one woman heard to shout "Give it him, give it the b——r," and another telling her companions to "get out your knives, we will give it to the b——r." Others in the crowd shouted against the "b——y police," calling them "b——y half-starved looking b——s." When one man managed to stab an officer, Ann Clements, one of the leaders of the crowd, shouted, "I hope the b——r is dead."[2]

Other witnesses made it clear that Ann Clements was most responsible for the crowd's breaking into the station courtyard. Mary Grenville, who had joined the crowd some time before, said that Clements and two others were the first to begin jumping at the gate to break it open. Once inside with the mob, Clements went up to one of the prisoners, patted him on the back, and playfully said, "You b——r, I have pluck enough to release the whole of you." As if to further prove her mettle, Clements then "tucked up the sleeves of her gown and challenged to fight anybody," though no one took her up on the offer. The police arrested Clements for her role in leading the mob attack, but she served no sentence for her actions. Only one individual was convicted for the attack, although many who participated were known to the officers.

A striking feature of this case and many others like it was the willingness of individuals to challenge and even assault policemen they had known for years. Community members made little effort to hide or disguise their identities during such attacks, in spite of the potential consequences. In most neighborhoods, the police were not the unquestioned arbiters of disputes but had to compete with standards of acceptable behavior as defined by the community.[3] Attacks on policemen often began when constables were thought to have violated the norms of the working-class communities in which they patrolled. "Vagabond" and "half-starved" were common insults hurled at the police during such encounters, stressing both the constables' alienation from the local community and their low status within it.[4]

The hostility directed at policemen by the community was often mirrored by the intense skepticism directed at them by officials. The class and educational gulf between the police and the London magistrates was a constant source of tension in the 1830s and later. Although men of divergent backgrounds worked together in enterprises throughout London, the magistrates were unique in the degree to which they relied on working-class policemen not only for their labor but also for their judgments of complex situations. Before the coming of the Metropolitan Police, magistrates trained and supervised their own handful of constables; after 1829, however, they could be disinclined to trust the sometimes unknown men who brought a steadily increasing number of cases before them.[5] Juries, which were invariably made up of men of higher status than the constables, were also often suspicious of officers' motivations, especially when rewards, reimbursements, or payments were involved.

It is not surprising, then, that the increased application of the laws against sex between men created significant problems for the police. The rules governing "character evidence," on which many of these cases hinged, most often worked to the disadvantage of the constable when the defendant was a wealthy man. This predicament is just one example of the disadvantage all working-class men faced when proving character in court. Never did the tensions between working-class enforcement of the law and middle- and upper-class assumptions about character and the proper stance toward sex between men clash so powerfully as when a group of constables began a series of raids in Hyde Park to entrap men for soliciting sex with other men, arresting primarily upper- and middle-class men in the process. Through the exploration of this and other examples, this chapter demonstrates how class shaped the enforcement of laws related to sexual acts between men and the ambiguous role of the new working-class constable in this process.

Before the Metropolitan Police, law enforcement throughout England and Wales was controlled at the parish level, under the direction of the local magistrates. Magistrates personally supervised small forces of constables and beadles, who in turn supervised watchmen, all drawn from local property holders. Although a property holder might pay another man to fulfill his obligations to the watch, he was responsible for that individual's conduct, just as the magistrate was personally responsible for the constables under his direction.[6] Although some experimentation with a force of paid working-class constables had been carried out along the wharves in London in the early nineteenth century, because property holders were insufficient in this area to watch over the warehouses, until 1829 the system of policing remained under local control, structured by the bonds between upper-class magistrates and lesser property holders who knew one another.[7] The coming of the Metropolitan Police shifted the control of constables from the magistrates of London to the Home Office, vastly increased the number of constables, and drew them exclusively from the lower class.

Some recent scholars have minimized the degree of innovation represented by the replacement of the watch system with the Metropolitan Police, stressing instead the effects of changes that occurred at the parish level in at least some parts of London. The work of Elaine Reynolds in particular demonstrates how the watch improved in some areas in the early nineteenth century, with the number of watchmen patrolling the streets increasing steadily, if unevenly, through the 1820s. Some parishes, such as St. James's and Marylebone, were considered by contemporary observers to be policed extremely well, and a number of the reforms associated with the Metropolitan Police consisted of extending the most successful reforms in these parishes to the rest of London.[8]

It was in the West End parishes, which were considered the best policed in the early 1820s, that the highest concentration of police-court activity relating to sex between men occurred. Although information on cases before 1829 is limited, it appears that patterns of arrest were similar to those used later by the Metropolitan Police. Many arrests occurred after a sexual act was witnessed by a third party. Such was the case in 1823 when four teenage boys discovered Ambrose Henry Crofton, an educated gentleman, and William Clarke, a private soldier of the Grenadier Guards, engaged in sexual acts in a field one evening. The *Times* reported that once the boys had crept close enough to discover what the men were doing, "two of their party stole softly away, and informed the watchman."[9] In 1826 a constable followed Thomas Brewer into a secluded part of Kensington Gardens, where he saw that Brewer "began to take indecent liberties" with a young man.[10]

Other examples of watch arrests in the 1820s involved a watchman's being called in by a man who was the object of an unwanted sexual advance. In July 1822 Constable Staples was approached by two young men who wished to report the existence of a molly house at No. 5, Weymouth Street, Marylebone. One of the young men had recently arrived in London from the countryside, and he told the constable that he had been enticed to sleep there by a man who had promised to find him work.[11] In another case, George Barnard and Private Richard Green, after a disputed event that took place on a Kensington Street at 1:00 A.M., walked "arm-in-arm" to a nearby watch house, where Green charged his companion with an indecent assault.[12] Hugh Jones, a keeper of the Bell public house, went searching for a constable in January 1825 to arrest the young man who had accused him of "touch[ing] my p-v-t-s" in front of a print-shop window.[13]

The practice of using a concealed constable to entrap men for threatening to accuse of an infamous crime was also established before the formation of the Metropolitan Police. In 1825 Thomas Cozens, a chemist living just off Leicester Square, arranged for Constable Wainwright to be present when he discussed his alleged indecent assault on the young Joseph Mould. Mould brought a self-described "respectable stationer . . . [who] had brought up a large family" to speak for him in the negotiations, and once five pounds was demanded from Cozens to settle the matter, Constable Wainwright emerged from his hiding place and made his arrests.[14] A twenty-two-year-old man named Ballard found himself in a similar situation in 1825, although he sensed the trap before it was sprung. It was reported that after a few minutes he said of the money, "I only want to borrow it . . . Oh! never mind, take the 5s. back, and for God's sake let me go out."[15] These examples and many others indicate that whether on the streets, in the parks, or in private parlors, arrests for crimes related to sex between men followed the same patterns before and after the establishment of the Metropolitan Police.

Also consistent before and after 1829 were some of the ways in which arrested men sought to minimize their public exposure or avoid conviction once they appeared in the police court. The *Times* reported in 1825 that "scarcely a week passes but the magistrates of this [Queen Square] office have individuals brought before them, (and those of most respectable connexions in society), charged with indecent assaults on the sentries in the park; and not withstanding the exposure that always follows the parties, by the accusation made against them being published to the world, it does not act as a preventive to the perpetration of such revolting acts."[16] And yet exposure did *not* always follow: in this case, the accused man gave what was believed to be the false name of Thomas Williams. He was also, like a number of other men in the 1820s reports, flippant toward the magistrate and unimpressed by the gravity of the situation. Some men suspected of using fake names were held by magistrates until their identity was confirmed, but others were allowed bail, even when using such obviously fake names as John Tosier and Peter Frederick Wack. This pattern persisted through at least the 1860s.[17]

Wealthier men also regularly took advantage of the split between the initial police-court hearing and the criminal trial to evade prosecution. Although they were only misdemeanors, unnatural assaults could not be disposed of before the police courts but were sent on to the next session of London's criminal courts for trial. Bail was almost always allowed for these cases, and although magistrates usually made an effort to increase the bail for wealthier individuals, this practice allowed men to escape imprisonment for a price. William Dorrien was charged at Bow Street "by two young men belonging to the 72d Regiment of the

Highlanders with indecently assaulting them."[18] Dorrien was granted bail even though he attempted to lie about his identity and his wealth and was described by another gentleman as "a brutish man" tried previously for "brutish practices."[19] The police-court magistrate considered there to be sufficient evidence for a criminal trial and set Dorrien's bail at a steep £1,200, which Dorrien paid and then forfeited by failing to appear for his trial. The Rev. William Hayes, in a separate incident, also gave up his bail and disappeared between his police-court and criminal-court hearings in the 1820s, as did the more famous bishop of Clogher.[20]

Also consistent before and after 1829 was the likelihood that the police-court magistrate would reduce the charge to one of common assault and impose only a five-pound fine. This practice persisted in police courts in later decades. In 1850 the *Times* reported that "Thomas Barton was charged with having committed an indecent assault upon a young man named Joseph Baume, who, although a stranger, accompanied him into a public house to drink with him. There was no doubt of the indecent conduct imputed to the defendant, who was fined 5*l.*" In another example from 1846, George Robert Sizmur was thought guilty of sexually assaulting a fifteen-year-old shoemaker's apprentice, but the police-court magistrate was of "the opinion that it was better to deal summarily with such offenders, than to have the ears of the public polluted by the repetition of the evidence in another court. The magistrate then inflicted a fine of 5*l.*" In 1851, "James Caldwell, a short, thickset, well-dressed person, about 50 years of age, was placed at the bar before Alderman Wilson, charged with indecently assaulting several men on Monday night. The charge was fully proved, and the prisoner was fined 5*l.* The fine was immediately paid."[21] In all of these cases, the decision to reduce the charge from indecent assault to common assault, like the decision to set bail or proceed against a man believed to be using a fake name, was at the discretion of the magistrate.

These discretionary acts by magistrates do not leave traces in the official statistics gathered by the Home Office related to prosecutions for sex between men, but they were an important element of the enforcement of the law and an assertion of the magistrates' authority. With the coming of the Metropolitan Police, magistrates lost control of the constables to the Home Office. Yet they retained substantial autonomy within the system, and they also retained their skepticism toward some of the changes in it. The stricter enforcement of laws against petty crime that characterized the Metropolitan Police, in keeping with the liberal notion that a rigorously ordered environment could reform the behavior of the poor, did not fit well with the more paternalistic, Tory conception of the social order retained by many upper-class magistrates. Efforts to combat public drunkenness, rioting, and violent or bloody sports were a new mandate of the Metropolitan Police.[22] The older Tory social ideal may have severely restricted political participation, but it left unregulated a wide range of popular customs and behavior.[23] Under this system, urban riots and other forms of lower-class social disorder were seen not as the heralds of anarchy but rather as a means of displaying popular opinion, and they were usually allowed to run their course, even if they lasted for days.[24]

This view extended beyond the distribution of justice in the narrow sense. As Jennifer Davis has argued, magistrates' courts were not only forums for criminal disputes but also sources of charity that could be distributed at the discretion of the magistrate, in defiance of the Poor Law Guardians. Each court had a poor-box fund, and as the magistrates were not subject to pressure from parishes to keep the poor rates down, they were generally considered more compassionate than the Poor Law officials. After the mid-1830s, many of the magistrates viewed themselves as a mediating force between the poorest Londoners and an overly harsh police force and Poor Law Commission. At least through the mid-1860s, the magistrates' courts in London were seen by the working class as places where all manner of problems and disputes might be aired, not simply those that involved policing or prosecutions.[25] The magistrates often used their autonomy to oppose the liberal institutions being established and thus to try to preserve elements of the previous social order.

Greater skepticism toward the reforms may in part explain the drop in the conviction rate for crimes related to sex between men during the early years of the Metropolitan Police. Although many factors no doubt affected these statistics, the trend was pronounced. Between 1810 and 1819, more than 60 percent of criminal prosecutions for unnatural assault in London ended in conviction. Between 1820 and 1829 the conviction rate dropped to 52 percent; in the 1830s it was 44 percent; and by the 1840s it stood at only 37 percent.[26] At least part of this shift may be attributable to the uneasiness of the judiciary with the changes taking place.

Direct evidence of such uneasiness can be found in an 1835 letter to Home Secretary Lord John Russell penned by H. Wedgwood, the Union Hall magistrate before whom many such cases were tried. Wedgwood spent much of his letter discussing the shortcomings of the sodomy and unnatural-assault laws and their disproportionate impact on the lower classes. Arguing for the commutation of a death sentence passed on two men, Wedgwood wrote that

> there is a shocking inequality in this law in its operation upon the rich and the poor. It is the only crime where there is no injury done to any individual and in consequence it requires a very small expense to commit it in so private a manner and to take such precautions as shall render conviction impossible. It is also the only capital crime that is committed by rich men but owing to the circumstances I have mentioned they are never convicted. The detection of these degraded creatures was owing entirely to their poverty, they were unable to pay for privacy, and the room was so poor that what was going on inside was easily visible from without.[27]

In practice, it was usually wealthy men who benefited from the ameliorations of the law by magistrates. Yet statements like this one indicate that the general paternalistic tendency of magistrates to watch over the interests of the poor extended even to men who had sex with men, if only to ensure that justice was applied equally across different classes. This indicates that we need to look beyond simple class bias when attempting to explain why so many court cases seem to have acquitted middle- and upper-class men at the expense of their working-class partners. This bias is real, but it was more the result of unexamined assumptions governing legal procedures and ideas of what constituted masculine character.

The case identified by Wedgwood is not the best vehicle for exploring this issue, though, as the social class of the defendants makes it atypical. It was not cases involving two working-class men that appeared most commonly before the courts or generated the most extensive news coverage, even in the *Weekly Dispatch* and other working-class newspapers. Even less frequent were cases involving two middle- or upper-class men. By far the most common situation leading to an arrest and trial involved men of differing class backgrounds attempting a liaison in a space that was to some degree public and therefore subject to police observation and oversight.

In this respect the placing of the uniformed constable on the street in the 1830s as a deterrent to crime is somewhat ironic, as these men's relative youth, lone presence on empty streets at night, and obvious working-class status also made them targets for the wealthier men who approached other men on the street for sex. Cases involving the propositioning of a policeman occurred in every decade of this study,

with one of the most famous happening in 1833. This incident began
as Constable John Palmer was walking his beat about 1:00 A.M. on
an affluent Mayfair street, near Cavendish Square, when Charles
Baring Wall, an Oxford-educated MP for Guildford, came up to him
and began a conversation. Because many London publications such as
the *Weekly Dispatch,* the *Times,* and the *Annual Register* related the
events of the case in great detail, and because the scene recounted was
typical of many such encounters, it is worth reproducing at length.
Constable Palmer testified:

> He asked me what it was o'clock. I told him about a quarter to 1. He said
> "it's a b——y fine morning, is it not?" I said "Yes, Sir, it is a fine morn-
> ing." He then asked me of what religion I was. I told him I was of no reli-
> gion in particular, any more than the rest of us. He then said "D——n
> and —— all the —— religions, it is all a humbug; a parcel of boys (he
> said), 14 or 15 years of age, are sent to college, and brought up to govern
> the country." He asked what regiment I had belonged to, and whether I
> had belonged to the Guards. I said "No." He said "you're not allowed to
> take money, are you?" I said "No." He said "If I was to chuck a shilling
> on the pavement, would you pick it up?" I said "No." He said "D——n
> and —— the b——y system, I hate it, don't you?" I said I did not. With
> that I was going away; he caught hold of my hand and squeezed it, and
> put a shilling into it, and [Here the witness described what took place]
> I did not know what he meant, and I had scarcely time to speak before
> he put half-a-crown into my hand; I said something which I can't recol-
> lect; when he put the shilling into my hand he pulled his coat on one side,
> and (here the witness described a most disgusting action), he had hold of
> my hand, and again acted in an indecent manner. I took hold of him by
> the collar, and said "B—— you, do you think I am a —— or what?" I
> took hold of him by the collar, and said he should go to the watch-house.
> He said something which I can't recollect. I took him to the corner of
> Cavendish-square. He put another shilling into my hand, and said some-
> thing about his character, and wanted me to let him go. I said "No; I
> would sooner let a gang of burglars go than I would you."[28]

Of course the accuracy of Constable Palmer's statement was questioned at every turn by Wall's defense team, which the *Times* noted
was the best money could buy. Wealthy defendants always fared better
in such cases when they were moved to the Court of the King's Bench
and heard before a special jury, and Wall benefited from both of these
advantages.[29] Wall's defense team repeatedly argued for the impossibil-
ity of an educated and pious man such as Wall uttering the words and
performing the acts attributed to him by Constable Palmer, and they
further argued the dangers of having one lone policeman's word lead to

the conviction of a man like Wall. In his closing statement to the jury, the defending counsel, Sir J. Scarlett, disregarded the details of the case and instead argued more broadly that "if Mr. Wall should be convicted after the jury had heard the evidence . . . no man would be safe from such a charge—no man who walked the streets at 12 o'clock at night could secure himself from the designs of a policeman."[30]

The degree to which the proceedings had turned against Constable Palmer was evident at the end of the trial: the jury did not even allow the lord chief justice to finish his summary statements, indicating that further discussion was unnecessary. The jury did not leave the room but instead "turned round for a minute or two, and then returned a verdict of Not Guilty. . . . [O]ne of the jurymen said the jury were of the opinion that the defendant's character was entirely spotless."[31]

Although many aspects of the trial seem markedly unjust, the point is not to retry the case but rather to understand what it meant for the men involved. In their decision, the jury followed the instructions of the lord chief justice, who recounted the two criteria by which unnatural assault cases should be judged when they came down to one man's word against the other's. The first was the consistency of each story, and whether or not either man began to contradict himself with repeated retellings of the events. The desire to uncover inconsistencies in an opponent's testimony was the rationale behind the repeated questions over minor details that were a regular feature of these court cases. If a man failed to keep his story consistent in this way he usually lost his case, regardless of his social standing.[32]

It was when both men retold their stories consistently that the second criterion, that of character, came most strongly into play. Evidence of character was used in other court cases as well, but it carried the most weight in cases such as these, where physical evidence or corroborating witnesses were lacking. Character evidence could speak to the likelihood of a man's sexually desiring other men, because of how such acts were understood by the upper-class men who framed the laws. For upper-class lawmakers and juries, such desire in men of property and education was thought to be related to a general moral decay, the outcome of a long habit of indiscipline that led men to seek progressively more exotic forms of indulgence. Because a long-established pattern of dissolute behavior was considered a prerequisite to same-sex desire, evidence of good social standing was thought to disprove that a man felt such desires.[33] Such proof of character was not a foolproof guide to behavior: drunkenness and other forms of temporary loss of control might lead a man to commit a singular aberrant act. Even so, as one magistrate informed Robert Peel in a private letter on a similar case, "although character cannot answer a specific charge on oath, yet something must depend on the probability."[34]

In such cases, character evidence could determine the outcome. In this letter to Peel, the prosecutor in the case was described as "a servant out of place," and his lack of employment could be admitted as evidence of his suspect character and motivation for possible extortion. Lower-class men were thought to lack the self-discipline and personal restraint of their social betters and therefore more likely to instigate such acts, either for the gratification of base desires or for financial gain. Defendants were allowed to give evidence indicating such motivations or the general bad character of their accusers, and the character witnesses of poorer men were subject to being undermined by allegations that they were paid for their testimony. By contrast, the defendant in this case, John Aves, had twenty people speak for his character at his trial; many of them had known him for more than thirty years. Aves had a respectable job that brought him into contact with high officials in the Colonial Department and was married with a wife and children. In short, he had all the advantages of character evidence working in his favor, but ultimately these could not overcome the facts of the case. Aves had tried to entice the servant into a dark alley; the servant had called the police, and Aves had not denied making an indecent assault when the servant first accused him of it in front of the constable.[35] Such facts counted for more than character evidence in this case.

The disadvantages faced by all working-class men, including police officers, when it came to offering proof of character in this way seem to have had a dampening effect on policemen's desire to bring such charges. Constable Palmer observed in his cross-examination that "nothing of the same sort ever happened to me before: I have heard of similar things having happened to other policemen, but I never knew of any charge being made."[36] Another constable found himself in a similar situation after charging Charles Lucas with an indecent assault late one night in Duke Street, Grosvenor Square.[37] This case came down to one man's word against the other's, which gave extra weight to Lucas's witnesses who praised his "most excellent character," "his otherwise unspotted reputation," and the fact that he "lived on the happiest terms with his wife." In the courtroom the constable's manner was characterized as "flippant and unsatisfactory," and he lost his case. His fate may have been similar to that of another constable, who, after failing to prove in court that the "gentlemanly-looking" Nathaniel Archer had sexually assaulted him, heard it announced that "proceedings would be taken against the policeman." Another constable in a different case also began to feel the pressure as his testimony was undermined by the defense in the courtroom. It was reported that under cross-examination, the constable "became agitated and confused. After changing colour two or three times, he fell forward in a fainting state in the witness-box, and was led out of court."[38]

The consequences for losing such a case were serious, as Constable Teehan learned in 1865 when he was involved in a failed prosecution for unnatural assault against two middle-class men. The two men were observed in a court off Bell Street, Westminster, "behaving in the most indecent manner towards each other," but the key witness against them was an unemployed laborer by the name of Samuel Connor. As the arresting officer, Constable Teehan, perhaps knowing how these cases went in the courtroom, cautioned the working-class Connor "to be very careful of what he said, and to follow what he had said in his depositions, for if he did not, and the counsel got hold of it, he would be sure to get a jacketing." Teehan was right to be wary of the tactics of the defense team, but his warning was used against him as well. By the end of the trial, the jury was of the opinion that Constable Teehan and Samuel Connor had conspired to fabricate a false story. Constable Teehan was told in open court by the presiding magistrate that "the shuffling manner in which he had given his evidence was most disgraceful to him." The constable was dismissed from the Metropolitan Police, and Samuel Connor was tried and convicted of perjury and sentenced to nine months' imprisonment.[39]

According to Constable Teehan's wife, such a public indictment of his character was hard for her husband to bear. Before becoming a policeman he had served fifteen years in the military and had been decorated with the English medal, the Turkish medal, and the French medal for his service in the Crimean War. He had risen to the rank of sergeant, and two of the colonels under whom he had served had written him excellent testimonials. Because Teehan had trouble holding regular employment after his dismissal from the police, he and his family were impoverished.[40] He always professed his innocence in the case, and his wife clearly thought that the incident had "preyed on his mind" for all his remaining years.

Teehan died in 1868, a year before one of the middle-class men in the case was again arrested for engaging in sexual acts with another

man. Teehan therefore heard neither the reassessment of the verdict in
the earlier trial nor the gesture made by the magistrate of Westminster
police court to clear Teehan's name. The magistrate invited Teehan's
widow into the police court and stated to her "publicly that Constable
Teehan's character is entirely vindicated in the eyes of the public, as
well as those who knew him as a soldier and a policeman."[41] The magistrate did not admit a flaw in the system of prosecution or any courtroom bias against the constable and the laborer, but instead declared it
an "unfortunate mistake" and offered Teehan's widow five pounds in
compensation, which she accepted.[42]

Cases when an officer's word clashed with that of a respectable
middle- or upper-class man did not necessarily have to end with the
destruction of one man's reputation. A constable whose name was not
given in the newspaper report brought a highly respectable man into
court on charges of indecent assault in 1867. The constable claimed
that the gentleman had touched him in a public urinal, whereas the
defense team, who produced many character witnesses, argued for the
"improbability" of their client's doing such a thing. The court decided
in favor of the defendant, but they tried to not denigrate the character
of the constable. Instead, the judge and the jury agreed "that there
has been some misconception on the part of the officer, and not that
he has made any deliberate false statement." After the jury foreman
confirmed he was "anxious" to endorse that view, a not-guilty verdict
was returned, and the men left the courtroom with their reputations
intact.[43] A similar situation occurred in a case in 1850, when the court
could not reconcile the respectability of a defendant with an officer's
charge that he had attempted a sexual advance. The presiding magistrate told the jurors that they must explain their verdict, "for if they
thought that the police had given a false colouring or exaggerated the
matter, public safety demanded their instant dismissal." In response,
after declaring the accused man not guilty, the jury indicated that the
constable's statement "might have been an accident, and the police
deceived by appearances. They also thought that they (the police) had
done nothing more than their duty in bringing the charge forward,
and had not perjured themselves." The presiding magistrate "entirely
concurred" with the opinion of the jury, and in this case, again, all men
left the courtroom with their reputations intact.[44]

The fact that court cases involving the propositioning of on-duty
policemen were still occurring as late as 1867 becomes more understandable if we remember some of the most frequent assumptions about

the other men in uniform on the London streets. Before the formation of the Metropolitan Police, only soldiers were seen in uniform, especially around the royal and government buildings in the West End. Unlike the policemen, who were expected to display moral and sexual restraint, soldiers were considered dangerous and uncontrolled. The desperate poverty that often compelled men to join the army was perpetuated by the poor living conditions and dismal pay of common soldiers. These men were also often far from home, removed from their networks of friends and family, and thus less constrained by those social networks. A lone soldier in the public houses or on the streets of London at night was often assumed to be at liberty for only a short time and looking to make the most of it. Conspicuous in their uniforms, soldiers were often the objects of speculation and sexual fantasy for those who encountered them.

Such assumptions seem to have influenced William White, a barrister's clerk, when he spotted a soldier in Hyde Park around 9:00 P.M. on 29 October 1844. White had recognized the soldier by his regimentals, and the two men walked together, exchanging small talk. By White's own account, the soldier then touched White in a sexually suggestive way "outside my trowsers," and after White made no objection, the soldier suggested they leave the path for a darker section of the park. White agreed and followed the soldier. When they got to the more secluded area, White stated, the soldier "collared me . . . . [H]e then said 'You b—— b——, you shall not go till I have something from you,'" and searched his pockets for valuables.[45]

The soldier seemed to understand the assumptions White had made about him and manipulated them for his own ends. He was caught later that evening by the police, and the number of mismatched valuables on him indicated that he had gone through more than one set of gentlemen's pockets. By suggesting his sexual availability, the soldier increased his chances of success as a thief, as his victims lowered their guard and were also less likely to report the crime. He offered the arresting constable a fine silver watch and chain to release him and forget the whole thing, saying that "he knew the result of these cases" and did not want to face the court. The policeman declined, and the soldier's fears proved well-founded, as he was convicted for theft and transported for fifteen years.[46]

Other soldiers were not afraid to attempt such extortion even while on duty. Several fellow soldiers of Samuel Cooper, a private in the Second Battalion of the Scotch Fusilier Guards, had "heard him speak on different occasions of his having got money while on guard."[47] One such occasion occurred late at night while he was guarding the London residence of the Duchess of Kent: on that night a man came up to Private Cooper and, after some few words of small talk, "put his hand under his [Private Cooper's] great coat, on his private parts." Private Cooper collared the man and turned him in to the police, but he told some of his fellow soldiers back at the barracks that "if he could have got a sovereign the man might have gone to hell." In addition, Private Cooper lamented that the public nature of the place where he was on duty had prevented him from taking more advantage of the assault, and if it had occurred at one of the more secluded sentry posts where he sometimes worked, "he would have . . . got, money, rings, watch, and all."[48]

Private Cooper was willing to associate himself with situations involving sexual behavior between men so long as he was in control and benefited financially from it. To more respectable men, such actions demonstrated an extreme lack of masculine character and self-restraint; from the perspective of Private Cooper, such choices could be seen as a plausible strategy that compromised only men who were themselves lacking in masculine character, as he defined it. Private Cooper did not consider such behavior shameful; instead he bragged about it to his fellow soldiers. He did not feel compelled to distance himself from all associations with sex between men. His actions cannot be taken as representative of working-class men's attitudes, and the respectable married artisan would have had only disdain for his behavior. However, upper- and middle-class men were less likely to make such distinctions in their perception of the behavior of those of lower stations.

The evidence suggests that propositioning a policeman was a significantly more dangerous game than approaching a soldier and much more likely to lead to an arrest. The way a man might flirt with an officer but not necessarily open himself up to prosecution is indicated in the behavior of Henry Barnes, whose pattern was to drop suggestions but not do anything overt unless the officer responded. Several constables in the area around Greenwich Park had reported that "indecent assaults and inducements [had been] held out to them" by Barnes, but some of his most sustained efforts were directed at Constable Thomas Hicklin. During one attempt, Barnes had struck up a conversation with Hicklin, who was on his evening's patrol. As he said goodnight, Barnes told Hicklin that he lived just on the other side of the heath and "at the same time extending his hand towards [Constable Hicklin], and on shaking hands squeezed him in a very marked manner." The constable "detailed subsequent meetings with the prisoner and several assaults," but those incidents had not led to an arrest. Hicklin's superior felt that "the constable had in some degree encouraged the commission of the offence instead of preventing it, [and therefore] declined to take the charge."[49] Although eventually taken into custody, Barnes was able to escape conviction, in part by casting doubt on Constable Hicklin's character with the accusation that Hicklin had "demanded something from him for drink" as well.

Accusations of taking money for alcohol were especially tailored to play on upper- and middle-class men's anxieties about the working-class constable. Campaigns against alcohol were building among middle-class reformers in these years: alcohol consumption was thought by many to exemplify the lack of self-control among the lower classes and to be at the root of many social problems. Constables, as employees of a newly formed bureaucratic organization created by men sympathetic to the reform of lower-class morals, found themselves subject to innumerable moralizing regulations, among them a ban on alcohol consumption. Primarily for this reason, more than 50 percent of the men who joined the Metropolitan Police in the first two decades of the force left after less than a year.[50] Examining the nature of the job helps to explain why the figure of the policeman was resisted not only by the society onto which he was imposed but also by the very men who wore the uniform.

It is remarkable how much both the desired traits and the conditions of work of police constables mirrored those of female domestic servants. The ideal employee for both the police commissioners and the lady of the middle-class household was not a London native but a former agricultural worker from the countryside. Such individuals were considered easier to train and control. Both types of employers sought candidates who were relatively young; the police required in addition that recruits possess at least a rudimentary ability to read and write.[51]

Both jobs paid infamously low wages and required long hours of work. A starting constable in the 1830s was paid nineteen shillings a week, equivalent to the pay of a semiskilled worker and three shillings less than the nominal wage that their predecessors, the Bow Street Runners, had received seventy years before. The typical policeman in the mid-Victorian period worked a ten- to twelve-hour shift, and some areas outside London required as many as fourteen hours of patrolling per day.

Both jobs also required that the individual live under the supervision of the employer and meet certain standards of personal conduct and appearance. Policemen were required to live communally in barracks near the station house, overseen by their sergeants, so that they could be called out at any time for an emergency.[52] Exceptions were made for married officers, who were allowed to have private rooms near the barracks, but no married man with more than two children was allowed to be a policeman. Police officials considered the wages too low to support dependents, and it was not felt necessary to encourage family life for these men. One small exception to this general policy was the provision for the payment of a set fee for any policeman's wife wishing to take on the laundry duties for a barracks; the wife of the barracks sergeant always had first priority for this job. Laundry was an important duty, because high standards were set for the constables' appearance. In addition to stipulating compulsory monthly haircuts and rules governing facial hair, regulations decreed that a policeman begin the day in a clean and well-kept uniform.

The policeman's uniform, with its top hat and waistcoat, resembled the clothing worn by the middle-class businessman rather than the soldier. Yet this resemblance was only a suggestion; no one on the street would have confused the two. The policeman's hat was reinforced with stays so that it might be stood on to peer over fences and even used for protection. The policeman's blue waistcoat stood out against the somber tones worn by elite men, and a brass plate affixed to the collar gave a number by which the policeman could be identified. The collar was also reinforced with a thick band of leather, both to protect against strangulation and to improve the wearer's posture.[53] In a very real way, the uniform controlled the man inside.

Policemen were not allowed to wear civilian clothing, even when off-duty, until 1869. They were not allowed to be seen drinking, gambling, or fighting in public, because, like the maid in the middle-class home, the policeman was expected to reflect the moral standards of his employer. The upper- and middle-class ideal (or caricature) of sobriety, honesty, and rectitude became the template for the policeman's conduct. Just as pregnancy was considered the ultimate sign that the female domestic servant had failed to uphold the household's moral standards, so drunkenness represented a similar lapse from the masculine virtue of self-control for the policeman and was the cause of more than four out of five dismissals in the early years of the force.[54]

Much like domestic service for young women, serving on the

Metropolitan Police force was viewed as a stage through which a man might pass rather than a permanent profession. With their all-consuming and paternalistic structure, both jobs helped to ease the transition from rural to urban life for young people. Although policemen were often ostracized in working-class communities, a letter of character from serving as a police officer was extremely valuable for obtaining other work.[55] And although very few wanted the job for any length of time, enough men were willing to serve for a brief period to ensure that the police remained a visible presence on the London streets.

Men of working-class backgrounds accounted for not only all the constables on the streets but also all the posts within the new hierarchy, save for those at the very top. In part because of the fear that the new force might become a despotic "system of spies" on the Continental model, Peel ensured that once the structure and tone of the Metropolitan Police were set, he and later home secretaries exercised little direct control over the force. Within the Home Office was a permanent undersecretary for police, and this individual was the primary government liaison with the two police commissioners. Two upper-class men dominated the police-commissioner offices from the time of their creation into the late 1860s. Col. Charles Rowan had served in the army during the Napoleonic wars and was most responsible for the quasi-militaristic aspects of the new police; Richard Charles Mayne's chief qualifications were his eight years of service as a barrister and the fact that he was the son of a judge from a respected and well-connected family.[56]

The great divide in both class and education levels occurred between the commissioners and the superintendents who headed the divisions. In 1829 London was divided into seventeen police districts, each headed by a divisional superintendent directly responsible for at least two hundred men in as many as fourteen station houses.[57] Although positions of considerable power and responsibility, most of the superintendent positions were filled not by gentlemen or even propertied men but by men who had risen through the ranks. Although many had military experience, none had achieved a rank above that of sergeant major in the army.[58] Because of the low pay and heavy workload, Peel and Rowan felt that it was preferable to have ambitious lower-class men in the posts rather than sullen former military officers who would consider themselves to have taken a step down. Thus, although they were constrained by rules created by the government and the police commissioners, many decisions on policing were, at least in the initial stages, in the hands of working-class men. Just how significant that discretion might prove to be in cases involving unnatural assaults is evident in an extraordinary series of arrests made in Hyde Park during the spring of 1830.

If the Metropolitan Police aimed to curtail sexual liaisons between men, Hyde Park was a logical place to start. The court records available for the early nineteenth century make it clear that men caught alone in certain sections of the park at night were often seeking other men for sex. During his cross-examination in a later case, Robert Bendall was repeatedly grilled on this point. He responded to one line of questioning by saying, "I am not married—I do not often walk in the Park—I am quite sure of that—I have walked in the Park before, not at night, only about twice, I think—I had perhaps been in the Park as late as that, or about 10 o'clock, by myself, not more than that—I read the newspapers occasionally." When asked pointedly if he had "ever heard or read that at Hyde-park of a night sometimes persons have been doing things of a very filthy description," Bendall responded weakly that "it is that part of the paper I seldom read. . . . I have heard of it."[59] In a different trial, Matthias Cundale was grilled in a similar manner to determine whether he was the victim of or complicit with the sexual advances of another man. After questions over his marital status led to the assurance that he was "keeping company with a lady," he also assured the court that on his evening's walk he "did not go through the enclosure, or into the Park at all."[60] A generation before, because of associations with nighttime sexual activity, both homosexual and heterosexual, the home secretary had ordered Hyde Park and St. James's Park locked at night.[61] This association was also evident in pornographic works such as *The Boudoir,* which depicts exaggerated scenes of primarily heterosexual excess behind park walls after dark.[62]

The Metropolitan Police had not been in operation a full year before one of its seventeen divisions, the S Division, began a public campaign to curtail sex between men in Hyde Park. Policemen went into the park at night out of uniform and kept to areas such as the path parallel to Bayswater Road and just south of Marble Arch, where experience indicated that men came for sexual encounters with other men. An early article in the *Times* on the arrests appearing in late March 1830 announced that "four more of the miscreants who infest Hyde-park at night were brought up in custody from the watch-house . . . this makes 14 of the gang" that had been arrested thus far.[63] From that point on, the stories related to these arrests and trials appeared in the *Times* under the banner "The Hyde Park Gang."[64]

The plain-clothes officers dressed for this task as working-class men, and this choice affected the sort of man who would approach them, thus disproportionately ensnaring wealthier individuals hoping to use their economic advantage over other men. The stories related to the "Hyde Park Gang" show that the men arrested were well-off financially. A man giving the name of Frederick Sims was described as "a genteel-looking young man, fashionably dressed in a blue frock coat" with more than eighty pounds on him at the time of his arrest.[65] John Batson was described as "a well-dressed young man, about 35 years of age . . . indicted for an assault of a revolting description upon a police-officer." A man who gave his name as James Byrne was described as "a very respectable looking young man" employed as an audit-office clerk in India House. The *Times* provided a description of fewer than half of all the men who were arrested in the Hyde Park raids, but those that they did describe were often said to look "very respectable," "quite well connected," or " fashionably dressed."[66]

Many of the arrested men tried to give a false name and address. "Frederick Sims" was kept in custody for more than a week until he finally gave his correct name of Frederick Symons. He was then compelled to surrender a total of eight hundred pounds' bail.[67] The false name did seem to work for "James Byrne." Even though there was some doubt about the accuracy of his identity, the magistrate dealt with the case as a summary prosecution for common assault and did not send the case beyond the police court. The *Times* reported that "the magistrates, after consulting, fined the prisoner 5*l.*, the full penalty. The money was instantly paid, and the prisoner left the office with his friend, amidst the hootings of a crowd assembled outside."[68]

The men charged in the Hyde Park cases also tried various strategies to answer the officers' accusations. James Byrne argued "in his defense . . . if he had acted in the manner stated by the constable, it was from being in liquor." The evidence against Symons was described as "the worst of any," and "the prisoner attempted, in a most ingenious manner, to give a different meaning to the language he used, and said the assault was accidental."[69] Another man named Batson attempted no such elaborate lies but simply offered a substantial bribe to the arresting officer to release him after the attempted liaison went sour.[70]

Although none of these features were unusual in unnatural-assault cases, this particular group of trials was remarkable in that the strongest condemnations were directed at the police officers rather than the defendants. In one of the earlier cases, the *Times* noted that the defense counsel, "Mr. C. Phillips, and all the other gentlemen of the bar present, expressed the utmost indignation against the demoralizing system of policemen disguising themselves to ensnare to crime. Mr. C. Phillips remarked, that instead of a preventive police, such persons as the prosecutors deserved the designation of an accessorial police."[71] Coverage of the trials in the *Sun* also laid special emphasis on the fact that the arresting officers were in plain clothes.[72] At one trial, a defense attorney made an issue of the fact that one of the officers had been involved in four such arrests in the past two years. Batson's attorney "observed that very little credit was due to the testimony of witnesses, who acknowledged that they went into the Park in disguise for the avowed purpose of soliciting the commission of abominable crimes. Such a mode of employing police-officers was most degrading, and was calculated to bring the present [new] system into public odium."[73]

In no other unnatural-assault trials of this period were the arresting constables so vilified, even if from the perspective of the officers their actions might be justified. The officers of the S Division were enforcing the law against crimes publicly identified by many middle- and upper-class men as the worst possible, and they had devised an effective method. We need not assume that they set out to arrest disproportionate numbers of middle- and upper-class men in order to acknowledge that the system that they devised was biased in this direction. Like the other forms of class bias discussed earlier in relation to arrests for sex between men, the discrimination that occurred was the result of a series of unexamined assumptions on the part of the men who created and implemented a policy.

As in the Wall trial, many of the defense speeches centered on the need to protect propertied men from the conspiratorial designs of the police. The defense counsel Phillips cited previous Hyde Park cases to substantiate his claim that "police-constables brought forward cases for the mere purpose of obtaining the expenses attending prosecutions. No man who had observed the conduct of the new police in courts of justice could doubt the fact."[74] The effect of this questioning of motives was evident when, after a particularly vitriolic speech by one defense attorney, the *Times* reported that "the jury rose up as one man, and requested that none of the prosecutors [the policemen] in these cases should be allowed their expenses. The Chairman and Bench of Magistrates assented most cheerfully. Phillips observed that there would be no more disguises when it was found that nothing was made by it."[75]

The speeches condemning acts of sex between men were not printed in the newspapers in connection with the Hyde Park cases, and the question of the guilt of the defendants was sometimes given less prominence than the actions of the police. The one exception was a speech by Lord Chief Justice Thomas Denman, who presided over the last of the cases. He did not defend the police so much as question the overly lenient treatment that some of the Hyde Park defendants were given before the police courts. The *Times* reported that Denman

> had heard that the intervention of a jury in cases of this description had been dispensed with, and that certain magistrates, before whom these cases were brought, had, in their discretion, substituted a fine of 5*l.*, instead of sending the parties charged to be tried by a jury of their country. He could hardly credit this, and was willing to believe that some mistake had been made on the subject; but if the fact were true,— and he should regret to find it so,—then he was bound to say that such magistrates had not only acted illegally, but they were a disgrace to the bench, and contaminated the purity of justice.[76]

As in most of the Hyde Park cases, the above case resulted in a verdict of not guilty. Of the men sent on to the criminal courts, William Benton and Richard Milan were found guilty and sentenced to six months' imprisonment. Edward Butler, John Batson, Owen Barry, and Joseph Clarc were acquitted, although the *Times* reporter felt that Clarc's guilt had been clearly proved. Owen's acquittal was secured in part because "a number of his friends, male and female, attended to speak to his character."[77]

Many London men, including, it seems, Robert Peel, were introduced to the Hyde Park cases through their extensive coverage in the London newspapers. In a letter Peel wrote to Commissioner Rowan on 20 May 1830, he asked for further details about a number of police matters, including a request to "look at the comments attributed to Mr. Denman as to the conduct of the Police Officers of late at criminal trials."[78] Rowan returned Peel's letter the following day, noting the disagreement between magistrates and prosecutors over "the motives of the Police Constables in bringing forward these charges, and as to the propriety of their being out of their uniform in the Park for the purpose of detecting offenders." Yet Rowan did not take a stand on the legality or ethics of the issue, side-stepping the question by observing that "Mr. Mayne and myself thinking that public opinion appeared to be against the practice gave orders some time back that it should be discontinued."[79]

Rowan was frank about his willingness to terminate the operation when public opinion turned against it, despite the fact that he and Mayne directed the police to do a great deal that was wildly unpopular with the population, as shown by incidents like the assault on the police station discussed at the start of this chapter. But the men directing the Metropolitan Police, along with many of the other similarly educated men of the day, drew a distinction between the popular opinion expressed in a riot against a police station, and public opinion, which, according to Dror Wahrman and other scholars, was related more directly to the views of educated, propertied men.[80] The latter group was more outraged by the actions of the police in the Hyde Park cases because it was they who were most affected by this particular application of the law. Yet the Hyde Park cases should not be romanticized as an instance of working-class men using the mechanisms of the state for their own ends. Despite the predominance of working-class men in the Metropolitan Police, its rules and hierarchies were often sufficient to keep officers and divisional superintendents performing their tasks in the ways that served the ends of the middle and upper classes. If the men who had put together the Hyde Park arrests were disillusioned by their vilification for carrying out legitimate arrests, the police commissioners were less troubled. Few men stayed on the force for any length of time, and the reasons for this attrition had little effect on recruitment. Whenever a constable left his uniform empty, another could always be found to step into it.

It is this metaphor of filling the empty uniform on the street that perhaps best describes the Metropolitan Police in its first years of operation and illustrates most profound effects on the population. Save for a handful of men at the highest levels, almost no one in English society of any class wanted the Metropolitan Police when the force was first formed. The real battle in those early years was simply to keep the uniform on the street, to protect it from those in the upper and middle classes who wanted to abolish it, those in the working class who wanted to retaliate against it, and the men inside it who simply wanted to defect from it. Yet this was not a hopeless war of attrition for the men who created the force, because regardless of its effectiveness in detecting crime or apprehending criminals, every year that the uniform stayed on the street, it helped accomplish a broader goal.

Whatever the relative effectiveness of the watch and the Metropolitan

Police in the apprehension of criminals, the symbolic nature of the constable on the street changed with the coming of the new force. Unlike the
watch, the standardized and uniformed Metropolitan Police constable
was meant from the start to be visible in all parts of the city at all times
of the day and night. In its first years of operation, the Metropolitan
Police distributed a force of more than three thousand uniformed men
around London, and that number increased to more than five thousand
within twenty years.[81] Differences in the numbers of constables from
one police-court district to the next were minimized, and uniforms,
training, and a strict code of conduct were established in an attempt
to ensure uniformity across the force. The new uniform itself was a
ubiquitous presence on the London streets from 1829 onward, and this
innovation clearly set the new force apart from the watch.

The "Panopticism" chapter of Michel Foucault's *Discipline and
Punish* begins not with a description of institutional architecture, but
rather with a description of the transformation of city streets into a
disciplinary mechanism through observation, categorization, and
record-keeping. The greatest effect of the Metropolitan Police was not
that the policemen on the street increased what the state might observe
but that they increased the population's awareness of being observed.
In the example that began this chapter, the affront that caused Pearce
to attack Constable Cooper was the constable's imposing his gaze on
Pearce in what Pearce had felt to be private space. Constable Cooper
had made it clear he was going to bring no charges based on what he
saw, but Pearce perceived the observation and the knowledge gained by
it as themselves a violation.

Of critical importance for creating a system of mass discipline is
making policed individuals at least partially responsible for their own
regulation. Critical to that process is the creation of a perception of
ubiquitous and constant observation. The uniformed and visible Metropolitan Police constable was only a part of this process, but he was
a critical element in it, and it became increasingly important for the
regulation of sex between men in the years that followed.

CHAPTER 5

Unnatural-Assault Reporting in the London Press

He had not himself recently read in the newspapers of an account of a similar charge made by a policeman against a gentleman, nor had he heard any other person read any account of that transaction.[1]

He had never made such a charge against any person before, nor had he recently read himself nor heard read the particulars of a similar charge preferred by a policeman against a gentleman.[2]

He had not himself recently read in the newspapers any account of a similar charge made by a policeman against a gentleman, nor had he heard any other person read any account of such a transaction.[3]

The above three statements were printed in 1842 in the *Times,* the *Morning Post,* and the *Weekly Dispatch,* the leading papers for the middle, upper, and working classes respectively, and each in continuous publication from the start of the 1820s through the end of the 1860s. The statements concerned the trial of Private William Youl of the Coldstream Guards, who accused William Thomas Elder, "a middle-aged man of gentlemanly appearance," of making a sexual advance on him as he guarded the Tower of London. The defense attorney questioning Youl was trying to deflect suspicion away from Elder by implying that Youl had fabricated his charge and was attempting an extortion similar to one reported in the newspapers a few weeks before. Youl claimed to be unaware of that earlier case, although, like many men in nineteenth-century courtrooms, he was asked to speak of the relationship between his knowledge of unnatural assaults and what he had read in newspapers. Youl's statements were in turn printed in newspapers for other men to read.

The three articles are similar in overall length and wording. In this instance, and in many others, newspapers with very different audiences and political agendas often republished the same court report. Statements of editors are of little help in determining why this was so, as editors, like politicians, avoided discussing their professional decisions related to accounts of sex between men whenever possible. Although finding the same unnatural-assault story reproduced in upper-, middle-, and working-class newspapers makes clear that multiple groups within society were exposed to similar material, it also might flatten the picture, suggesting that class had no effect on newspaper presentation of these stories.

Comparing the tone of the different newspapers' coverage rarely yields significant differences. Much more revealing is to map their patterns of reporting over decades. Such mapping reveals significant differences in the reporting of the *Times,* the *Weekly Dispatch,* and the *Morning Post.* The clearest distinctions are found in the amount of coverage of cases involving sex between men and the type of story covered most often. These patterns also align with those found in other Whig, Tory, and Radical newspapers and reinforce class-based differences in the understanding of sex between men evident elsewhere. The liberal daily press published the greatest number of accounts of sex between men between 1820 and 1870, in part, it seems, because the imperatives of political liberalism compelled those editors more than others to deal with even distasteful matters if doing so was in the public interest.

This survey covers a fifty-year period between the years when the working class first began to read newspapers en masse and the time when the "new journalism" of the later nineteenth century changed the rules for reporting sex between men.[4] The scandal trials of the late nineteenth century did not break a silence on sex between men, as the more than one thousand newspaper reports on this topic published between 1820 and 1870 attest. Rather, those late-nineteenth-century cases marked a new way of politicizing sex between men. The Boulton and Park prosecution, the Dublin Castle Affair, the Cleveland Street Scandal, and even the trials of Oscar Wilde can be better understood if we know something about the earlier conventions of newspaper reporting on sex between men and how those patterns varied with the social class of the audience.

Despite their editorial differences, the leading papers had many common features. The most basic was their physical shape and appearance, which for most of the eighteenth century consisted of one large sheet of paper, folded in the center to make four pages. Originally two columns of text appeared on each page, but as sheet size increased and printing technology improved, the number of columns and thus the total amount of text in a newspaper rose. By the 1760s most newspapers were printed with four columns per page. In 1819 the *Times* was the first major newspaper to move to a five-column format; just over ten years later, it again led the other London papers by becoming the first to adopt an eight-page, six-column layout that it kept until the 1860s.[5]

Other elements were also consistent across most London newspapers. The different categories of news, such as foreign intelligence, domestic intelligence, shipping news, and other business information were included even in papers that catered to a "fashionable" or "radical" readership. All the papers also included some courtroom reporting, which was considered to be informative, entertaining, and relatively easy to collect. Typography did little to visually distinguish one section or story from the next, or to indicate that one story was more important than another. With the exception of masthead embellishments, there were no regular illustrations in London newspapers until the second half of the nineteenth century, and within a given category of news, one report typically followed another with no visual separation. The primary methods of drawing extra attention to a given report involved placement or length.

The central feature of most newspapers, regardless of their target audience, was parliamentary proceedings. In some papers, these reports occupied more than half the issue, often squeezing out other regular features during times of particularly important debates. Such strong popular interest was perhaps inspired by the degree to which real political power was at issue in parliamentary debate during these years, as well as by the importance of the issues decided in Parliament between the Napoleonic wars and the Reform Act of 1867.[6] The right of the public to know the substance of the debates in Parliament, as opposed to being presented only with the results of those debates, was won through a series of struggles in the 1770s, with the upper class finally acquiescing to note taking in the House of Commons from 1783. For much of the early nineteenth century, knowledge of the disagreements among the powerful still had the feel of a newly won freedom, and the fourth estate, as guardians of a public trust, jealously protected this prerogative.

The conventions of courtroom reporting changed in the early nineteenth century. In her work on trial coverage of sexual assaults on women from 1770 to 1845, Anna Clark has noted that the regular reporting of these cases in newspapers began only in the first decades of the nineteenth century.[7] Clark contends that these stories acted as cautionary tales for women, providing negative examples of women in public space at a time when the range of acceptable public activities for women was becoming more circumscribed. Newspaper reporting was not used in the eighteenth century to disseminate warnings to the popular classes because "eighteenth-century journalism, unlike its later counterpart, was not read by ordinary people."[8] Eighteenth-century crime reporting tended to focus on highway robberies of gentlemen rather than sexual assaults of any kind. Clark thus demonstrates that eighteenth- and nineteenth-century journalism tailored trial reporting to the perceived interests of its audience.

A newspaper's level of court reporting was determined by its size and circulation. The numbers of police and criminal courts in London increased steadily in the first half of the nineteenth century, so that by midcentury more than two dozen separate venues generated court cases.[9] It was a relatively simple matter for a paper to dispatch a reporter to a given courtroom, but only the largest papers could send reporters to the majority of the London courts. Many papers thus relied on the same court report, and smaller papers often picked up a court story after it was first covered by a larger daily newspaper. Thus larger papers had greater influence over which stories received the broadest coverage.

Magistrates and judges also exerted some control over newspaper court reporting, occasionally talking directly to reporters from the bench and requesting that they include certain details in their reports. One Bow Street magistrate, Mr. Halls, after reading an article in the *Morning Herald* that commented on one of his decisions, "called for the person who reports for that journal, and addressed him to this effect:— 'I address you, Sir, not because I consider you a responsible person for the articles contained in the paper you represent, but because, in your capacity as reporter, you have access to the editor, and can, therefore, convey to him the observations which I feel myself called upon to make, in consequence of a leading article in this day's number of the *Herald*, founded upon the report of a case decided by me on Tuesday last.'"[10]

Magistrates also knew that a particularly forceful or moralizing speech delivered at the end of a reported case would likely be reprinted at length in the newspapers and thus could benefit the public as well as the defendant in the courtroom.

In spite of these conventions of cooperation, though, decisions over what to publish rested mainly with the reporters and newspapers. One magistrate, Thomas Henry, complained that "in every police court there are fifty to sixty cases in a day, and the reporters, perhaps, select the one case which would most likely interest the public."[11] Henry considered that too often stories were chosen because they reinforced popular stereotypes of the criminal or played on public sentiment.

But even when the cases chosen might seem sensational, they still often served a greater public interest. The *Times* explained its reporting on cases involving sex between men in part on the grounds that these cases regularly came before the courts, and therefore potential jurymen needed to be informed about the relevant laws and practices.[12] After a report of several paragraphs concerning such a case, the *Times* declined to provide any information on the next case heard before the court because it was "of no public interest"—unlike, presumably, the case it had just discussed.[13] Two years after increasing its coverage of unnatural assaults, the *Morning Post* also declared that it was still "at all times reluctant to bring cases of this description before the public" for the most part because "it would be an act of injustice in any way to mix up the name of a highly respectable individual with so atrocious an accusation, to which . . . innocent parties are at all times exposed."[14] Yet despite this professed reluctance, the *Morning Post* continued to publish these stories, and the events of 1842 made clear that knowledge of them could be of great importance to upper-class men. Editors seem to have been genuinely reluctant to discuss sex between men in their publications, but other concerns, such as the professional obligation to serve the public interest, overcame this reticence.

This obligation remained consistent even as the composition of the newspaper-reading public was changing. In 1790 there were twenty-three London newspapers: fourteen dailies, seven triweeklies, and two weeklies. By 1811 that total had increased to fifty-two, with much of the difference accounted for by new Sunday papers aimed at the working class.[15] Although the number of weeklies continued to increase, by 1855 the number of daily papers in London had fallen from fourteen to ten, even though total circulation continued to increase. This consolidation was largely due to the dominance of the *Times*, which in 1814 became the first newspaper to adopt a steam-driven printing press, capable of producing 1,000 impressions per hour. By the 1840s, circulation of the *Times* had reached 40,000 issues a day, four times that of the nearest rival, and it led the other London papers in adopting the new editorial and technological processes that would later be seen as defining nineteenth-century journalism.[16]

The main rivals to the *Times* were weekly publications, although in the first half of the nineteenth century weeklies were often short-lived. Sales of the *Political Register* rose to more than 40,000 per week in the 1810s, although this total fell sharply after the rise in the stamp duty tripled its cost in 1820. Because of its content and the reputation of its editor, William Cobbett, *Cobbett's Weekly Register* was considered one of the more influential radical stamped weeklies, with a circulation of approximately 13,000 copies per week in the early 1830s.[17] The *Weekly Dispatch* was the most successful weekly paper in the 1840s, with a circulation of more than 50,000 at a time when most of the other Sunday papers sold between 10,000 and 30,000 copies. It was described in the 1840s as radical, anti–Poor Law, anti-Episcopal, and addressed "chiefly to the operatives and artizans [sic], to whose feelings and comprehensions its strong, rough, unceremonious mode of dealing with principals and potentates, and 'powers that be,' seems peculiarly appropriate."[18]

Newspaper readership often far exceeded the number of copies printed. Papers were rented by the hour, circulated in subscription libraries, and read aloud in public houses, coffeehouses, and workshops.[19] Roger Schofield has estimated that one-third of the London population had regular access to the contents of newspapers in the 1780s and into the first decades of the nineteenth century. The most significant increase in readership seems to have occurred in the 1830s, so that by the 1840s five-sixths of the London population had regular access to newspapers.[20] Thus the first half of the nineteenth century saw not only a dramatic rise in the amount of newspaper reporting of sex between men but also a huge increase in the number of people exposed to that reporting.

Most of the statistical information on newspaper circulation relates to the stamped newspapers; it is more difficult to track the development and influence of the more clandestine, unstamped publications. The most successful unstamped radical newspaper from the early 1830s was the weekly *Poor Man's Guardian*, with a circulation of between 12,000 and 15,000. Radical unstamped newspapers proliferated during times of political unrest in the 1810s, 1830s, and 1840s, with a substantial dropping-off of production of titles in the less tumultuous 1820s.[21] The government often avoided prosecution of these newspapers, in large part because the publicity associated with such trials often benefited the newspapers in question. In a discussion of the Chartist press in 1838, Home Secretary John Russell wrote that "so long as mere violence of language is employed without effect, it is better, I believe, not to add to the importance of these mob leaders by prosecutions."[22] The content of these newspapers was often inflammatory, but their brief print runs and small circulation limited their influence.

One of the unstamped radical weekly publications with an editorial policy perhaps furthest from the goals of the government during its short run was the *Black Dwarf*.[23] Like other unstamped weeklies, this paper did not have a regular section devoted to trials as most other newspapers did, but instead it occasionally gave prominence to a particular case that reinforced a political message. A representative example of the court cases covered in the *Black Dwarf* not involving charges of sex between men was published in 1822. It centered on a probably apocryphal letter from a young boy about to be transported for a petty theft. In the letter, the boy claimed he had never been taught that picking pockets was wrong, and that on his street the most successful thieves were most admired. He stated that he had never been taught of God or Christianity, "and I thought these words, like many others, were only useful to swear by."[24] The boy recounted that he had worked hard to become good at "my calling" of picking pockets, and he ended his letter (which he says he dictated to a fellow prisoner) by stating that at least "the savages [in Australia, his destination] would have taken care of my education, have taught me to shoot and hunt and fish, and would have taught me how to be a great and good man—but the Christians have not done so."[25] The theme of indignation at the upper ranks, who spoke of Christian obligations to the poor but then did little to fulfill them, was sustained as the author of the article railed against the fact that picking a pocket is a transportable offense, but that "the pillage of a nation" was rewarded with military and civilian honors, wealth, and dignity. This young boy "could never hope to be a rogue on so large a scale as to sin with impunity. . . . He was silly enough to steal from hand to mouth. The importance of stealing enough to silence accusation, or to bribe justice from her course, never occurred to his simple inexperience."[26]

The two themes of animosity toward authority and the call to protect the lower orders pervaded the *Black Dwarf*'s coverage of the most
widely discussed unnatural-assault arrest that occurred during its life-
time. In one of its later articles on the 1822 bishop of Clogher case, in
which an Irish Anglican bishop was discovered in a London public house
committing "unnatural acts" with a soldier, the *Black Dwarf* editorial-
ist expressed his fury over the fact that "this wretch was BAILED, for
the *express purpose of escaping from the laws*, of *settling his pecuniary
affairs*, and carrying away from wretched Ireland the sum of £150,000,
to spend in his abominable debaucheries abroad."[27] The author faulted
the Crown for not seizing Clogher's assets and not dispatching any
Bow Street officers to track him down. The author went on to argue
that "the poor wretches under sentence of death in Newgate: and those
who are now almost daily arrested on such charges, have just reason
to complain that they are not bailed by the bishop's friends, and sent
after the bishop, who has money enough to keep them all, and who
would, of course, be delighted with their company. . . . Three miserable
devils are to be executed, for the offense which has been screened from
punishment in the person of the Bishop."[28]

The *Black Dwarf* kept the Clogher controversy alive by alluding to
the bishop in another unnatural-assault trial to which he had no connection. The article centered on a soldier, George Kelly, who attempted
to take sexual advantage of a younger man in St. James's Park.[29] No
one involved in this case knew the bishop of Clogher or had any direct
connection to him, yet the *Black Dwarf*'s reporter framed the article by
writing that "I should not wonder, if any trial took place, that the soldier would boldly defend himself, as a follower of the bishop; and plead
that the bishop's example completely exonerated him from all blame."
The article goes on to say that the soldier, "as a poor, ignorant fellow,
might be expected to follow the precedent set him by his betters among
the respectable ranks of society, who are held out by all our politic
monitors as persons to whom we must pay an implicit obedience."[30]

Implicit in the *Black Dwarf* article is the idea that a man of weak
character who is easily led, as soldiers were assumed to be, might be
tempted into sexual acts with other men. The bishop of Clogher is presented as already beyond the pale of depravity: the greatest concern is
expressed for those with whom he might come into contact. This view
becomes clearer still when the author asks the reader to "only think,
Sir, of the influence of a Bishop among the uninformed and ignorant
loyalists!—The 'proneness to iniquity,' and the 'innate depravity' of

human nature, worked upon by a Bishop! Mercy on us! What may we not fear?"[31] Yet if figures like the bishop carry the potential to corrupt others, it is the character of working-class men outside the military that, according to the *Black Dwarf,* will act as the bulwark against the malevolent influence. Near the end of the piece, the author declares that "whatever mischief his Unholiness of Clogher may have effected among the higher orders, and the military, the people have escaped the contagion; and hold him and his disciples in detestation."[32]

The coverage of the bishop of Clogher case in the *Black Dwarf* expounded at length on the abuse of privilege, another theme that was one of the hallmarks of that publication. The amount of space a paper devoted to a story was strongly related to the interests of the readerships that it cultivated. Conversely, a paper like the *Patriot,* sympathetic to the monarchy and its government and not wishing to embarrass it or the established church, devoted very little space to the case and referred to the bishop of Clogher simply as an "unhappy person."[33]

By and large, though, the working-class papers did not attempt to make political hay of cases of sex between men. The attention and invective focused by the *Black Dwarf* on the bishop of Clogher case had no parallel in other popular working-class weeklies, such as *Cobbett's Weekly Register* or *Bell's Weekly Messenger. Cobbett's* does not appear to have taken notice of even the most sensational unnatural-assault cases. It featured no article on the Hyde Park cases from the spring of 1830 or the MP Charles Baring Wall's arrest and trial in May 1833. There was a discussion of courtroom proceedings in the issues of late May 1833, but it centered on the cases arising from the worker demonstrations at Coldbath Fields.[34] The *Poor Man's Guardian,* an unstamped "penny paper for the people," did not discuss any such trials during its run in the 1830s. Less surprisingly, publications created with the express purpose of improving the morals of the working class, such as the *Penny Magazine* and the *Moral Reformer,* both published by the Society for the Distribution of Useful Knowledge in the 1830s, included nothing in the way of unnatural-assault trial coverage. The *London Phalanx,* a short-lived weekly socialist newspaper dedicated to disseminating the utopian theories of Charles Fourier, also had nothing in the way of unnatural-assault coverage.[35]

Representative of unnatural-assault reporting in the weekly newspapers with more limited coverage were reports in *The Man: A Rational Advocate* on the case of Captain Henry Nicholls in 1833. On 18 August, the *Man* published the news of Nicholls's execution, relating that he had been tried and convicted at a recent Surrey Assizes "of an unnatural offence." The two-paragraph story noted that he "was a remarkable fine-looking man," that he had served in the Peninsular War, and that he was of a "very respectable family," although no member of that family had visited him during his time of incarceration.[36] This report appears to be the first report in the *Man* of cases involving Nicholls and his associates, although the article appears to assume that the reader was aware of the details surrounding his arrest. By this point Nicholls and several other military men and civilians had been the focus of many stories in the daily papers. It was alleged that they worked to procure young men and boys for a brothel patronized by high-ranking men.[37] Nicholls and several others were convicted for both murder and crimes related to sex between men, with great attention in the daily papers given to their executions.

Other working-class newspapers, such as the *Weekly Dispatch,* more closely matched the daily newspapers in the amount of unnatural-assault coverage they carried. Between January 1824 and December 1825, for example, the *Times* published thirty-seven separate reports of sex between men, and the *Weekly Dispatch* published at least twenty-five. The stories in the *Times* were generally longer than those in the *Weekly Dispatch,* although there were exceptions. The *Weekly Dispatch* published six stories that the *Times* did not; all but one of these stories involved only working-class litigants. Overall, a higher proportion of the coverage in the *Weekly Dispatch* consisted of stories involving only working-class men.

Similar patterns appeared a quarter century later. Between July 1851 and June 1852, the *Times* published at least twelve stories regarding sex between men, while the *Weekly Dispatch* published nine. Often the length and wording of the reports were almost identical. Only one story appearing in the *Weekly Dispatch* was longer than the corresponding report in the *Times,* but the additional detail related to an earlier theft and did not provide details of the unnatural assault in question.[38] Two stories appearing in the *Weekly Dispatch* did not appear in the *Times:* one described a case involving only working-class individuals. In that case, a working-class man awoke one night to find two unknown men in his house. One was in his kitchen, assaulting a female servant, while the other, a soldier, was asleep in the bed of his nephew. The householder said that he "endeavoured to rouse him; but, finding that impracticable without some gentle stimulant, I went downstairs for the horsewhip, and on my return I applied it to his shoulders, which soon induced him to open his eyes. (Laughter.)"[39]

These trends identified for the years 1824–25 and 1850–51 generally hold throughout the fifty-year period surveyed. The *Weekly Dispatch* regularly published between one-half and one-third as many stories related to sex between men as the *Times* did. The majority of those stories were drawn from the same court case, if not the same court report, as the *Times* stories. If a case was covered by the *Weekly Dispatch* but not the *Times*, it was most likely to be one involving only working-class men, or one in which a working-class father defended his son against unwanted advances from a man of higher social station. The *Weekly Dispatch* was also much more inclined to preface its reports of sex between men with headlines like "A Miscreant," "A Nasty Fellow," "A Beast," or "Shocking Depravity." The *Times* generally maintained an objective tone.

The differences between the papers are most evident from the story each paper covered most heavily between 1820 and 1870. For the *Times*, this was the 1870 arrest and initial prosecution of Boulton and Park. For the *Weekly Dispatch*, although it also covered this trial extensively, the events of 1842 produced a greater spike in its coverage of sex between men, as table 1 illustrates. Even more pronounced was the increase in coverage for 1842 in the *Morning Post*. For the *Morning Post*, in fact, 1842 seems to mark a watershed in its reporting of cases involving sex between men. Thus the events of 1842 were apparently of particular importance to upper-class men.

Newspapers targeted at the upper class displayed unique patterns in their reporting of sex between men. Although sometimes criticized for their lack of serious news, the fashionable papers did carry political and business news. What distinguished fashionable West End papers— aside from an editorial policy favoring economic protectionism, the established church, and Tory politics—was generous coverage of the royal court, along with columns on the activities of members of the peerage and gentry. One such item published in the "News Raisonée" section of the *John Bull* Sunday newspaper on 14 May 1826 read as follows. "Mr. Heber's complaint, for which he is recommended to travel, is said to have been produced by an over addiction to *Hartshorn*."[40] This single sentence appeared surrounded by similar short observations about prominent individuals and events in and around London. Although the mention of hartshorn might have alluded simply to the ammonium compound then used medicinally and in smelling salts, the

TABLE I. COMPARISON OF REPORTING ON SEX BETWEEN MEN IN THE *WEEKLY DISPATCH* AND THE *TIMES*, 1820–1870

	Reports in the *Weekly Dispatch*	Reports in the *Times*	Control group 1	Control group 2
1815			6	9
1816			0	17
1817			12	13
1818		1	8	8
1819		0	21	28
1820	0	2	8	10
1821	0	0	5	9
1822	3	8	17	19
1823	3	7	16	20
1824	2	4	10	10
1825[a]	24	34	21	21
1826	9	22	9	9
1827	7	12	24	23
1828	3	11	29	31
1829	5	11	14	16
1830	0	20	16	45
1831	5	6	21	20
1832	6	10	47	23
1833	17	25	39	45
1834	1	3	39	38
1835	3	5	32	27
1836	6	10	47	45
1837	1	2	27	21
1838	4	5	32	27
1839	6	11	30	28
1840	8	6	17	20
1841	5	16	7	29
1842	20	29	15	23
1843	15	38	21	21
1844	5	22	28	34
1845	1	9	21	21
1846	8	18	24	30
1847	4	15	17	18
1848	3	7	6	25
1849	4	10	0	24
1850	10	26	0	31
1851	11	17	5	19
1852	1	4	2	7
1853	1	8	5	9

TABLE I *(continued)*

	Reports in the *Weekly Dispatch*	Reports in the *Times*	Control group 1	Control group 2
1854	2	7	3	10
1855	2	2	6	19
1856	3	6	6	17
1857	2	5	2	21
1858	2	9	6	14
1859	0	3	4	8
1860	3	6	7	11
1861	2	4	6	10
1862	6	15	5	17
1863	5	15	13	14
1864	3	11	2	11
1865	1	5	7	9
1866	2	9	10	—
1867	0	6	1	3
1868	0	2	6	10
1869	3	14	5	14
1870	17	44	15	22
Totals	254	597	802	1,083

NOTE: Control group 1 consists of criminal trials for which individual names and trial dates are available from court documents. Control group 2 consists of criminal trials for sex between men in London and Middlesex.

[a] The significant spike in coverage in 1825 is connected with the change in the laws related to threatening to accuse of an infamous crime.

capitalization and italicization of the word suggested a double meaning. It was only because a man named Hartshorn took offense at the published statement that we know it to be a veiled reference to an alleged extended sexual relationship between the man's seventeen-year-old son and Richard Heber, MP. Rumors surrounding the two men had apparently grown after their return from a drawing expedition to the eastern Mediterranean, and the editor of the *John Bull* stated later at his trial that he published his jibe as an effort to shame the men into less obvious behavior.[41]

The senior Hartshorn felt the innuendo against his son and his family to be both public enough and direct enough to require legal redress. The *John Bull* was well known for its willingness to publish defamatory reports, having been founded specifically to attack the reputation of Queen Caroline during George IV's effort to divorce her in 1820.[42] At the ensuing libel trial, the editor of the *John Bull* built his defense around the assertion that his statement was true and was borne out by the public behavior of the two men. He was thus demonstrating a way in which publicity could be used against a class of men who could most easily afford to "purchase their privacy." This example shows one of the ways in which upper-class men policed their own, exposing the acts of men whose wealth might otherwise have rendered them immune to public disclosure.

Heber and Hartshorn were both upper-class men, and by taking a few precautions, they could largely escape the observations that would have led to their arrest. The vast majority of references to sex between men that can be positively identified in upper-class newspapers, however, deal with other kinds of relationships: situations involving a significant class divide and meetings in spaces that were to some degree public. These sorts of stories dominate the coverage in all newspapers, as men acting entirely in private were unlikely to be arrested. A closer examination of the *Morning Post*'s reporting, however, reveals other patterns that seem to reflect more directly the concerns of upper-class men.

According to a comprehensive survey published in 1847 of all British newspapers, the *Morning Post* was "the paper of the beau monde, the journal of the fashionable world."[43] Although its law and police-court coverage was limited in the 1820s, it later expanded to match that of other daily newspapers. This change occurred even before the paper's adoption in the 1840s of an eight-page format, which gave it an overall size comparable to that of the leading liberal dailies. For these reasons, the *Morning Post* provides a suitable vehicle for exploring long-term patterns in the representation of sex between men as presented to the upper class.

The *Morning Post*'s coverage of trials centering on sex between men was analyzed for twenty-five of the fifty years between 1820 and 1870 (see table 2). In these years, there were 471 instances in which an individual's name, the trial date, and trial location were obtained from state records: these form the control group of the table. In these years, the *Times* covered 321 cases heard in the criminal courts or police courts.

Table 2 shows a significant increase in the *Morning Post*'s coverage of unnatural-assault cases beginning in 1842. Many notable incidents before 1842 were either not mentioned or given only cursory coverage: stories covering these events average only seventeen lines. The Hyde Park cases of 1830, for example, seem to have been reported only in a

TABLE 2. COMPARISON OF REPORTING ON SEX
BETWEEN MEN IN THE *MORNING POST*,
THE *TIMES*, AND THE *WEEKLY DISPATCH*,
SELECTED YEARS

	Reports in the *Morning Post*	Reports in the *Weekly Dispatch*	Reports in the *Times*	Control group
1827	0	7	12	24
1830	4	0	20	16
1831	0	5	6	21
1832	3	6	10	47
1833	1	17	25	39
1834	0	1	3	39
1835	1	3	5	32
1837	0	1	2	27
1838	0	4	5	39
1839	1	6	11	30
1840	4	8	6	17
1842	11	20	29	15
1844	7	5	22	28
1846	9	8	18	24
1848	4	3	7	6
1850	8	10	26	0
1852	3	1	4	2
1854	2	2	7	3
1856	4	3	6	6
1858	7	2	9	6
1860	2	3	6	7
1863	5	5	15	13
1866	1	2	9	10
1869	10	3	14	5
1870	17	17	44	15
Totals	*104*	*142*	*321*	*471*

NOTE: The control group consists of criminal trials for which individual names and trial dates are available from court documents.

short account of one of the criminal trials at Westminster. The stories of sex between men that do appear before 1842 were not discussed in significant detail.

The increased coverage in 1842 began with the Youl case, with which this chapter opens, and culminated with the months-long series of events related to the charges of indecent assault and false accusation between John Ellis Churchill and William Stringer. From this point forward, the average story in *The Morning Post* involving sex between men was sixty lines long. In 1842 it was generally only the Saturday issue of the *Morning Post* that ran to eight pages, and so the first expanded unnatural-assault coverage appeared in the four-page newspaper.

The most striking evidence that this increase in coverage related to editorial policy and to the anxieties that these events generated among upper-class men centers on the type of story singled out for attention after that date. One-quarter of the reports in the years 1842 to 1870 focused on extortion charges similar to those at the center of the events of 1842. Of the remaining articles, five involved clergymen, seven focused on cross-dressers, and four were given over to questioning police methods. Compared to what can be recovered from the *Times,* the *Weekly Dispatch,* and the surviving court records, after 1842, extortion cases and cases involving upper-class men (who were usually victorious) were much more common in the pages of the *Morning Post* than they were either in the courtrooms or in the middle- and working-class newspapers.

Of course, arguments based on the absence of certain types of evidence are always problematic and susceptible to refutation by further research. In his pioneering works, Jeffrey Weeks relied on printed versions of the annual *Palmer's Index to the* Times in order to identify newspaper reports related to sex between men. More recently, scholars have been able to make use of electronic indexes and even databases that allow for full-text searching. These new and powerful tools are, however, still imperfect. Full-text searching of names and keywords very often misses information, so that multiple search techniques are still needed. As recently as three years ago, a study argued that all papers save the *Times* were silent on the coverage of sex between men in the 1850s and 1860s, but the search methods employed for this study have yielded different results.[44] Future studies may turn up additional material. For now, what can safely be said is that such coverage was plentiful in the upper-class papers; it favored stories highlighting the defeat of extortionists who preyed on the upper class; and in no case between 1820 and 1870 did the interests of upper-class men seem as threatened as in the Churchill and Stringer case of 1842.

This case was broadly similar to the many others involving competing accusations of two men who met in a public space, but it highlighted the dangers and capriciousness of the state system in adjudicating guilt and innocence more than most, and it also exposed a more intense threat to respectable men. It started with a report of a minor trial for unnatural assault, initially covered by many papers including the *Times*, the *Morning Chronicle*, and the *Weekly Dispatch* in their respective law sections for 13 August 1842. A "respectable-looking" man named William Stringer testified that he was walking through Hyde Park at about 9:15 P.M., "when on passing a clump of trees he saw two men in an indecent situation."[45] He said he sprang on the two men, one of whom got away. The man he caught, named John Ellis Churchill, allegedly begged to be let go and indicated that he was a gentleman and would give Stringer any amount of money.

Churchill, described as a "well-dressed" young man, next gave his version of the story. He said that while walking through the park at night, a young man came up to him and asked him the way to Oxford Street. Churchill said he would show him, as he was going the same way. As they were walking together, Stringer came upon them and accused them "of having committed a most opprobrious crime."[46] At this point, Churchill said, he began to suspect that the young man asking for directions was in league with Stringer, as he was giving Churchill advice to go quietly with his accuser and not resist. The young man had run away before Stringer and Churchill found a group of policemen.

This was the extent of the first day's coverage. It was most unusual that the papers described both men as well-dressed and gave roughly equal amounts of space to each man's story. Often reports recounted in detail only the story of the individual whom either the reporter or the magistrate seemed to view as the innocent party. A later report indicated that the magistrate had initially believed Stringer, and that if anything the first day's hearing had gone against Churchill, even though he was known to be the nephew of a member of Parliament. Still, there seemed little else remarkable about this report. This was the sort of case where the subsequent police court hearings and later criminal trial might as easily be reported as not.

Yet this was not to be one of the stories that disappeared. In the second day's coverage, on the following Monday, the *Times* and the *Morning Chronicle* devoted a half-column each to the story, and the tone of the writing began to shift in favor of Churchill. One of Churchill's friends had discovered that Stringer had lied about working at the firm of Sheppard and Sutton.[47] As a result, Churchill made a countercharge against Stringer for assaulting him in the park. Two days later, as the case was still unfolding in the Marlborough Street police court, the story received its first coverage in the *Times* outside the law section. Closer to the front of the paper, adjacent to the parliamentary proceedings and foreign intelligence sections, appeared a lengthy letter to the editor. It stated in part:

> The prosecutor swears before a magistrate that he saw the defendant committing the supposed offense, and that he seized him and gave him in charge to a policeman. The defendant, on the other hand, claims that the prosecutor assaulted him and made a false charge against him for the purpose of extorting money. The evidence, then, is simply oath against oath. Now, Sir, let me ask, if this be the law of England, what security is there for any man's reputation! . . . It appears that a gentleman cannot walk in safety through Hyde-park unless he be strong enough to knock down any blackguard who may find it more convenient to lay his betters under contribution in this legal and authorized manner than to subject himself to the penalties due to highway robberies.
>
> Signed "A Solicitor"[48]

The matter grew in importance, with a full column of text devoted to the proceedings in the next day's law sections of the *Morning Chronicle,* the *Times,* and the *Morning Post;* even more appeared in the following day's edition of the *Weekly Dispatch.* The *Satirist* took note of the case on 28 August 1842, opening its report with the observation that the investigations of Churchill's friends revealed that he was the victim of "a gang of miscreants who lived by the practice of making revolting charges against respectable individuals with a view to extortion and robbery."[49]

By 23 August there was no question as to where the reporters' sympathies lay. Several reports opened by noting that "ever since Mr. Churchill was charged by [Stringer] on Friday fortnight, with indecent behavior with another person in Hyde-park, he and his friends, assisted by the police, have been unremitting in their efforts to trace the conspiracy to the bottom."[50] That day's report revealed that Churchill's friends had succeeded in apprehending and placing at the bar William Newstead, "a good looking, well dressed young man" who had worked with Stringer on that first night in Hyde Park. Churchill's attorney told the court that he could prove that Newstead and Stringer were "intimate companions, and he had too much cause to fear that the present was not the first case of the kind they had been concerned in together for the purposes of extorting money." He also indicated that he could prove that the men were "connected with a number of persons concerned in similar conspiracies."[51]

That proof came from one of Newstead and Stringer's friends, who had decided to cooperate with the police. Frederick Clark "admitted that he had frequently been in company with the prisoners and their companions . . . [and] there were a great many more in the gang."[52] It was also revealed that Stringer went by multiple aliases, and that he had illegally returned from a sentence of transportation.[53] The mother of another friend, Eliza Fitzgerald, was also brought in to testify, and both she and Clark were provided with lodging at the house of a policeman before the trial, "to prevent [their] being tampered with, or threatened by any of the prisoner's companions."[54] Near the end of the report, which took up nearly three-quarters of a column in the *Times,* the magistrate was quoted as observing that "a more foul or detestable conspiracy he had never heard of."[55]

Information from the friend whose cooperation had led to Newstead's capture also led to the apprehension of William Fitzgerald, Eliza's son and a close friend of the two accused men. William Fitzgerald was brought into the Bow Street police station not on a charge related to his connection with Stringer and Newstead but instead for an extortion he had carried out on his own months before, against a man named Henry Watson. Watson initially had no intention of pressing charges against Fitzgerald, almost certainly because of the degree to which he had compromised himself in the encounter. It was the police who pulled a visibly reluctant Watson into the courtroom and forced him to recount his actions.

Watson told the court that he "was looking at some prints in the window of a shop in the Strand" when Fitzgerald came up to him and commented that "the pictures looked very fine." Fitzgerald then said "I beg your pardon, Sir, you appear to be a judge of these things, I am a poor man, and have some pictures at home for which I wish to find a purchaser."[56] Watson agreed to take a look at them and accompanied Fitzgerald to the room he occupied in the area of Drury Lane. When in the room, Watson said he inquired about the pictures, to which Fitzgerald allegedly responded, "Oh d—— your eyes! I have no prints or pictures here." After further abusive statements, Fitzgerald then said "You b——, unless you give me all the money you have, I'll tear your linen, and accuse you of an assault with intent, &c."[57] Watson gave Fitzgerald the only shilling then in his possession, but he was not able to escape before Fitzgerald had torn his shirt and trousers. The delay in prosecution, Watson said, was due to the fact that he had gone "raving mad from the shock which he had received, and was consequently unable to attend and give evidence."[58]

The courts and by extension the newspapers almost always only dealt with cases of failed extortions, in which one of the two parties was able to construct an innocent enough interpretation of his actions to risk making an appeal to the law. The case between Fitzgerald and Watson is one of the few recorded examples of an almost completely successful extortion, one that came to light for reasons only indirectly related to the original incident. Watson had voluntarily gone to the lodging of a man he had known only for a matter of minutes, and Watson's discomfort on the stand strongly indicates that he knew that his excuse for doing so was a thin one. It is unlikely that Watson would ever have taken the case to court if not forced to do so by the police.

The day after Watson's testimony appeared in many newspapers, the *Times* published a letter to the editor on the incident that read in part: "Charges of a most unfounded character, to the nature of which it is impossible to more particularly allude, have lately been brought for purposes of extortion against respectable individuals. It appears that these accusations emanate from a gang of miscreants who derive their abominable livelihood from thus infamously practicing on the fears of those victims. . . . Good God, Sir, in what frightful peril, then, do we all stand? Who knows if his own turn may not be the next to fall within the scope of this atrocious villainy?"[59] The letter ends with several paragraphs arguing for the return of hanging for any man found guilty of making a false claim related to unnatural assaults.

The newspaper drama surrounding this particular "band of miscreants" ended with the following day's coverage of the Central Criminal Court proceedings. Stringer, Newstead, and Fitzgerald were tried before the same judge and sentenced together, even though the case against Fitzgerald was separate from those against his two friends.[60] The coverage that day in the *Times* was more than two columns; that of the *Morning Post*, the *Morning Chronicle*, and the *Weekly Dispatch* was nearly as extensive. Each report noted that "the jury, without hesitating for a moment, returned a verdict of Guilty against [the] prisoners." The *Morning Post*, in celebration of this verdict against the extortionists, further reported that "the verdict was received with applause by the persons in the Court." The *Times* and the *Morning Chronicle* also reported the applause but restored order and seriousness to their representations of the courtroom by adding that these "loud marks of approbation . . . were of course instantly suppressed by the Court."[61] The *Weekly Dispatch*, though not sympathetic to the convicted men, perhaps saw less reason to celebrate and made no mention of the applause.

At the end of the trial the judge, Baron Rolfe, "addressing the prisoners, said they had been convicted upon the clearest evidence of one of the foulest and most serious offenses known to the law; that they were prowling about the park in the evening for the purpose of concocting such charges there could be no doubt whatever."[62] Because Stringer had been previously convicted of a felony and returned early from his sentence of seven years' transportation, he was sentenced to transportation for life. Newstead was transported for fifteen years, and Fitzgerald for thirteen. Several weeks later the trial of another man alleged to be connected with Stringer, Fitzgerald, and Newstead generated further substantial court reports and an additional letter to the editor in the *Times*.[63]

This was the most shocking and most extensively reported of the cases in 1842, although it was part of a wave of similar incidents. Churchill's plight was seized on because it seemed to show how closely a man well placed in society had come to being wrongly convicted of unnatural interest, with only the efforts of his friends averting this fate. The anger and fear felt by respectable men was reflected in the coverage of the *Morning Post* and even the *Times*, although these emotions were more evident in the letters to the editor of the *Times* than in its reporting. The greatest single difference in the coverage of these events among the newspapers surveyed was not that the *Weekly Dispatch* was tepid in its support of the conviction but rather that its reporting portrayed Watson, the working-class hairdresser who had followed Fitzgerald to his lodgings to view the prints, in a more sympathetic light than did other publications. Watson was represented as an additional victim of Stringer, Newstead, and Fitzgerald rather than as a compromised man less worthy than Churchill of respect.

The extensive coverage of this case was less unusual for the *Times* than for the other papers. Not only did the *Times* regularly publish more stories related to sex between men than any other paper, but it also published more stories centering on men of different class backgrounds who first encountered one another in a public space. In this respect the *Times* surpassed other leading liberal dailies as well. Although not particularly evident in the coverage of the Stringer and Fitzgerald case, the variation between the *Times* and other liberal daily newspapers, such as the *Morning Chronicle,* was pronounced. The *Morning Chronicle* did not print the police-court reports of the 1830 Hyde Park cases, even though it regularly covered the Queen Square Police Court, where most of the Hyde Park hearings took place.[64] Its first article on this topic covered one of the related criminal trials; it clearly assumed that the incidents were already known to the reader.[65]

Although the *Morning Chronicle* failed to report the Hyde Park police court hearings, it included other unnatural-assault coverage from the police courts that month, including the "Apprehension of a Gang of Miscreants" at the Bull public house.[66] There are some slight differences in emphasis in the *Times* and the *Morning Chronicle* coverage of this molly-house raid, but each article listed the same defendants in the same order, and each related similar details concerning how the two prosecuting soldiers encountered men with "rouged cheeks and hair in ringlets."[67]

Like the *Times*, the *Morning Chronicle* covered the resulting criminal trial with a short report; unlike the *Times*, the *Morning Chronicle* failed to mention another unnatural-assault case heard in the same court on the same day. The *Times* related to its readers in a separate report that "George Dymond was indicted for an indecent assault upon a lad of the name of John Hart. He was found guilty, and sentenced to six months' imprisonment in the House of Corrections."[68] This was a more innocuous story of one man who tried to take advantage of another when the opportunity presented itself.

Although in isolation this difference means little, it illustrates the *Times*'s more extensive coverage of this sort of case. The other liberal daily papers, including the *Morning Chronicle,* published less of this material than did the *Times,* but as much if not more than did the *Weekly Dispatch,* at least in the first half of the nineteenth century. As tables 1 and 2 show, from 1830 through at least 1870 the *Times* covered only a fraction of all the unnatural-assault cases that appeared before the London criminal and police courts, yet it seems to have published at least twice as many of these reports as any of the other London papers did. The *Times* was more likely to cover those cases that pitted middle- and upper-class men against working-class men, where the contest came down to one man's word against another's.[69] This finding raises the question of why the liberal press in general and the *Times* specifically were responsible for so much of this reporting, and the related question of what meanings such reporting had for newspaper readerships.

Addressing the second question first, two early nineteenth-century works demonstrate the impact that unnatural-assault reporting could have on men who strongly identified with feelings of same-sex desire. Both consist of collections of newspaper clippings, spanning decades, of precisely these stories. The first is an unpublished collection compiled by William Beckford, born into one of the wealthiest and most power-ful eighteenth-century families, who faced a period of ostracism and social exile when his sexual relationship with another young man of his own class was discovered.[70] The second and far more interesting work is an eighty-page privately printed poem in defense of same-sex desire written in the style of Lord Byron, titled *Don Leon*.[71] Like Beckford, the anonymous author collected clippings from the newspapers of unnatural-assault trials, but he integrated this material into his own creative work, using the clippings as footnote material.

We know little about the author of *Don Leon*, except that he most likely composed the work while living in Paris: many of the newspaper accounts of sex between men that he used were reprints of reports pub-lished in an English-language newspaper, *Galignani's Messenger*, origi-nating in Paris. The examples used in the poem are dated between 1822 and 1850, which may have been a period of enforced exile. The style and language of the poem indicate that the author was a man well-read in the classics and in the romantic poetry of his day, and we can infer that he was wealthy enough to escape adversity by crossing the Channel.[72]

The poem demonstrates that the author recognized himself in the men described in the newspaper clippings. He used them to argue that sex between men was common in London, and that "it will not be difficult, within the compass of a single year, to select from police reports cases enough to force from the strongest stickler at the moral-ity of this churchgoing generation an avowal that no class of English society has been exempt from the stain."[73] The stories also showed that prejudice against these acts easily became brutal and arbitrary, as when one man slit his own throat in Brighton rather than be subjected to a mob attack.[74] Most remarkably, though, the author did not allow the bleakness of the newspaper stories to set the tone for his poem. They provided proof of the existence of men like himself, and from that base he was able to construct an imaginative and hopeful epic. After recounting the acceptance of such acts in ancient Greece and Rome and modern Constantinople, he added:

This little spot, which constitutes our isle,
Is not the world! Its censure or its smile
Can never reason's fabric overthrow,
And make a crime of what is not really so.[75]

Don Leon's most important message may be its implicit warn-ing against making assumptions about how individuals interpreted accounts of unnatural assault. Newspaper editors always presented sexual acts between men in a negative light, and none of them intended their reporting to be a basis for the validation of such sexual desires. Readers, however, do what they want with texts.

Yet the author of *Don Leon* was atypical. The statements by Private Youl that opened this chapter most likely better exemplify the effects of this coverage on the population at large, as do the other statements of men who decided on levels of extortion. Much of the population apparently derived its information and opinions about such acts from the newspapers: some aspiring extortionists set the amounts of their blackmail payments on the basis of newspaper accounts they had read.[76] Similarly, the *Times* remarked, in relation to another unnatural-assault case, that "most members of the general public had seen the reports in the papers, and had taken an interest in the question."[77] In a different extortion trial, Henry Tiddiman was asked if he knew another man who had also recently been involved in a court case involving sex between men. Tiddiman replied that he did not know the other man personally but did "remember reading an account of it in the paper."[78] Later in the same trial, it was recalled that one of the extortionists had used the threat of publicity by observing that this "was a most infamous affair, and, if it got into the papers, would cause more sensation than Greenacre's murder."[79] Another man, George Johnson, who had once been robbed by Levy Le Grand, came forward to testify against him after seeing Le Grand's name in the newspaper in connection with another case of unnatural assault on a young man.[80] Men were expected to know enough from newspaper accounts to avoid Hyde Park at night, and on the witness stand they were usually not allowed to claim ignorance of its reputation as a site for sexual encounters between men. These newspaper stories were the primary medium for a message that was otherwise problematic to disseminate to the public, and they succeeded in making most men in London aware of it.

But why did the liberal papers generally, and the *Times* specifically, lead the way in this type of coverage? One answer might focus on the problematic nature of liberal, middle-class masculine identity, building on the work of historians who have argued that the early nineteenth century was a period of heightened anxiety for men of this rank.[81] Often sedentary in their occupations, frequently relying on the work and resources of their wives for material support, and defining themselves through religious belief, with its tendency to effeminize, middle-class men were often more detached from established signifiers of masculinity than were men of other classes.[82] Although such an argument has merits, a more positive explanation for the wider coverage of these stories in the liberal newspapers centers on the strengths inherent in middle-class male identity.

Liberal ideology was based on the power of reason. A respectable man's reason and morals guided his actions, especially in the first half of the nineteenth century, when a belief in reason and intellectual progress could still be completely compatible with and even reinforced by a literal interpretation of the Bible. Before this alliance of faith and reason was broken in the later nineteenth century, it provided a powerful and distinctive worldview, a basis on which middle-class men could build their identity and from which they could challenge the upper-class monopoly on political and social power.[83] The *Times* was the leading proponent of such liberal reform in the public sphere, and it often tailored its reporting to support its political goals. From its watershed coverage of the Peterloo Massacre in 1819, in which it opposed the tactics employed by the government, the *Times* was considered by politicians and the public alike as a decisive force in English politics.[84] In the debates over Catholic emancipation, the Reform Act of 1832, Poor Law reform, and the Factory Acts, the *Times* supported its liberal goals with prominent leading articles and oblique references to the injustices of current policies.[85]

The influence of the *Times* was demonstrated when a politically weakened Duke of Wellington, on the formation of his new ministry in November 1834, attempted to negotiate with the editor of the *Times,* Thomas Barnes, about the support he could expect from the paper. Barnes's first response, in keeping with his position of supporting liberal policies regardless of party, was to inform the new ministry that it need only put forward sensible policies to enjoy his paper's support.[86] At that critical moment, the *Times,* in the masculine middle-class manner, rejected the role of client to a powerful upper-class patron and the trading of personal allegiance in return for future rewards. It continued to base its editorial policy on the dictates of a liberal philosophy, based on the demands of reason, morality, and civic responsibility.[87]

The *Times* also aimed to cultivate civic responsibility in its readership. Newspaper editors hoped that their law reports would influence individual readers to curtail improvident behavior, as in an 1853 article on embezzlement:

Every now and then our law reporters supply us with notes of a trial which afford us some little glance behind the scenes, and a pretty insight into life about town it is. For a few weeks or days the exposure hangs in the public recollection, and then, like other warnings, is forgotten. The private bill discounters and money-lenders drive their ignoble trade, and the dupes flock into their nets as merrily as ever. What, then, it may be said, is the use of commenting upon cases of this kind? We certainly do not expect that any words of ours will avail to check the iniquitous system in question; but it may just happen that one paulo-post-future dupe may read these few lines and hesitate ere he affix his name to a document which will most infallibly lead to his great and enduring embarrassment, if not to his permanent ruin.[88]

Stories from the 1810s and 1820s remarked on the power of the press to educate and enlighten people and to foster a sense of connection among readers. The newspapers themselves encouraged readers to believe that they had a close relationship with other readers, and most newspapers claimed to represent public opinion in some way.[89]

The attention to sex between men in the liberal newspapers was meant to serve a necessary civic function. As the leading liberal newspaper, the *Times* was inclined to present a more complete picture of sex between men in London than the circumscribed views of the *Weekly Dispatch* or the *Morning Post*. By not singling out for special emphasis extortion cases, as did the *Morning Post,* or cross-dressers or working-class fathers supporting their sons, as did the *Weekly Dispatch,* the *Times* presented a more representative picture of sex between men in London, one that reflected the most common types of prosecutions. Printing dispassionate stories of middle-class men caught in degrading acts was a hard and unpleasant choice, but a choice mandated by the paper's liberal philosophy.

Although such editorial decisions were in the hands of a small number of men, the competitive nature of the nineteenth-century newspaper market makes it possible to read greater significance into these decisions. In the eighteenth century, newspapers had often been influenced by direct payments from the government or from other political interest groups. After the first decades of the nineteenth century, this practice all but ceased. As newspaper circulation and gross receipts steadily increased, external payments became inconsequential.[90] A paper unable to cultivate a readership for its views did not last long, no matter how powerful the men who backed it. Government attempts to cultivate alternative papers for the working classes, such as the *White Dwarf* or the *Anti-Cobbett,* met with little success.[91] As Lord Liverpool wrote to Castlereagh in 1815, "No paper that has any character, and consequently an established sale, will accept money from the Government; and, indeed, their profits are so enormous in all critical times, when their support is most necessary, that no pecuniary assistance that Government could offer would really be worth their acceptance."[92] If the readership of the *Times* had been offended by the frequency of unnatural-assault stories, it could have switched to other successful and reputable liberal papers that had less such coverage. These reports would not have continued as consistently or for as long as they did if they had been offensive to their readers. The liberal ideals that led editors to print these stories were shared by the readers. Thus liberal political philosophy set the tone for the reporting of sex between men in the years between 1820 and 1870.

It might be argued that class politics was a factor in the four spikes in the publication of stories related to sex between men. The 1825 increase in stories was related to the change in the laws on extortion, in the context of the increased use of the laws related to unnatural assault. The other three spikes, in 1833, 1842, and 1850, all seem to follow episodes of intense class-based political upheaval, coming after the Reform Act of 1832 excluded workers from the expanded franchise, after the failure of the second Chartist petition in the midst of a severe economic downturn, and in the wake of the failed third Chartist petition and coinciding with the Continental revolutions of 1848. Because the spikes in reporting do not directly correspond to spikes in prosecutions, the threat posed by sex between men as it was depicted in the press was not a simple reflection of more vigorous enforcement of the laws. But these cases did not become politicized in the mid-nineteenth century as later cases did. Neither Feargus O'Connor nor any other working-class radical leader made an issue of them at Chartist rallies. They were not yet material for politics as they would be later in the century.

The coming of the new journalism coincided with efforts by individuals and groups to use cases of sex between men for political purposes.[93] Morris Kaplan has shown that in the 1889 Cleveland Street Scandal, editors refused to allow upper-class men to escape justice as they had regularly done earlier in the century, and their decision helped to create a public sensation.[94] Kaplan's close reading of the newspaper reports from that incident demonstrates that it was the abuse of class privilege rather than merely sex between men that caused outrage. In the 1884 Dublin Castle Affair, the Irish nationalist press seized an opportunity to humiliate its political enemies by making public the sexual activities of British officials in Ireland.[95] Even the prosecution of Oscar Wilde proceeded as it did in part because of political concerns.[96]

But even though it was not the new journalism, the journalism of the 1820s evidenced significant innovations of its own. Political liberalism was itself a new and dynamic force in the 1820s. Middle-class liberals were the insurgents then, and their form of reporting challenged the status quo. Liberalism believed in the power of reason to overturn the inefficiencies of an "Old Corruption" that founded power on birth and patronage rather than on merit and individual ability. Rational liberalism could lead men to conclusions that were extremely unpopular, but the mark of truly respectable masculinity was to have the courage of one's convictions, to follow logic to its conclusion, and to be strong enough to live even with uncomfortable or unpopular conclusions. Jeremy Bentham, who founded a uniquely British version of the liberal philosophy, came to the conclusion that discrimination against sex between men was not intellectually justifiable, although he kept these conclusions secret.[97] John Stuart Mill was braver when his liberal philosophy led him, against the views of many of his class, to conclude as early as the 1860s that women should exercise the vote on equal terms with men. He lost his seat in Parliament in part because of his public defense of women's suffrage. Mill also espoused equal treatment under the law for Britain's Jamaican subjects of African descent, and for this stance he was publicly ridiculed by Thomas Carlyle.[98]

For Mill, Bentham, and other reforming liberals, decisions had to be based on reason and facts, and distasteful matters had to be dealt with in a forthright manner. If liberal papers dealt with sex acts between men more candidly and extensively than working- or upper-class newspapers did, it was because the imperatives of political liberalism dictated it. To shrink from the responsibility to publish these stories would have been to fail the test of character for the respectable man.

PART THREE

Implications

CHAPTER 6

Patterns within the Changes

In the 1820s and early 1830s, as previous chapters discuss, a series of state reforms altered and intensified policing of sexual acts between men. This outcome was not the main motivation of the reforms, and the men making them largely avoided the public discussion of such practices. For this reason, the historical records are fewer in this area than for other categories of legislated change, such as the Poor Law reform of 1834, the regulation of prostitution, or the extension of the franchise. Nevertheless, the policing of sex between men was brought into line with nineteenth-century patterns of law enforcement, which entailed reduced but more consistently applied penalties and more pervasive policing. This approach replaced the eighteenth-century pattern of rare but spectacular prosecutions coupled with severe punishments.

This greater state scrutiny led to an increase in the amount of newspaper coverage of court cases focusing on sex between men from the 1820s onward, with the extent of reporting determined by the editorial policies of individual newspapers. The liberal daily newspapers, and especially the *Times*, had the most extensive coverage. Statements from the period, largely recorded in newspaper accounts and trial documents, indicate that there was a substantial public awareness of the new laws and the new practices concerning the policing of sex between men by the early 1830s, with this awareness often created by the newspapers themselves.

Because of the reticence of so many to speak on this topic, understanding the social effects of these changes requires identifying the less obvious patterns of enforcement of the laws. The laws regulating sex between men, like almost all laws, were not implemented exactly as written, and discrepancies between the law and actual practice reveal important limits to the state's power and individuals' tacit assumptions about the intent of such laws. As written, the law could have been used to curtail more behavior than was prosecuted in practice. Enforcement was confined largely to the public spaces patrolled by the police and those private spaces where the state was called in by a complainant.

One set of otherwise unarticulated assumptions became evident during the prosecution brought by the wife of Edward Berry against her husband in the early 1830s. As she entered the courtroom in the spring of 1833, Mrs. Berry had good reason to believe that her case was similar to many other recent trials. Although none of the other prosecutions presented in the newspapers involved a wife's charging her husband with sodomy, she nevertheless recognized the crime of unnatural assault described in those accounts as similar to what her husband had done to her. If the newspaper reports were any guide, Mrs. Berry had a significant chance of winning her case.

Her own experience in court was dramatically different. The majority of newspaper stories described contests between two individuals, in which one person's word was weighed against another's. Without additional witnesses to the act, it was left to the magistrate or the jury to judge the validity of the competing stories, basing their decisions on the individuals' character and the consistency of their stories under close questioning. In the Berry case, her husband was never called on to present his side of the story, as the judge announced that it was quite unnecessary. The *Times* and the *Weekly Dispatch* reported that "as the evidence of the prosecutrix was unsupported by any other testimony, and she being *particeps criminis,* the learned judge directed an acquittal without calling upon the prisoner for his defense. He was immediately discharged."[1] To add insult to injury, Mrs. Berry was "hooted and pelted" as she left the courtroom by a crowd that had gathered to witness the event.[2]

Under the sodomy and unnatural-assault laws as they were then interpreted, Mrs. Berry's status as a participant in the act did not necessarily disqualify her from testifying. Questions of evidence fell to the judges, who had wide latitude in deciding who was an admissible witness.[3] The fact that the Berrys were husband and wife might seem a significant factor, but the judge made no reference to this point when he dismissed the case. The police-court magistrate who sent the case up to the criminal court had come to the conclusion that Mrs. Berry's case was worth pursuing.

It was almost certainly because Mrs. Berry was a woman that she and her case were not taken seriously. This seems to be the only criminal trial in London between 1820 and 1870 in which a woman attempted to prosecute a man for sodomy, and the only such trial occurring anywhere in the country reported in the *Times* or the *Weekly Dispatch* over that period.[4] Its uniqueness cannot be attributed to a long-standing interpretation of the sodomy laws, as a handful of cases with women complainants went to trial in the eighteenth century, and their details were recorded in the session papers of the Old Bailey.[5] Mrs. Berry's treatment by the men of the courtroom was not what Englishwomen of past generations could have expected, and it therefore highlights one of the changes occurring in the early nineteenth century.

Mrs. Berry initially felt that the law was on her side, but was abruptly made to feel otherwise when the trial began. A group of working-class policemen also thought they were acting appropriately when they attempted to entrap gentlemen in Hyde Park who were soliciting sex from other men, but that practice too was quickly condemned and halted. Both of these boundary-setting events occurred between the late 1820s and the early 1830s, when the policing, prosecuting, and reporting of infamous crimes were in flux, and both indicate something about the assumptions held by the men who oversaw the revision, interpretation, and implementation of the laws.

In attempting to discern the motivations of these men, examining the fractured nature of social, political, and economic power among them can be instructive. The decision to brusquely dismiss Mrs. Berry's case was made by a magistrate, functioning as arbiter of the laws of England as he understood them. The decision to report this outcome in the newspaper was made by the staffs of at least two companies known to take pride in their independence from the state. Both the *Times* and the *Weekly Dispatch* reproduced not only the judge's derogatory statements but also the details of Mrs. Berry's humiliation by the assembled crowd. Because the goals of the judge, the newspapers, and the crowd overlapped, their common message was amplified and widely disseminated.

It is possible to interrogate patterns of omission in the regulation of unnatural assaults because several important types of records survive in substantial quantities. First are the records of the London criminal courts, which provide a comprehensive list of trials occurring at those venues, although they lack much in specific detail in cases related to sexual crimes. With regard to the Berry case, these records demonstrate that there were no other women listed as prosecutors for cases involving sodomy or attempted sodomy. The second source is newspaper records, which allow us to compare the content of a given paper to the court records and to the contents of other newspapers to show what aspects of infamous crime they publicized or failed to publicize. Such analysis reveals patterns of omission and emphasis. The first such pattern is that although women were active in cases arising from sex between men, they could not use the unnatural-assault laws to defend their own bodies. These laws were invoked to defend a certain conception of masculinity rather than to protect all individuals from physical abuse.

The next pattern of omission, even more surprising, is that the nineteenth-century prosecutions of sexual acts between men were not directed against the men who habitually engaged in such acts. Both the molly house and the cross-dressed man were hallmarks of a homosexual subculture, and yet these spaces and individuals are mentioned in only around 4 percent of the hundreds of trials and newspaper court reports concerning sex between men from the 1820s through the 1860s.

The eighteenth-century pattern of molly-house raids, discussed in previous chapters, abated in the mid-1820s through to 1830: such raids are not discussed in court records or newspaper articles after 1830. In 1825 the Barley Mow public house, just off the Strand, was raided after it became known to a magistrate that "a gang of detestable wretches" regularly met there. The magistrate, who still controlled constables at this time, directed his men to infiltrate the house and collect evidence against the men. The Bull public house was raided in the spring of 1830, during the first year of the new Metropolitan Police, at the same time that another division of the new force was conducting its ill-fated raids on men soliciting sex from men in Hyde Park.[6] Many stories about these molly-house raids appeared in the *Times*, the *Morning Chronicle*, and the *Weekly Dispatch*, but it becomes very difficult to identify similar incidents in later years. Rather than assume that these places ceased to exist, it seems likely that raids on them were curtailed, just as the police discontinued sending plain-clothes officers into Hyde Park at night in the face of public disapproval.

As the eighteenth-century material shows, raids took time and resources: the molly houses had to be infiltrated, and undercover individuals had to visit repeatedly before they were trusted enough to be allowed into the back or upper rooms where illicit activity occurred. For the 1825 Barley Mow raid, the chief magistrate at Bow Street ordered two of his patrol "to go to the house, and mix with the company, and endeavor to ascertain if there was any ground for the suspicions." The officers were "obliged for some time to be patient witnesses of them, in order to get a sufficient knowledge of the principal actors to enable them to support a case against them."[7]

If the new system of enforcement was really focused on rooting out the most persistent and blatant forms of sex between men, such places should have received greater attention; but infiltration, entrapment, and spying were not commonly used after 1830. Moreover, mollies could turn their meeting spaces into protected private spaces with their own systems of surveillance, as they seem to have done with the Druids' Hall in the 1850s.

Molly houses were raided in the eighteenth century because the publicity generated served the interests of those carrying out the raids. The Metropolitan Police of the 1830s had no such incentives. National honor was already being invoked in infamous crime trials: if such decadent places were discovered, their existence was a discredit to the authorities. And even after long-term surveillance at the Barley Mow, the resulting prosecutions were disappointing. Although it was reported that "scenes of the most horrible kind took place," and twenty-five men in the large crowd gathered there were arrested, only seven men were actually charged. Of these, six were convicted, but their sentences were short: twelve months' imprisonment in the House of Correction.[8] Although molly-house raids seemed to expose a high level of depravity, the resulting punishments were no greater than those for casual incidents in the streets.

Law enforcement in 1830 and after, then, was not about stamping out sex between men regardless of location. As H. G. Cocks and Sean Brady have found for different periods in the nineteenth century, there was no specific mandate for actively investigating sex between men; instead, Cocks observes, there was "a policy of de facto toleration of private offences by the police."[9] This policy helps to explain the experience of men such as Jack Saul, a male prostitute working out of the brothel at the center of the Cleveland Street Affair, who claimed that he had supported himself through prostitution with male clients for years and that he had never been interfered with by the police in all that time. Without the private vice societies of the eighteenth century to finance investigations, much private behavior between consenting individuals occurred out of the public eye. For many reasons, then, the laws against sex between men were not actively enforced against the spaces most closely associated with that behavior.

After 1830, even prosecutions of cross-dressed men were uncommon. Ever since Jeffrey Weeks described the cross-dressing, selective use of makeup, and stylized male dress that characterized the nineteenth-century male prostitute, such figures have been central to scholarly generalizations about how male homosexual behavior was understood and publicly represented in this period.[10] A handful of vivid sources from the period, such as *Yokel's Preceptor,* an anonymous 1850s guide to the less respectable entertainments of London, include descriptions of mollies and of associated incidents.[11] It was observed early in *Yokel's Preceptor* that "the increase of these monsters in the shape of men, commonly called Margeries, Pooffs, &c. of late years, in the great metropolis, renders it necessary for the safety of the public, which they should be made known."[12] The author warns that "the Quadrant, Fleet-street, Holborn, The Strand, &c., are actually thronged with them! Nay it is not long since, in the neighborhood of Charing Cross, they posted bills in the windows of several respectable public houses, cautioning the public to "Beware of Sods."[13] Readers are advised that "pooffs . . . generally congregate around the picture shops" and that "a great many of them flock to the saloons and boxes of the theaters, coffee-houses, &c."[14] In these statements, the author puts forward a picture similar to that in a letter sent to the Home Office in 1827, which described the "swarms of lads who carry on the infamous occupation of catamites" who "infest" the porticos of London's theaters.[15] The guidebook author felt that these men could be identified on the street by their "effeminate manner" and "fancy dress" and had to be watched out for, as they regularly tried to pick up men on the streets. In the author's opinion, the laws were inadequate to stop them: "The wretches are too well paid . . . being principally, it is well known, supported by their rich companions—to care a jot about a few months imprisonment."[16]

Despite such descriptions, painted and powdered men are absent from the vast majority of stories centering on sex between men in the newspapers. Many of the stories in the *Times,* the *Morning Post,* and the *Weekly Dispatch* discussing sex between men were set in the same locations mentioned in the guidebook, yet only on the rarest occasions does a cross-dressed molly seem to have been present. One of the very few articles on a police-court trial centering on such a man provides clues as to why these stories were not more common.

The *Morning Post*, the *Times*, and the *Weekly Dispatch* each opened its report in March 1846 by observing that "a young man named John Travers, who was dressed as a female, was charged with loitering in the public streets, supposed for some unlawful purpose."[17] According to the arresting officer, Travers had been frequently seen in the area of Pall Mall East, especially on the streets near the clubhouses of St. James's. The constable had seen him about twenty times in the area late at night and spoken to him on several occasions. Because the officer had assumed Travers was a woman, nothing had come of these earlier talks, and the officer had simply asked Travers to "move on." The constable did not become suspicious of Travers until he heard a rumor that a man in women's clothes was in the habit of frequenting his beat. Shortly thereafter, the constable came upon Travers talking to "an elderly gentleman" in the street at about 1:00 A.M. on a Saturday night and took him into custody. "The prisoner resisted him, and denied that he was of the male sex; but when called upon to account for his conduct in court, he attributed it to a mere frolic, stating that he had made a bet with a friend that he would pass undetected in his disguise."[18]

The three newspapers made clear that the court assumed that Travers's cross-dressing was linked to acts of sex between men. It was reported that "Inspector Partridge said, that from what had come to his knowledge, he was satisfied that the object of the prisoner and his associates, in frequenting the streets and parks, was either to steal or to obtain money by practices of the most revolting and unnatural character." It was also reported that the presiding magistrate, Mr. Hall, felt that

> it was impossible, after hearing the evidence of the inspector and the two constables, to suppose that the prisoner had assumed the garb of a woman in a mere frolic. He had been seen upwards of 20 times lurking about in the dark and narrow passages, and frequently in conversation with other men. Every one who had had any experience in life, and knew to what extent vices and crimes of the most abominable nature prevailed in this large town, must deduce from these circumstances the most unfavourable conclusions. To protect the public, therefore, from the injuries which these men inflicted on society, he should require the prisoner to enter into his own recognizances for 50*l.*, and to furnish two sureties of 25*l.* each, to be of good behavior for six months, or be committed in default.[19]

The magistrate intended to punish Travers harshly; but after accusing Travers of engaging in sex between men, there was little the court could do beyond revealing his name and setting a high bail. Although almost all of the men in the courtroom assumed that Travers's intention that night was to have sex with another man, the old man had not lodged a complaint against Travers, and the constable had not seen him engaging in any sexual acts. Under the law there was little he could be charged with. At the end of the hearing the *Times,* the *Morning Post,* and the *Weekly Dispatch* reported that Travers "put on his bonnet, leaped out of the dock, and retired amid the execrations of the court."[20]

That a man so bluntly accused of engaging in sex between men could walk out of the room, bonnet and all, could not be construed as a victory for the law. The newspaper reports opened by noting that "this was the second or third case of the kind which has been brought under the notice of the Court within the past few weeks," but neither of the other stories seem to have been printed, perhaps because they presented a similarly mixed message.[21]

More successful prosecutions stemmed from cases in which otherwise respectable men fended off advances from cross-dressed male prostitutes, but such cases were almost never reported. A distinctive characteristic of the unnatural-assault stories printed most often in the newspapers was that they showed not just a guilty party punished but also an innocent man vindicated. The stories were written from the perspective of the man who had won his case and who was proved respectable by rejecting the advances of another man. In such accounts, each man could proffer an innocent interpretation of his actions, but in cases involving a cross-dressed man, usually neither man could. As with the molly houses, the cross-dressed male prostitute did not disappear from London in the early to mid-nineteenth century, but such men were not the primary focus of concern for the state or for the newspapers.

When separated from its association with sex between men, cross-dressing could be presented in a light and diversionary manner in the newspapers.[22] Examples of this type of story in the *Times,* the *Weekly Dispatch,* and the *Morning Post* include an account of a "respectable" student named Louis Hillingsworth caught attending a church service wearing female attire in 1841.[23] Another young man named Thomas Francis Druce was reported to have gone to the Holborn Casino "very effectively" disguised as a woman in 1855.[24] In 1858 an Italian, Antonio La Rosa, was arrested as he took a casual daytime stroll in women's clothes along the streets in the West End.[25] When confronted, La Rosa, speaking through a translator, claimed that the dress was actually intended for the woman he was to marry in a few weeks' time and that he had only put it on to help in the alterations process. He expressed some astonishment that doing this had led to his arrest. The cross-dressed man arrested in the Holborn Casino claimed that what he had done was only "for a lark," and Hillingsworth's school friends came to court with him and verbally attacked the arresting officer for even taking notice of the matter.

The general tone of these articles was jocular. The *Times* reported that while trying to determine the gender of the man attending the church service, the investigating officer approached a woman who worked as a pew opener. She was reported to have "laughingly" relayed her suspicions to the officer.[26] Before describing in detail Thomas Druce's hair and make-up, a court reporter offered the young man a backhanded compliment by noting that "the appearance of the defendant created no little amusement in court, for the delusion [sic] was almost perfect."[27] Readers of the report on La Rosa's case were treated to a full description of his outfit. The article noted that the "defendant was dressed in very gay and fashionable attire, the skirts of a pink muslin dress being duly expanded by means of crinoline and hoops, his legs inserted in lace drawers and military-heeled boots, his by no means handsome face partly concealed by ringlets, and his hands enveloped in light kid gloves."[28]

The lightness in tone of these pieces was mirrored in the mild sentences imposed. While the hundred pounds Thomas Druce had to personally surrender was no small amount, his income and respectable occupation meant that he had little trouble raising it on short notice. The money was to be held by the court for twelve months, after which time it would be returned, provided that he had "kept the peace" by not publicly cross-dressing again. For attending a church service while cross-dressed, Lewis Hillingsworth received only a stern lecture from the bench. La Rosa also paid no money, but he was made to remove his wife's dress and had to send for male attire to wear out of the court building.

The only references made to sex between men within these reports came in their concluding paragraphs, which each contained long admonitions from the respective magistrates disdaining the men's "foolish behavior." In the Holborn Casino case, the magistrate "lectured the defendant in strong terms upon the impropriety of his conduct and reminded him that persons often assumed women's attire for felonies and other still more disgraceful purposes, although there was no reason to suppose that anything of the kind was designed in the present

instance."[29] The specter of the cross-dressing molly was also invoked
in the lecture from the bench to La Rosa. The magistrate "directed the
interpreter to tell the defendant that people were in the habit of attiring
themselves in women's clothes for very evil purposes, and he would
certainly be committed if the frolic were repeated."[30] As long as infamous crime seemed remote from the case, stories of male cross-dressing
could be lingered over and enjoyed by reporter and reader alike.

In one incident reported in the *Weekly Dispatch,* the *Morning Post,*
and the *Times* in 1858, the cross-dressing young man was clearly implicated in engaging in sexual acts with other men, yet the events were
presented as spectacle and narrated in rich detail. The case, however,
is anomalous because the central actor was not an Englishman but a
twenty-year-old West Indian of African descent identifying himself as
Eliza Scott.

The *Morning Post,* the *Weekly Dispatch,* and the *Times* related the
excited mood in the courtroom and also created anticipation about
their own reports when they observed that "an immense crowd of persons assembled yesterday" to witness the trial.[31] The crowd had gathered "in consequence of the report that an American slave in women's
clothes was to be brought before Alderman Gibbs . . . and out walked a
person in woman's attire, accompanied by a policeman. The questionable woman was dressed in a light cotton gown with stripes and a straw
bonnet, and certainly had a most feminine appearance."[32] Constable
J. W. Tanner stated that during the previous week he had often seen
Scott walking around the Fenchurch Street area, from about 9:00 in
the evening till about 1:00 or 2:00 in the morning, and always in the
dress he was wearing in the courtroom. The constable remarked that he
had "considered that [Scott] was a woman, and that he belonged to the
wretched clan who live by prostitution."[33] Another police officer said
that he had known Scott to live at No. 5 Angel Gardens for nearly six
months, and had always seen him dressed as a woman. "The prisoner
walked the neighborhood of the Thames-tunnel and Ratcliffe-highway,
and I have frequently seen him with sailors, and always considered him
to be a woman." Constable Tanner finally apprehended Scott at 11:45
on a Saturday night, while Scott was walking along Fenchurch Street
in women's clothes. The constable told the court that "as I was taking
'him' to the station house he resisted in a most violent manner, and
attempted to escape. I charged him at the station-house with having
annoyed gentlemen in Fenchurch-street, having seen him frequently
following and addressing respectable persons in that locality."[34]

Constable Tanner's decision to arrest Scott was sparked by a complaint from a respectable man in the area. That man told the court that Scott

> came up in his present dress of a woman and asked me if I was good-natured. I of course thought he was a woman, and we walked together. As we went into a more retired place the prisoner lifted a veil, which was fastened to the bonnet, and then I for the first time observed that the face was that of a person of colour. I soon suspected, from the growth of the beard, that I was speaking to a man, and as soon as I saw a metropolitan policeman I gave him in charge; but the constable refused to take the charge; and the prisoner then began to load me with abuse and to declare loudly that 'he' was a woman and would prove that fact upon the spot. [35]

Constable Tanner's initial reluctance to arrest Scott most likely stemmed from the fact that Scott had not made a physical advance or overt proposition to the complainant. Without any such move, the prosecution would have had as weak a case against Scott as they had had against John Travers. As late as 1837, arguments between constables and their sergeants over whether a "flashily dressed" man on the streets should be arrested were still being referred to the police commissioners for resolution, indicating the ambiguity that persisted in these matters more than eight years after the founding of the Metropolitan Police.[36] Ultimately Scott was convicted not because of the gentleman's complaint but because he had resisted Constable Tanner's attempt to arrest him.

Although the *Times,* the *Morning Post,* and the *Weekly Dispatch* usually presented narratives from the perspective of the man proved respectable by the court, this case was different. Eliza Scott's story was presented in his own words. At the police court, Scott stated, "I am almost a stranger to London and have been here only about six months. . . . The captain who brought me over was to have seen me back again, but he is gone away without me, and I never could get any place. He promised positively to take me back to America, but he never did so. I was a slave in America and ran away to the West Indies."[37] It was also said that he "got his living by washing, ironing, and cleaning, and attending people who were ill, more particularly those afflicted with rheumatism, whom he had the skill of curing by friction and an application of Indian herbs. He had been brought to this country from New York by the captain . . . to attend him in his illness."[38]

The facts that Scott cross-dressed, did not seem averse to sexual acts between men, and had skills in healing ailments all suggest that he considered himself a *jin bandaa,* although that word does not occur in the evidence.[39] The Bantu term was used by some men of African origin to describe cross-dressed and otherwise culturally feminized men who mediated between the physical and the spiritual worlds. In Angola, these men tended to band together in communities. They were respected by others and were responsible for performing traditional burials and other ceremonies. James Sweet has argued that "cultural feminization rendered [these men] more likely to be penetrated by the spirits," and that the cross-dressed medicine man who was sexually available to other men was a cultural role that persisted in many central and southern African societies into the twentieth century.[40] Portuguese records for sixteenth- and seventeenth-century Brazil record the persistence of individuals identifying as *jin bandaa* among slave populations in the New World, despite the attempts by the Catholic church to suppress their spiritual and sexual practices. Although Scott may have encountered English cross-dressed prostitutes while in London, it seems most likely that he was not imitating them but rather taking advantage of the English cultural form of the molly to achieve the more pressing personal goal of raising money to return home.

Distinctions can also be drawn between what Scott said and what was said about him. When asked further about the captain who had brought him to London, Scott replied simply that "he did not perform his promise, and I have nothing more to say."[41] This forthright statement of disdain for a man who had broken his word was in keeping with what any respectable individual might say, but Scott was never characterized in this way. In paraphrasing Scott, the reporter wrote that he "in a very mincing effeminate tone of voice, made a long rambling statement, denying that he had laid hands upon the prosecutor, but most artfully avoiding any allusion to his having worn female apparel."[42] A long explanation by Scott was characterized as "rambling" rather than complete, and his well-crafted argument could only be "artful" rather than intelligent. Racial difference placed Scott at a sufficient remove to allow Englishmen to be amused by this case without drawing inferences concerning themselves. Respectable masculinity was defined against men of other races and nations, as well as against men who lacked character and self-control. The case of Scott, who embodied both effeminate behavior and racial difference, only confirmed the idea among respectable Englishmen that the two were linked.[43]

The ways in which the Englishmen responded to Scott in person are also important. Two of the three witnesses against him were police officers, whose job gave them legitimate reason for having seen Scott frequently on the streets. The only other Englishman shown encountering Scott claimed to have believed he was speaking to a woman: once the (literal) veil had been removed, he reacted as a respectable Englishman should.

In a second case of sex between an Englishman and a foreigner, the Englishman behaved much less respectably, and the reading public of London consequently learned almost nothing of the event. The incident occurred in 1849, when a young English tradesman voluntarily accompanied a Turkish seaman back to his ship. Only the *Times* seems to have covered the Central Criminal Court proceedings, and it did so in two sentences: "Hassan, a Lascar seaman, belonging to the Turkish Government, and John Rowbottom, aged 18, a paper-stainer, were convicted of attempting to commit a nameless offence. The court sentenced them to 12 months' imprisonment and hard labour."[44]

Hassan and Rowbottom were caught together on the Egyptian frigate *Sharkyeh* by Metropolitan Police officers who were following up on reports that a Turkish sailor had been seen returning from the West End with a local Englishman. The two men had been together on the ship for nearly a day before their arrest, although they had had no previous acquaintance. The *Times* and other newspapers were able to remain silent on the details of the case and its implications, but the Home Office was compelled to deal extensively with the matter. Unlike Eliza Scott, who was an isolated individual in a foreign land, Hassan was a Turkish subject and had been taken from an Egyptian ship. As a formidable naval trading power in its own right, the Ottoman state had an investment in protecting its subjects while in foreign lands, and from the time of Hassan's arrest, Admiral Hafiz Bey, the commander of the *Sharkyeh,* attempted to intervene with the Home Office to stop the criminal trial and have his crewman returned.

Hafiz Bey's first attempt to free Hassan occurred immediately after the police court hearing on the day after the arrest. He assumed that the Home Office would have the power to override the decision of the police court. In response, H. Waddington, the undersecretary at the Home Office, told him "that while [he] appreciated [his] motives in making the application," a criminal trial could not be canceled after a police-court hearing had determined that it should be held.[45] In this, Undersecretary Waddington was slightly misrepresenting the powers of the government. It would have been possible for the attorney general to prevent the magistrate's decision from leading directly to a criminal trial, but this was done only under the most exceptional circumstances, as it was considered an abuse of executive power. With Hassan's case neither in the papers nor of great diplomatic concern, the Home Office was not willing to recommend such an intervention.

The diplomatic pressure on the British government increased when the Turkish ambassador in London became involved. The Foreign Office forwarded the ambassador's letter to the Home Office for consideration, with an attachment letter that made clear Foreign Secretary Palmerston's disdain for its arguments. It stated that "Lord Palmerston cannot recommend [the Home Secretary] to comply with the request of the Turkish ambassador, which would obviously in its results be an entire remission of the sentence, inasmuch as the man would be at liberty during his voyage home, and would in all probability not be punished at all after his return to Turkey."[46]

There was more at stake here than a desire to see Hassan himself punished: the letter later makes clear the deterrent effect that Hassan's punishment was intended to have on other Turkish nationals in England. The letter addressed the fact that "the annually increasing intercourse between the Turkish Dominions and the United Kingdom seems to point out the expediency of not allowing Turkish subjects to suppose that they can with impunity introduce the habits of their own country into this; and Lord Palmerston would therefore recommend that the man in question should as an example to his countrymen be made to undergo the whole amount of the punishment to which he has been sentenced."[47]

Palmerston's desire to have this case serve as an example was not shared by the judge who presided over Hassan's criminal trial, and who registered his opinion privately with the home secretary. Concerning Hassan, the judge told the home secretary that "the poor fellow has behaved very well here; and much as we must all abhor and detest the crime of which he has been found guilty, and I would give every Englishman the fullest sentence, yet perhaps with these poor unhappy wretches, they do not feel it any crime." The presiding judge concluded his letter by arguing that if there were any way to ensure that Hassan would face some form of punishment in his homeland, "it would be much better" for him to be returned to the Turkish authorities.[48]

The best indication of what sort of treatment awaited Hassan if he were returned to his countrymen is found not in the letter of the Turkish ambassador but in the further correspondence of Hafiz Bey. He put forward a practical solution that addressed the concerns on both sides of the dispute, assuring the Home Office officials not only that Hassan would be confined on the return voyage but that on the ship's arrival in Egypt, "the term of imprisonment which would be unexpired . . . will be re-imposed in Alexandria as a punishment for his having been absent from his military duties and that a communication to that effect would be made to Her Majesty's Consul in Egypt."[49]

With this proposal Hafiz Bey addressed the concerns of his English counterparts without necessarily registering his agreement with the assumptions that lay behind them. It is difficult to say what exactly tipped opinion within the Home Office in favor of Hassan's release, but a particularly pointed argument made by Hafiz Bey may have had a significant influence. He rightly observed that under English law, Hassan would have to be released in one year's time, at which point he would be stranded in London. Hassan should be returned to the *Sharkyeh* before it sailed for Alexandria in a few days, "not with a view of withdrawing him from punishment," he said, but to take him home so that he would not be alone on the English streets with no means of supporting himself after his eventual release.[50]

The discussion of differing norms of sexual behavior had little to do with the ultimate resolution. Although the home secretary and the undersecretary exchanged notes to the effect that Turks were not interested in prosecuting sexual acts such as Hassan and Rowbottom had committed, they did not make these points to the Turkish officials.[51] For their part, neither Hafiz Bey nor the Turkish ambassador expressed an opinion on the morality of sex between men. Only Foreign Secretary Palmerston put forth a platitude about Turkish "habits," unlike the home secretary who regularly reviewed petitions and statistics documenting sexual acts between English men.[52]

The sexual habits of foreigners were invoked in newspaper reports even less frequently than cross-dressers were, and even then they were mentioned only when the Englishmen involved were shown to have behaved appropriately. When two otherwise conventionally masculine Frenchmen were arrested in Hyde Park in 1829 for indecent assault on an Englishman, the judge found fault only with the Frenchmen; but he treated them leniently, explaining "that they escaped a severer sentence for this most aggravated assault, because, as they were natives of a country in which the crime to which it referred was not visited with the punishment which it would deserve, they might be supposed, from their ignorance of the language of England and its customs, to labour under some disadvantage."[53] Allowances could be made for foreigners, provided their behavior helped to heighten the contrast between respectable English masculinity and decadent foreign practices. Because there was no way that the story of Hassan and Rowbottom could be framed to cast English masculinity in a complimentary light, it was for the most part ignored by the papers.

That the Rowbottom and Hassan case was mentioned at all in the *Times* is surprising, given the men's lower-class status and their arrest at the London Docks. Its singularity draws attention to an additional geographic and class pattern evident in both law enforcement and newspaper reporting. Comparing the frequency of infamous-crime arrests across London's police-court districts shows that the Marlborough Street police court, between Regent's Park and St. James's Park in the West End, had nearly three times more hearings that were reported in the press than any other. Second was the Marylebone district, also located in the West End, in the northern section of Mayfair.[54] This geographic pattern is amplified by the reporting patterns of the newspapers for the upper and middle classes. It was not, therefore, in the East End neighborhoods of the "dangerous classes" but instead in the wealthier parts of the city that the policing of sex between men was most intense and most intensely followed. However, this pattern becomes evident only from statistics for multiple decades, and the higher arrest rates in these areas were not concentrated enough to draw public attention or indignation.

In all likelihood this geographic pattern had its origins in the higher numbers of police patrolling affluent areas to protect property and suppress prostitution. The police most regularly disrupted sexual encounters between men that were opportunistic, that occurred in public space, and that were leveraged with proffering or promising payments or gifts. Such encounters were most common in the West End, where the wealthy and poor lived in close proximity. Soldiers, who were frequently implicated in such incidents, were also concentrated near the government and royal properties of the West End. Court cases arising from these encounters involved wealthier and poorer men in the roles of both prosecutor and defendant, thus veiling signs of overt class bias. Many of the more than two hundred cases reported in the *Times* not mentioned in the *Weekly Dispatch* were of this type. Most of the cases appearing in the *Morning Post* after 1842 also conformed to this pattern, although the *Morning Post* focused almost exclusively on cases in which the wealthier man was proved innocent.[55]

Even when they successfully defended themselves, working-class participants in these cases were often presented as the objects of the discussion rather than as its subjects. The clearest way to reveal the assumptions about class difference that structured trials for sexual acts between men is to look at examples in which this difference was not present: the extremely rare cases involving men of middle- or upper-class status accusing one another of sexual advances. Examining the usually unspoken assumptions that come to the surface in these cases reveals the uniquely problematic nature of male same-sex desire for respectable masculinity.

The events leading to one such case began with the appearance of George Rogers at the Westminster police court to face charges made by two soldiers of attempted unnatural assault. As a result of his court appearance and the publication of his name and address in the news-papers, Rogers received anonymous letters from several individuals. One of these, from Edward Whitehurst, written on 25 October 1862, put forward "a proposal of an infamous character" and then indicated that "if Mr. Rogers is really desirous," he should come to the top of Constitution Hill on the following day at 6:00 P.M. and wait under the archway while wearing white kid gloves—at which point, the cor-respondent wrote, he would introduce himself.[56]

Rogers did not go to the meeting place in the park, but Whitehurst was not dissuaded. He wrote to Rogers a second letter on 30 October and a third shortly thereafter, both making similar proposals to meet. The second letter postulated that Rogers must not have attended at the first suggested time because of a prior engagement, and the third letter speculated that Rogers might have been sick. A fourth letter made a further excuse for Rogers's previous absences, indicating that the still-anonymous writer knew from additional newspaper reports that Rogers had recently moved to a new address. Whitehurst, after postulating that Rogers may have not received his letters in time for the meetings on the previous occasions, again suggested that they meet at a time and place similar to the one first proposed.

By now Rogers had handed the letters to the police. The police encouraged Rogers to keep the fourth meeting suggested by this most persistent of anonymous correspondents, accompanied by police con-stables who would be hidden around the arch. With the trap set, Rogers donned the white kid gloves and set out for Constitution Hill. At the designated time, Whitehurst passed by Rogers several times before asking him, "Are you Mr. Rogers?" After answering in the affirmative, Rogers walked with Whitehurst "arm-in-arm along Constitution-hill" to a spot where the concealed policemen could easily hear them. Whitehurst, unaware of the danger he was in, "proposed that he and Mr. Rogers should dine together on the following day (Tuesday) at a hotel where they should pass the night." Whitehurst's suspicions were apparently not raised even when Rogers produced one of Whitehurst's letters to him there on the path and got him to confirm aloud that it was in his own handwriting. Neither did Whitehurst hesitate to write his real name and address in Rogers's pocket-book when asked to do so. Not only did Rogers convey these confidences to the police, but he also recounted the intimate details of Whitehurst's plans for their evening together in the hotel, a conversation that the newspapers declared "utterly unfit for publication."[57]

This case differed from the many others that elicited one or two reports and were quickly disposed of because both parties in this case were men of respectability and high status. For this reason, neither the defense nor the prosecution could be undermined by witnesses of inferior character or accusations of extortion. Moreover, both men could afford excellent legal representation. Although the dispute between Whitehurst and Rogers did not become a scandal on the same scale as cases like that of George Dawson Lowndes in the 1840s, it was the subject of more than a dozen separate reports in the *Times*.

A protracted courtroom contest might seem unexpected in this case, given the evidence against Whitehurst, but as a solicitor and a man of "high standing" and "respectable position," he refused to back down. On 7 November 1862, Whitehurst wrote a letter to the *Times* indicating that he would fight the charge, and that he was "thankful to say that those who best know me have suspended their judgment until they have heard the whole case, and I ask your readers to do the same."[58] This aggressive attempt to influence his representation in the newspapers was complemented by the sympathetic opinion expressed in the courtroom by the prosecuting attorneys. One of them, Mr. Sleigh, observed at the start of one hearing that "it is a distressing duty imposed upon me by the nature of my profession to conduct a case against one who up to the present has been regarded as a most respectable member of his profession and of the community."[59] The other prosecuting attorney, Mr. Smyth, on a different day, "expressed his greatest regret at having to prefer so serious a charge against a gentleman of respectable position."[60] As might be expected, the witnesses that Whitehurst himself called were at least as complimentary as the prosecuting counsel. Past character mattered a great deal in these cases, and Whitehurst seemed to have that advantage firmly on his side.

But although Rogers had been compromised by his association with soldiers and unnatural-assault charges, he also had the advantages of good family and character: he was described in the courtroom as "a young gentleman of wealth and position." Rogers was currently in school, but he was also on the verge of securing a military commission in the 5th Dragoon Guards. Major General Windham of the guards, who had been asked by Rogers's uncle, Thomas Blake, to obtain a commission for him, was told that Rogers was well suited "by fortune, habits, and education" to becoming a commissioned officer. A teacher of Rogers's also wrote to the *Times* to state that Rogers had exhibited no questionable behavior at school, although the teacher was also clearly concerned about the mention of his school in connection with the case. Although he did not criticize Rogers personally, the teacher further added that he hoped "other young men may see the serious and fatal consequences of getting intoxicated and getting into low company," as had apparently happened in the initial incident between Rogers and the soldiers.[61]

Rogers's involvement with the soldiers in the Queen and Prince Albert Public House in Knightsbridge was more typical of the way these cases usually played out. Rogers had accused the soldiers of taking his watch, and they in turn accused him of attempting a sexual advance. The charges against Rogers were dismissed, it was said, because there was no evidence to corroborate the soldiers' story. As we have seen, under other circumstances two men's testimony might well have been enough to lead to a conviction, but the soldiers especially were of "low character," and Rogers was not. Rogers admitted to being drunk and not using good judgment on that evening, and this admission allowed his version of events to prevail.

Thus Rogers went into the courtroom in his subsequent contest against Whitehurst with his own reputation largely intact. His account could not simply be discredited or disposed of. The case between the two men with similar advantages of wealth and character provides a unique opportunity to see how a court resolved such a dispute in the absence of the usual class imbalance.

The justification Whitehurst used to reconcile his character with his actions was fascinating. Rather than admit to the feelings of same-

sex desire that his letters indicated, Whitehurst instead argued that
his only motive was to put Rogers's character to the test. The *Times*
relayed that "the letters which Mr. Whitehurst had written Mr. Rogers,
and which it was alleged were intended to incite him to the commission of an unnatural offence, were written, not in secret, but openly
and avowedly, with the knowledge of other persons, with the view of
testing the character of the prosecutor."[62] The effort was an attempt
to lay a trap for Rogers, Whitehurst's defense argued, and his actions
would be perfectly legitimate if he were a police officer or a private
investigator.[63]

But Whitehurst was neither of these, and he therefore had no
legitimate reason to conduct such an investigation and lay such a trap.
Indeed, in the final summation at the police court, the presiding magistrate asserted that Whitehurst had committed a crime by his incitement
of Rogers to commit an unnatural offense. Also, Whitehurst's claim
that he had carried out his actions with the knowledge of his office
staff was called into serious question, although without impugning
the character of the office clerk who confirmed that Whitehurst had
included appointments with Rogers in the office daily calendars. What
remained, therefore, were multiple, explicit letters of one respectable
man's sexual interest in another respectable man, and a longer conversation to this effect overheard by constables and confirmed by Rogers.
The evidence against Whitehurst seemed overwhelming.

And yet Whitehurst was not convicted. The prosecuting attorneys
repeatedly praised Whitehurst as a man of character, and the magistrate in his summation stated that he did not believe that Whitehurst
really intended to carry out the sexual act with Rogers. The magistrate
seemed most concerned about Whitehurst's publication of obscene
libels in the form of the four letters sent to Rogers, and the discussion
of this matter took up the majority of his recorded closing statement.
Whitehurst's legal team later successfully petitioned to have the case
moved from the Central Criminal Court to the Court of the Queen's
Bench, to be heard before a special jury, and this move delayed the
criminal trial for more than a year. When that trial was finally held on
26 November 1863, Rogers did not show up to pursue the case, and it
was dismissed.[64]

In an editorial, the *Times* lamented for Whitehurst's sake that
the trial had not taken place, and that "all the statements made by
Mr. Rogers . . . and the two police-officers remain unretracted, the
comments of [the magistrate] Mr. Corrie remain unanswered, and the

character of Mr. Whitehurst remains uncleared, except by charitable inference, that inference being only one of the two that might be drawn from the same circumstances."[65] The *Times* laid the blame for the lack of resolution mainly on Whitehurst, whose request that the case be moved to the Court of the Queen's Bench had caused the delay. The editorial asked whether, had the trial taken place a month after the police-court hearing, as would normally have been the case, there would be "any reason to doubt that the prosecutor and his witnesses would have appeared, and a verdict been obtained." It also argued that only "ill-natured people" would assume that Whitehurst planned the delay to escape justice. The *Times* did remark that the prosecution's "voluntary non-appearance is as great a mystery as the omission to bind them over in their recognizances," but it was also stated that "this mystery we do not seek to penetrate."[66]

No one, it seemed, really wanted to penetrate the questions of this case. If the *Times* expressed concern that neither man had been proved innocent, no respectable man had been proved guilty, either. None of the men involved in the police-court hearing, even the prosecution, seemed to want to find Whitehurst guilty, save for Rogers, whose reputation was at stake. Whitehurst's defense was implausible and possibly inadmissible for legal reasons. In defense of his own judgments in the case, the magistrate stated in his summation that "if I was wrong in admitting that evidence I have erred on the right side."[67]

The amazing aspect of Whitehurst's defense was that it entirely removed male same-sex desire from the motivations of the two respectable protagonists in a court case that centered on allegations of those acts. All sexual desire for other men was displaced onto the common soldiers who had originally made the charge against Rogers, and they were the only participants whose characters were tarnished. When Rogers and Whitehurst met, the argument ran, each man was simply attempting to capture a rogue. The magistrate accepted that neither man at the meeting on Constitution Hill desired other men; the *Times* saw no need to penetrate the mystery; and this class-affirming fiction became the final version of the story. The very few other published cases that involved charges of sexual acts between two men of middle- or upper-class status also ended in similar denials of desire.

Cases involving two respectable men were infrequently prosecuted and publicized for a second reason: two men of equal status could more easily resolve tensions arising from affronted honor without recourse to the courts. While attending the opera, William Graves stood in the midst

of a considerable crowd as twenty-five-year-old John Cairn, whom he
did not know, "stood beside him . . . [and] laid his hands upon him in
a very indecent manner." Graves said he let it pass, thinking it an accident, but then Cairn "again assaulted him in a more indecent manner
than on the first occasion." Graves left the theater for a short while,
but on his return he saw Cairn approach another man in a way Graves
thought suspicious, and that other man later confirmed to Graves that
Cairn had "been behaving with great indelicacy towards him" as well.
Three times, the other man said, Cairn had placed "his hand against
him in a very indecent manner," and three times he had "struck his
hand away with an opera-glass." Shortly after this Cairn came back up
to Graves, and "placing his arms on his shoulders, pressed very close
against him."[68]

Both Cairn and Graves were respectable young men in a space surrounded largely by men of their own class. In explaining why he had
originally decided not to take the matter to the police, Graves said he
"would have been satisfied with the thrashing which he had given"
to the other man, which amounted to grabbing him roughly by the
collar and shouting at him. Graves cited "the danger of making such
a charge unless there was other evidence besides my own to support
it," combined with the satisfaction that his own personal honor had
been defended.[69] In a different case in 1853 involving two respectable
men, the prosecutor expressed his desire to let the case drop for similar
reasons, although the magistrate did not allow it.[70] In another case,
a solicitor in Lincoln's Inn was willing to drop his charge of indecent
assault against an elderly man "of very genteel appearance" after the
older man apologized.[71] Perhaps most revealing of the rules of behavior that existed between men of the same class was in an exchange
between two such men in 1850. John M'Dougal, twenty years old,
picked up a younger man on the Strand and brought him back to his
nearby rooms, sparking an incident that led both of them to court.
Although M'Dougal had been the aggressor in this attempted sexual
encounter, he was also the one to lash out in anger at the younger man
in court. "Turning to the complainant, [M'Dougal] said he must be a
person of no mind or confidence to go and disclose what had taken
place between them in private."[72]

All of these men were counting to some degree on the discretion of
their peers. As discussed by John Tosh, upper- and middle-class men
could expect a certain amount of confidentiality in their private dealings. Alone among men of their own class, as they might be at the opera,

in a private home, or even during a prearranged meeting on a secluded path, a shove and a shout could end an incident that elsewhere, and involving a man of a lower class, could have easily led to a court case. It was not that physical intimacy between men was more tolerated among these adult men, as it was among adolescent upper- and middle-class boys in public schools, but rather that these men were less willing, or perhaps had less reason, to take their social peers to court and expose their private affairs. In a similar way, other examples demonstrate that working-class men were more likely to settle such disputes privately between themselves.

Even so, men did not necessarily take such affronts lightly, as is clear from an incident between two respectable men that occurred in 1842. Samuel Nathan was looking at paintings at Foster's auction rooms in Pall Mall one evening when he was approached by three other men: Richard Mountain and his friends Thomas Rason and William Davey. It is unknown exactly what had transpired between the men before this meeting, but according to an uninvolved witness, the first thing Mountain said on approaching Nathan was, "Did you mean to say that I was a **** gentleman?" to which Nathan responded, "Yes, you are a s——, you know you are; it is right enough."[73] On hearing this response, Mountain "appeared very angry and very excited." He turned to his friend Rason and said, "You hear what he says, and you know I am not." He then asked Rason to go and relate the story to a policeman so that Nathan could be taken in on a charge of slander. Mountain and his friends left Foster's together, apparently to find a policeman, but returned about twenty minutes later without one. On seeing them return, Nathan nudged Mountain with his finger, and said, "How is your temper now? what I said is right enough; it is right enough; you know you are so." Mountain then turned to his friend Rason and said, "Tom, I can't stand this any longer; I must go and have something to drink." On hearing this, Nathan said, "Oh, something to drink, aye, something to drink; *stand* something to drink, and we will say no more about it."[74]

The four men then walked out of the auction rooms together, but no sooner had they cleared the door than Mountain "seized Nathan by the collar with one hand, and [struck] him over the eye with the other." Mountain's friend Davey tried to stop the beating, saying he could not see the need for it, but Mountain broke free and delivered a succession of blows to Nathan's head. The noise and shouts attracted the attention of the other men who were still in the auction rooms, some of whom made it into the hallway in time to witness Mountain's final blows on Nathan as he dropped to the floor. Nathan later died from the brutal beating. Although Mountain, Rason, and Davey were all found guilty of "feloniously killing and slaying" Samuel Nathan, they were "recommended to mercy on account of the provocation," and each was sentenced to six months' imprisonment.[75] The short sentences suggest sympathy for Mountain's desire to defend his reputation.

Sex between men and the suggestion of it most often happened around the edges, in the twilight moments of men's lives, and in such circumstances it could bring about ambiguous responses.[76] But when such incidents were brought into the open, respectable men were expected to defend their honor, and those who did not were suspect. The magistrate in another case remarked that he "was only surprised that the prosecutor when accosted by the prisoner did not knock him down."[77] An established physician stated in court in another case that "if such an abominable charge had been made against himself when he was younger and a stronger man than he now was, and when, perhaps, he did not know the law quite as well as he did at present, he should have knocked down the fellow who made it."[78] Another young man entered court saying that he had been very "shocked and disgusted" by another man's fondling him in a sexually explicit way in front of a picture-shop window, but the fact that he did not strike the attacker down, and that he let the "assault" continue for five minutes, undermined his assertions of indignation.[79] A violent response to a sexual proposition from another man was considered natural and understandable for a respectable man.

If caught in the act, respectable men were likely to claim that their actions did not reflect their true character. The friends of James Caldwell, a fifty-year-old Presbyterian minister, did not dispute that Caldwell had indecently assaulted four men on a single night, but they argued that he had had two glasses of brandy and water that evening and was so unused to the effects of drink that it "destroy[ed] all consciousness of what subsequently occurred."[80] He was otherwise a man "of very vigorous intellect, and stood high in the estimation of his congregation and everyone who knew him in his native town." The Rev. Thomas Reynolds also used alcohol as his excuse for "inciting a boy, named Daniel Collins, to commit a disgusting crime."[81] On another occasion David Azuley, a clerk to an attorney, was "indecently assaulted" in the pit of the Haymarket Theater by a man who claimed later that he was "intoxicated, and . . . had no recollection of what had occurred."[82]

Still other respectable men simply claimed that their actions were out of character and inexplicable. William Wilson, "a well dressed gentlemanly-looking young man," had come up to Police Constable Martin Palmer three times around 3:00 A.M., each time asking for directions to a different location in the area around Oxford Street and Manchester Square. On the third occasion, "he seized hold of [Constable Palmer] in an indecent manner, accompanying the act with language which left no doubt on the witness's mind of his intentions." Wilson was not drunk at the time, and when confronted with a report of his actions at the station house, responded simply, "Yes, that is all right; I had forgotten myself."[83] Samuel Miller did not claim that he was drunk on the night he indecently assaulted several men, but rather that "he was unconscious of what he did."[84] Miller, after making indecent assaults on at least four separate occasions, offered only that "it was an act of sudden impulse he could not account for."[85] James Rowton, a forty-five-year-old private tutor, when asked why he had indecently assaulted an office boy in a railway station, said "he had done what he did on the impulse of the moment."[86] Other men claimed that a spasm or a seizure had in fact been responsible for their actions. As implausible as these excuses seem, they were often believed, or at least accepted in the courtrooms. Court officials and other respectable individuals had a strong desire to deny the existence of such feelings in men of good standing of their social class, and this view tacitly influenced the interpretation and implementation of the unnatural-assault laws.

These patterns in the new system of policing sex between men indicate that the law was not applied as assiduously as it might have been. The new methods of regulation did not extend to the protection of women's bodies, and they did not rigorously prosecute the men who seemed most obviously or strongly drawn to other men for sex. Both the molly houses and the male cross-dressers seeking sex with other men were largely exempted from arrest. Both the policing and the reporting of such cases favored the more affluent West End neighborhoods, and the arrests of foreigners who were thought to follow very different mores were only rarely covered. The new arrests and the publicity generated by them related mainly to men who were considered conventionally masculine and who could usually make a plausible argument for their innocence. Couples charged with sexual acts were most often cross-class, yet it was the behavior of the wealthier man that was most often the focus of concern. In the handful of cases pitting two equally respectable men of middle- or upper-class status against one another, the law found it extremely difficult to reach a conclusion. This final pattern points to the ways in which respectability and sexual desire for other men were seen as fundamentally incompatible.

This incompatibility was a problem not only when an otherwise respectable man publicly exhibited desire for another man, but also for the individual himself. There were many ways to disavow same-sex desire in the face of an accusation, and officials seemed willing to accept even the most implausible of explanations. But the conscience of a respectable man would not be satisfied by an implausible explanation simply because it was accepted by others. A nineteenth-century man of character did not gain his sense of masculine status and self-worth from the opinion of others, as he would if his reputation played a greater role in his self-image. Any excuse vigorously defended, however implausible, might get a man of otherwise good character out of a conviction for sex between men; yet in earnestly proclaiming a lie, or vigorously defending an untruth, a man would no longer be respectable in his own eyes. His peers might never know, his reputation might remain intact, but he would know that he had compromised his character.

For the man of character who felt sexual desire for members of his own sex, this was both a contradiction and a growing concern as the nineteenth century progressed. The value of inner feelings as a guide to right action only increased as the religious idea that man at his core was corrupt and tainted by base desires emanating from original sin continued to wane. At the same time, what had been the specifically middle-class formulation of masculine respectability, arrayed against distinct upper- and working-class formulations, was gaining influence as the century progressed. It was also the case that if a man of character felt desire for other men, there was an increasing amount of material within the public sphere to inform him of the regular prosecution of such acts when perpetrated by men of similar status. These factors put such men of character in an increasingly untenable and contradictory position as the tensions between inner desires and society's expectations increased. Liberal reason and rationality held out the promise that such contradictions need not be allowed to stand, yet respectability and sexual desire for men could not be reconciled.

The prospects for a positive identity incorporating the concepts of character and same-sex desire in Britain were extremely remote by the close of the 1860s. The cultural texts that structured the middle-class notion of respectability, including patterns of religious belief and the middle-class conception of character, did not permit such a positive interpretation to be either publicly voiced or privately held. Medical opinion in Britain only reinforced the negative interpretation of sex between men, stressing that such acts stemmed from uncontrolled lust and accelerated moral decay. And yet new ways of understanding same-sex desire did develop in the final decades of the nineteenth century, allowing some men to reconcile these internal desires with the concept of character. The final chapter explores some of those developments.

CHAPTER 7

Conclusion

Character and Medicine

Michel Foucault famously argued that the late nineteenth century saw a discernible shift in the state's regulation of sexual acts between men. Previously the law had punished individuals for specific acts, but increasingly the medical and state authorities on the continent focused on "the homosexual" as "a personage, a past, a case history, and a childhood, in addition to being a type of life, a life form, and a morphology, with an indiscreet anatomy and possibly a mysterious physiology."[1] According to many scholars, this new identity category was later appropriated by the individuals who felt same-sex desire, who used it as a basis for the assertion of positive self-understandings and rejected its original connotations as a marker of disease and debility.

Although this thesis has been highly influential, there have been many calls for its revision.[2] Critics have called for greater attention to how the ideas associated with the field first called "sexology" in 1902 were disseminated in society, and particularly to what readers did with the medical and cultural texts they encountered. They have also called for greater efforts to understand the ways individuals understood their sexuality independent of these specialized and unevenly distributed medical texts. In addition, variations in national legal systems and cultures need to be taken into account in a way not reflected in Foucault's work. Most scholars still credit Foucault with profoundly important insights that have shaped the study of the history of sexuality, but there is also a desire to move beyond his impressionistic and generalized narrative to better understand how ideas and discourses influenced individuals' understandings of their own sexuality.

One scholar who has successfully taken up this challenge is Harry Oosterhuis in *Stepchildren of Nature*.[3] Oosterhuis was the first scholar to gain access to the personal papers of Richard von Krafft-Ebing, the Viennese psychiatrist who wrote the most influential nineteenth-century study of the nature of sexual desire between men. Through these previously unexamined sources, Oosterhuis was able to explore the evolution of Krafft-Ebing's thought and has established that there was a dialogue between Krafft-Ebing and the hundreds of individuals, primarily middle-class, who made up his case studies. Patients did not passively accept the categories assigned to them: many challenged Krafft-Ebing's initial characterizations of their conditions, and Krafft-Ebing in turn modified the clinical categories and the argument of *Psychopathia Sexualis* over its many editions in response to the evidence they presented.[4] Although these individuals worked to modify the language of science, they also often adopted it to describe themselves, in order to provide a new and more positive interpretation of their internal desires. The work of Oosterhuis has provided a significant advance in the area of "who knew what when" in relation to sexology and shows the value of approaches that link well-known cultural texts to individual experience.[5]

While Oosterhuis has added to our understanding of the role of medical categories in shaping sexual identities, Sean Brady, Matt Cook, H. G. Cocks, and Morris Kaplan have all described the very limited impact that these medical theories had in nineteenth-century Britain. Works like *Psychopathia Sexualis* constituted a new and powerful set of cultural texts through which the Britons who knew of them could interpret their desires, just as ancient literature had done for Anne Lister at the start of the century and newspaper clippings had done for the author of *Don Leon*. But many of the works of sexology had only a limited circulation in Britain, and British medical opinion remained openly hostile to arguments that seemed to dilute the moral objection to sex between men.[6] As late as 1895, Oscar Wilde derived no benefit from invoking the language of sexology to justify his own behavior in a private letter to the Home Office.[7] By that time, the testimony of medical professionals had been successfully deployed in trials related to sex between men for decades in France and in German-speaking states.[8] Yet in Britain, ways of thinking about sex between men stemming from new medical research influenced only those educated men who sought it out, and these views had no significant role in influencing state practices or procedures until well into the twentieth century.

This new medical thinking was, however, informed by assumptions related to respectable masculinity that made it relevant to the British men who read it. When some of the premises of the medical literature are examined closely, the writings most influential in the 1890s constitute much less of a break than previously believed with understandings of sex between men in early to mid-nineteenth-century Britain. The roles of class and character in shaping the interpretation of a man's sexual acts were reflected in both the legal and the medical formulations, with both finding the same-sex desire of respectable men the most problematic manifestation, and the most in need of extraordinary efforts to explain. Although all of the major works of sexology were generated outside Britain before Havelock Ellis and John Addington Symonds wrote *Sexual Inversion* in 1897, those works spoke to underlying characteristics of masculine character that were applicable to the British experience, in part because of the common liberal understanding of the self that underpinned middle-class masculine identity in late nineteenth-century Britain and Europe.[9] Especially as the work of Krafft-Ebing evolved in dialogue between doctor and patient, medical theories involving identity and sex between men became as much about preserving older notions of identity based on character as they were about creating new identities based on sexuality. Recognizing this theme in the earlier medical texts makes it possible to appreciate the ways in which the first major British contribution to the field, that of Havelock Ellis and John Addington Symonds, ironically represents the most significant rupture with how British culture understood sex between men to come out of nineteenth-century medicine.

In the early nineteenth century, if medical opinion was sought in a case involving sex between men, it was generally related to the search for physical proof of the sexual act rather than the psychological motivation for it. In a typical instance in 1806, a surgeon by the name of McMahon, attached to the Fifth Regiment of Foot, was brought in to examine William Hawkes, a young man only recently assigned to the regiment, for signs of sodomy.[10] It was alleged that a fellow soldier, John Bourke, "took some liberties with Hawkes" as the two men slept in the barracks. The surgeon said he "found some appearances in the fundament which induced him to think that a penetration had been effected," and this became a central piece of evidence in the trial that followed. Similar evidence was used in trials in 1842 and 1844.[11]

Much less often, a physician was called in to speak to the state of mind of a defendant, as occurred in the 1820s when a Dr. Veitch attended the police-court hearing of John Grossett Muirhead, Esq., the sixty-five-year-old brother-in-law of the Duke of Atholl. Muirhead was charged with sexually assaulting two young men, each around sixteen years of age, and because he was "connected with some of the first families," the very unusual step was taken of holding his hearing in the private chambers of the Marlborough Street police court. Muirhead's defense team was not able to make their case around the question of the character of the two young male working-class accusers, as lawyers for upper-class men would typically do, because "the books, papers, &c., found upon [Muirhead] consisted of a collection of the most abominable indecencies, in point of language and prints, that can be conceived; together with other things too shocking to describe."[12] Muirhead used these materials to seduce young men, and he therefore had no basis for denying his sustained interest in sex between men.

Dr. Veitch was called in to provide an alternative defense by offering a psychological explanation for Muirhead's actions. The doctor "declared it as his opinion, that the conduct of the prisoner arose out of a strange fatuity, that sometimes seized on men in a very advanced stage of life."[13] This defense reflected the idea that the very old, like the very young, might lose the ability to control their baser passions, and that their uncontrolled lusts might be directed toward young men as well as toward women. Although other men in the early to mid-nineteenth century argued that alcohol, seizures, or other factors caused them to temporarily "forget themselves," Muirhead's use of medical testimony to explain his desires was unusual. It seems that only Muirhead's position in society, coupled with the desire of upper-class men to publicly deny that any of their number were capable of such acts when of sound mind, led to its admission in this case.[14]

In Britain, medical examinations in such cases were carried out mainly to discern whether sex between men had just occurred, whereas on the Continent, such examinations were also conducted to determine whether such acts had been repeatedly engaged in. This approach had developed under the influence of writers like Ambroise Tardieu, a prominent practitioner of forensic medicine in Paris and a frequent witness at criminal trials. Tardieu's 1857 *étude médical-légale sur les attentats aux moeurs* (Medico-legal studies on offences against public decency) claimed that sexual desire between men was caused by either seduction or debauchery, and that "pederasts" were also more prone to criminal behavior than were other men.[15] He further claimed that the shape of the penis and anus was affected by repeated acts of anal intercourse and that these signs could be discerned by the expert.[16] Pederasts, Tardieu argued, could be identified by distinguishing features, but not because they had been born with them. Instead, their actions over time left marks on the body.

After their arrest for cross-dressing in 1870, Ernest Boulton and Frederick Park were subjected to medical examinations intended to find evidence of repeated homosexual acts, but the circumstances indicate how exceptional such examinations were in Britain. James Thomas Paul, the surgeon at the police station where the men were first taken, carried out the examination on his own initiative, saying that he did so because he had recently read of such procedures in a French medical text.[17] Although his inspection had lasted less than a minute in a poorly lit room, Paul reported at the police court hearing that each man revealed signs of repeated sexual acts with other men. The physician's testimony was contradicted by other English medical men, and the scientific validity and usefulness of such examinations were questioned in the courtroom. Dr. Frederick Le Gros Clark declared that he "could never have imagined that the offence alleged is so common as to have come within the frequent experience of any practitioner," and other men expressed pride that such matters were poorly understood in Britain. The lord chief justice presiding over the trial instructed the jury to assign no weight to the prosecution's medical evidence, which he declared to be entirely discredited.[18] Claims that medical examinations could detect regular acts of anal intercourse were not a factor at other British trials.

Nevertheless, the idea of a connection between a man's actions and character and his physical characteristics was common. George Mosse has argued that in the early nineteenth century the idea was current among respectable men. A man's actions were determined by his character, and character could be read on the body of the individual.[19] Negative changes might accumulate over time on the body of an immoral man, just as a robust and manly carriage was seen as the external expression of an inner morality. Respectable men were not thought to be immune from temptation, as all souls were burdened with dark desires that must be resisted. The ability to control or deny such desires, including sexual desire for other men, was one of the tests of a man's character.

If sodomites were thought recognizable by their physical characteristics, as when one man declared of another that "you can see sodomy printed on his face," it was not because they were thought to have been born with those traits.[20] A sallow complexion, weakness of frame or demeanor, and uncontrolled nervous movements were all physical markers of the sodomite, but they stemmed from a man's repeated actions rather than his birth.[21] Men became sodomites over time because of what they did, not because of the way they were born.

It was not even necessarily sexual desire for another man so much as other suspect behaviors that led men into sodomy. Regular masturbation, for example, was believed to create nervous excitement that was damaging to health, as well as reduce the sexual act to a matter of base gratification rather than a solemn mystery.[22] The uncontrolled sexual pursuit of women might lead as well to physical exhaustion and, over time, to a greater willingness to pursue a wider range of sexual objects to satisfy an overstimulated libido.

These ideas are manifested not only in the medical literature and high culture but also, much more explicitly, in those works that dealt with sex directly and at length. Pornographic works, although not widely disseminated, provide a depiction of behaviors and beliefs that are often only suggested in other sources. Well-studied works in this genre, including *My Secret Life* (1888) and *The Pearl* (1879–80), depict oversexed male protagonists who are primary interested in women but who are on occasion willing to have sex with young men as a way of adding to their store of experiences.[23] These depictions of homosexual acts as an extension of unrestrained heterosexual lust are in keeping with the eighteenth- and early nineteenth-century works that argue for a continuum, rather than a break, between these forms of sexual excess. In another such story from the period, previously unexamined in the secondary literature, these themes, and their connection to notions of masculine character, are especially pronounced. For this reason it is worth looking at the story "The Three Chums" in some detail.

The narrative of "The Three Chums," published in installments in *The Boudoir: A Magazine of Scandal, Facetiae, &c.* in 1860, links notions of character, sexuality, and respectability.[24] The magazine itself consisted of about a dozen serial stories and features, each between three and eight pages in length. There were almost no descriptions of acts of sex between men in any of the stories, even where they might be expected, as in the recurring section titled "Choice Letter from the Greek of Aristenetus." "The Three Chums," which runs to nearly one hundred pages in total, contains only two scenes that depict acts of sex between men. Both of these confirm patterns and attitudes identified by Mosse and other scholars.

"The Three Chums" is a variation on a popular genre of story centering on an experienced Londoner taking a friend from the country on a series of sprees around the city at night. The narrator, Charlie, with whom the reader is most invited to identify, has come to London to have adventures with his friends Henry and Frank before the three men go off to school in the next term and embark on the serious study that will secure their future professional and respectable status. Each installment graphically describes their sexual acts with women they meet in public houses, music halls, theaters, and on the streets of London. Such behavior does not disqualify them from respectability in their own minds because a rigid separation is maintained between these nighttime activities and their daytime lives, and it is also clear that they plan to curtail such sprees after the summer.

One night the three friends stay in Green Park past the ten o'clock closing of the gates. In the midst of scenes of heterosexual excess, the three young men come upon a contest over erect penis size between a police officer and a soldier, with the prize money being furnished by a wealthy older man. After the policeman is declared the winner, the author writes that "the bobby had his quid, and the old fellow walked off, as we supposed, to grope the soldier, who went with him."[25]

The three young men express no disdain over what they have witnessed: it is presented as simply one more "unblushing indecency" occurring in the park. This is in part because the working-class soldier and policemen are represented as both masculine and sexually interested in women as well. The only man in the scene who exhibits same-sex desire is the old man, who is represented in a way that distances his sexual desires from the protagonists in three ways. First, because he is old, he is judged less capable of controlling his lusts, and the young protagonists do not see themselves reflected in his actions. Secondly, the economic leverage that tempts the soldier and the constable is no inducement to the three relatively affluent protagonists. Finally, the three friends are never themselves directly propositioned: they are observers and not participants in the scene. These three factors allow the protagonists and the reader alike to enjoy the spectacle without feeling implicated in it.[26]

In the final installment of the story, the three friends seem to face the consequences of their actions more directly. The opening of the installment finds them in a dense crowd on brightly lit Regent Street, where the groping of passers-by is the apparent purpose of almost everyone in the crowd. The only such encounter fully described is one in which "the three friends had immense fun with a modest old lady and her daughter, who, though awfully indignant, were perfectly helpless."[27] Of the more than one hundred sexual acts depicted in the story, this is the first that is represented as nonconsensual: it suggests that the character of the protagonists has been affected by their actions to date. The pleasure they now take in forcing themselves on modest women foreshadows the more ominous transformation that awaits them.

Farther down Regent Street, they notice a large van parked on the side of the street. After standing up on a wheel to peer inside, they see "two old swells" and six young women engaging in sexual acts. The three friends enter the van at the invitation of the two older men and proceed to get drunk on champagne and engage in sexual acts with the women inside. The van takes the party to a private house, where most of the group is carried in, already unconscious from alcohol. On waking up in the strange house early in the following morning, Charlie noted that he "was not quite so drunk but he had a dim recollection of curious liberties which the old gents took with his naked person, and for a day or two afterwards Frank and Harry as well as himself confessed to feeling rather stretched and sore, as if their rear virginity had been ravished when they were helpless to prevent what they afterwards felt disgusted at."[28]

Thus, at the end of a long series of ever more exotic sexual experiments, the friends break the final taboo by engaging in sex with men. This act is presented as somewhere near the end of a continuum of illicit activities that they had long been exploring. Like many of the men mentioned in the courtroom accounts, Charlie seeks to evade personal responsibility for such acts through the excuses of intoxication and lack of consent.[29]

For Charlie, the act has humiliating consequences. He is awakened from his drunken slumber by smelling salts administered by the beautiful niece of the two old swells. She hastily takes Charlie off to an adjacent room and explains to him that her two uncles have cheated her out of her father's fortune. The house and all the wealth that the uncles have squandered on their decadent adventures are not their own. She has awakened him because she feels him to be a man of good character, or, "at least, I am sure you are not one of the filthy unnatural fellows my uncles usually bring here, I have not the least doubt you three have been tricked, made tipsy and outraged by them!"[30]

The two talk further, and, after establishing a bond of mutual
respect and recognition, they attempt the first sexual encounter in
the story that involves a single couple in a private bedroom. The scene
clearly mirrors the marital sex that Charlie anticipates; but for the
first time in the narrative, Charlie is unable to perform sexually. He is
distraught, but the kind words and soft touch of the respectable niece
restore him.[31] After a simple, mutually satisfying sexual encounter,
Charlie gathers his clothes, wakes his sleeping friends, and quits the
house in the early hours of the morning. The final scene shows Charlie
home alone with a cup of tea, resolving that his sprees are now over
because it is time "to study, and rise in my profession."[32]

Despite the clandestine nature of the magazine in which it appeared,
the story reflects assumptions about the sexuality of respectable men.
Charlie is sexually indulgent in his youth, but he keeps his adventures
separate from his family and public life. Moreover, he knows enough
to stop before the marks of excess and dissipation become permanent
on his own body, as they have for the two uncles. That the uncles
are presented as equally and indiscriminately interested in men and
women, that they are ugly, and that they have lived extravagantly
from an income that they had not earned, are highly relevant.[33] For
all its shortcomings as a historical source, "The Three Chums" incor-
porates the ideas expressed in Tardieu and many other early medical
writings on sex between men. Among respectable men and physicians
in nineteenth-century Britain, moral failure, or even "moral insanity,"
and same-sex desire were linked.[34]

The belief in this connection was part of the reason that respectable men found it so hard to believe that men of otherwise good
character would engage in sex with other men. Several defendants
invoked the argument in court that because they were respectable
men, they could not possibly have contemplated or committed unnatural acts. Edward Peckham, a middle-aged man who was the superintendent of the Fine Arts Commission and arranged exhibitions of
paintings in Westminster Hall and other locations, "asked . . . if it
was likely that a man in his station of life and public capacity would
do such a thing as that imputed to him by the soldier."[35] After noting
that Benjamin Smith was "very respectable" and had been "some
years in the service of Messrs. Rothschild, and they had so high an
opinion of his morality and general propriety of conduct," it was
then argued that "it could hardly be imagined" that he would "in
broad day commit such an assault upon an entire stranger and then

walk quietly away," as he was accused of doing.[36] In the 1867 trial
"of a gentleman whose name we omit . . . Mr. Coleridge rested the
defence on the improbability of the defendant, who would be proved
to have borne the character of a moral, pure-minded man, suddenly
committing such an offence upon an officer of the police."[37] The
magistrate at a Marylebone police-court hearing remarked that the
case he was hearing "was one of a most painful nature" because it
involved charges of sex between two men who both seemed to be of
high character.[38]

With this view in mind, we need to take a fresh look at the reception
of *Psychopathia Sexualis* by at least some Britons in the final decades
of the nineteenth century. By most accounts, the book was dismissed
or condemned by the British medical community as promoting deca-
dence and immorality, an opinion that did not begin to change until
after World War I.[39] Recent work by Ivan Crozier has shown that
Continental theories did have supporters in British medical communities in the 1880s and 1890s, but even these supporters were reluctant to
speak at length on these theories, and "anxieties about sex continued to
be the main point made in the English medical press."[40] To the degree
that there was any medical consensus on the topic of sex between men,
it was still largely the view of men like William Acton, who argued in
the 1860s that such acts resulted from a lack of self-control and had
dire health consequences.[41] Although *Psychopathia Sexualis* was not
without detractors on the Continent, with groups such as the German
Purity League criticizing the book "as a serious undermining of the
moral order," its many editions enjoyed strong sales in France and in
German-speaking countries.[42]

Because the book circulated mostly in Europe, the changes it underwent in successive editions, in response to the concerns of its readership, were effected largely by European correspondents. The 1886
edition was published with only 45 case studies in 110 pages, but by
the twelfth edition, published in 1903, there were 238 numbered and
several dozen unnumbered case studies, analyzed in 437 pages.[43] In the
second edition, Krafft-Ebing added material to differentiate between
individuals who had inborn feelings of contrary sexual feeling and
those who developed such desires later in life. By the fourth edition, in
1889, he had further differentiated the concept of inborn inversion in
men into four distinct categories.[44] These categories evolved in response
to readers' reactions, but with only "one or two notable exceptions"
Krafft-Ebing received none of this correspondence from Britain.[45]

Of the two main forms of inversion described in Krafft-Ebing's work, British readers would have been more familiar with the concept of acquired inversion. Like many in nineteenth-century Britain and Europe, Krafft-Ebing felt that a man could develop sexual desire for other men through prolonged abrogation of self-control. More surprising to British readers was Krafft-Ebing's postulation that there were congenital inverts, who felt "antipathic sexual instinct" from childhood. Krafft-Ebing's understanding of this category was influenced by those who had contacted him, including Karl Ulrichs, a German lawyer from Hanover who had felt sexual desires for other men since childhood and who began the first lobbying effort in European history to repeal certain laws against sex between men.[46]

On the surface, the creation of the category of the congenital invert would seem to sever the link between same-sex desire and respectability, but in fact notions of character and adherence to the norms of respectable middle-class masculinity remain central to the diagnosis of a healthy invert in the multiple editions of Krafft-Ebing's work. Those reading it in late nineteenth-century Britain, such as George Ives or Edward Carpenter, would have encountered a text that treated these issues in ways they found familiar.

Understanding the role played by the middle-class conception of character in categories established by Krafft-Ebing requires paying careful attention to the highly structured arrangement of his case studies in the later editions of his book. The section "Antipathic Sexuality" is divided into two main parts, dealing with "acquired" and "congenital" feelings of desire for those of the same sex. Of the four subsections discussing congenital inversion, the first is reserved for men who have some desire for women but stronger feelings for other men; the final category describes the individual seemingly most defined by "antipathic sexual instinct." Ostensibly these categories lay out a continuum of types, from healthy to more debilitated or diseased, but they also form a continuum of styles of masculinity, from the respectable to the contemptible. Within this schema, effeminacy, rather than sexual desire for other men, is the primary marker of the diseased individual.

For the first category of congenital inverts, men who also have weak sexual feelings for women, Krafft-Ebing suggests that medical treatments would allow them to marry and join conventional society. These men are represented as having steady employment and being conventionally masculine in other ways, and they are not represented as being tainted with hereditary problems.[47]

The next section, "Homo-Sexual Individuals, or Urnings," describes those who have feelings exclusively for members of their own sex and whose "anomaly" is "limited to the vita sexualis, and does not more deeply and seriously affect the character and mental personality."[48] These men are described as being conventionally masculine in all ways except in their sexual desire for other men, and their personalities and heredities are also represented as being free of degeneracy and other taints. All of the healthy urnings in this section demonstrate both their mental soundness and their masculine self-control by exhibiting no desire to participate in active or passive anal or oral sex. Instead, they might engage in touch and mutual masturbation with another mature man, with one man explicitly stating that he "confined himself entirely to acts not proscribed by the law of the land."[49] The choice of an immature sexual partner, eschewed by the healthy urnings in this section, is viewed as a sign of degeneracy. "Unlike the old and decrepit debauchees, who prefer boys (and indulge in pederasty by preference), [the sexual desire of healthy urnings] seems never to be directed to immature males."[50]

All but one of the men described in the nine case studies of healthy urnings had respectable and highly skilled jobs, as well as respected positions in their communities. These men were described by Krafft-Ebing to be "masculine in every respect," showing "refined thought," and with "no signs of degeneration." In the last case study of the section, Krafft-Ebing allows one of these healthy urnings, a successful physician, to speak at some length in his own defense, telling Krafft-Ebing that "the majority of 'aunts' like myself, in no way regret their abnormality, but would be sorry if the condition were to be changed; and, moreover, since the congenital condition, according to my own and all other experience, cannot be influenced, all our hope rests upon the possibility of the change of the laws with reference to it, so that only rape or the commission of public offence, when this can be proved at the same time, shall be punishable."[51]

The placement of this long quote at this point in Krafft-Ebing's book is revealing. The standard of behavior that denoted a healthy urning was not dissimilar from the standard a middle-class man needed to follow to be considered respectable. Respectable masculine status was not something that an individual was entitled to simply because he was born a man; rather, it had to be earned. Although a man might be designated an "urning" by birth, the designation of "respectable" derived from an individual's choices and actions. This conflation of the categories of health and respectability runs throughout Krafft-Ebing's work on homosexuality.

The designation of respectable urning was difficult to maintain. All men were subject to debility based on their actions, and urnings were in a particularly precarious position. Masturbation could degrade the sexual instinct of all men, but enforced abstinence could also damage health, and such abstinence was often forced on urnings attempting to be respectable. As a result, many urnings fell victim to debility and degeneration though their inability to either control their actions or find healthy outlets for their natural sexual urges. The perils of this dilemma, along with the role that hereditary taint might play in the process, are shown in Krafft-Ebing's final two categories within this section.

The third category comprises congenital inverts who were also effeminate. An urning who was effeminate, or desired to play a passive role in sexual or other social relations, lost the designation as healthy and was discussed in terms of degeneration. Krafft-Ebing does not write that effeminacy was innate in urnings but rather that it represents "deeper acquired degenerations of the original anomaly" brought on perhaps by masturbation, and "analogous to the signs of progressive degeneration observed in acquired sexual inversion" of non-urning men.[52] Passivity and effeminacy were therefore acquired traits, and they disqualified any man, urning or not, from being considered respectable.

All of the men described in this third section demonstrate some level of sexual excess, nervous disorder, or tainted family history.[53] They were also, to varying degrees, removed by their actions from the norms of respectable masculinity. These were the congenital inverts who desired anal and oral sex, who were promiscuous, and who were concerned with pleasing other men. In the successive case studies, such characteristics become more common, as do the designations of degeneration and ill-health.

The final category in this section, "Androgyny," is meant to describe a medical condition, but in fact the sole case study in this category describes an individual presented not so much as diseased as the antithesis of respectable middle-class masculinity. "Mr. v. H." was thirty years old, and like many in the "Effemination" category, he was described as being drawn to girls' games and clothes from an early age. Like the effeminates, he also had a history of masturbation, but the consequences of these characteristics were far more extreme than for the effeminates. Although not of the respectable occupations, the effeminates were at least able to support themselves and function independently in the world. Their sex drives may have been turned toward pleasing other men and toward acts that were illegal in some European countries, but they did at least demonstrate strong sexual urges. The representative of the "Androgyny" category, by contrast, had "an indolent, effeminate, dreamy habit of thought [that] had become more and more noticeable ever since puberty. All efforts to induce the patient to take up an earnest pursuit in life were in vain. His intellectual functions, though formally quite undisturbed, were never equal to the motive of an independent character, and the higher ideals of life. He remained dependent, an overgrown child; and nothing more clearly indicated his original abnormal condition than an actual incapability to take care of money."[54]

This is also the only case study in which Krafft-Ebing repeatedly mentions that the subject was lying to him, indicating that Mr. v. H. was not even of sufficient moral character to be forthright with his physician. He considered himself an aesthete, wished to discuss paintings and poetry, and also had a "shy, effeminate manner . . . the swimming, neuropathic expression of the eyes; the traces of powder and paint; [and] curtailed cut clothing, with the bosom-like prominence of the upper garments."[55]

From these descriptions, Mr. v. H. seems to have had far less sex with men than the physician previously quoted. But Mr. v. H. was considered diseased, whereas the physician was healthy. Again, the true markers of disease for Krafft-Ebing were the lack of masculine self-control and the absence of the characteristics of masculine respectability.

Another group of case studies involves men with antipathic sexual instinct who were not urnings. Those men were born with sexual desires exclusively for women, but they were so degraded in their sexual instincts, through tainted heredity or lack of self-control, that they came to desire men as well as women, or men exclusively.[56] This category includes men like the uncles in "The Three Chums" and those analyzed by George Mosse, whose base actions were thought to have permanently influenced their bodies and their character. The flaw that led to their acquired inversion was the lack of self-control.

Worldwide, many cultural roles allowed for sex between men with some degree of social sanction or social toleration, and Havelock Ellis and John Addington Symonds listed many of them in the opening chapter of Sexual Inversion. Examples from China, Japan, India, and the Americas were described, as were patterns in southern Europe and among the lower classes in Britain.[57] Nevertheless, rationales from other parts of the world or the lower classes could not be taken as a sanction or an excuse for such behavior among respectable middle-class men. Middle- and upper-class European men considered themselves superior to the men of other cultures, and well above the lower classes within their own borders. These other examples were to be defined against, not held up as models to be emulated.

Respectable men needed a justification for homosexual acts drawing on systems of authority that had value among them, such as science. *Psychopathia Sexualis* provided such justifications although, for some, it strained the limits of what science could be invoked to justify. But for those who knew of the idea of the congenital invert, it provided a way of understanding their desires that did not require them to acknowledge moral weakness, to identify with foreign cultures or the lower classes, or to independently construct a positive self-understanding out of fragmentary pieces of texts, like Anne Lister or the author of *Don Leon*.

This identity of the respectable invert was also defined against the ribald urban subculture of the molly houses and the cross-dressers, and this is perhaps the point at which a divide, recently identified by other scholars, began to widen. In their studies of homosexuality in London in the late nineteenth and twentieth centuries, Matt Cook and Matt Houlbrook have argued that the class divide between "queans" and "queers" was omnipresent. Discreet and respectable middle-class queers defined themselves against the flamboyant and public working-class queans, with the two groups inhabiting separate spaces within the city. At one extreme was the West End gentleman's club described in Cook's work, where respectable queers met and socialized discreetly, free of police interference; at the other end of the spectrum were the cafés around Piccadilly Circus, where working-class queans in powder and paint flirted more publicly and faced greater harassment.[58] Cook regards these men's experiences as so disparate as to require discussion in separate chapters. Houlbrook has argued that it was the repudiation of the conduct of the working-class quean by the middle-class queer that led to the legalization of private consensual sexual acts between adult men in 1967.[59] This argument contrasts with the view of the eighteenth-century molly house as an egalitarian space, where men of different class backgrounds mixed, class barriers were relaxed, and a spirit of camaraderie prevailed among men across class lines because of a shared clandestine sexuality.[60]

These two positions may be reconcilable in light of the change that occurred in the decades that separate the extensive documentation of the molly house in the eighteenth and early nineteenth centuries and Cook's study of the late nineteenth century. Respectability among queers, as found by Cook and Houlbrook, is a particular cultural form that grew out of the late eighteenth- and early nineteenth-century understanding of middle-class respectability described most thoroughly by Leonore Davidoff and Catherine Hall. Evidence from the molly houses is sparse for the nineteenth century, but it may be that a broader cultural shift, the rise of respectable society, is responsible for this fracturing of the social experience.

If men who had sex with men were defining themselves against one another in new ways in the late nineteenth century, it is in part because politics was more involved by the late nineteenth century. The respectable queers were invoking a new liberal discourse of political rights, or at least the right to toleration within a liberal political framework. In the liberal tradition, a man earned inclusion through his actions, and this was the underlying theme of British politics throughout the century. It should not be surprising that respectable middle-class liberal men might be drawn to this logic, or that they might use it to justify separating themselves from other men who did not exhibit the masculine self-restraint that they respected and imposed on themselves. Liberal logic did not create political change in early to mid-eighteenth-century Britain, and consequently it provided less of a rationale for creating divisions within groups in society, but by the end of the nineteenth century it was a powerful political force.[61] The camaraderie of the eighteenth-century molly house may well have been an outgrowth of eighteenth-century politics, just as the segregation of some spaces in London associated with sex between men in the late nineteenth century might reflect the class politics of that time.

This emphasis on actions and character as the core of a man's identity was itself a cultural artifact of a specific time and place, and it too was subject to change and challenge. One such challenge can be seen in the next milestone in sexology's study of homosexuality, which was also the first to be written by Englishmen. *Sexual Inversion*, by Havelock Ellis and John Addington Symonds, was published two years after the Oscar Wilde trials, and it demonstrated a significant break with both Krafft-Ebing's analysis and most other published works on the origins and nature of sexual desire between men. Ellis and Symonds began their work with a survey of the current medical opinion on the nature of sexual inversion, noting the debate that existed between the proponents of acquired and congenital inversion, and stated that "before the study of inversion was placed on a scientific basis all cases were of course regarded as acquired."[62]

Acknowledging the dominance of Krafft-Ebing's formulation, they disputed many of his key points. Based on their own case studies, they considered congenital inversion to be the norm and acquired inversion to be extremely rare, occurring only in old men of failing sexual powers and a very few young men who had debauched themselves with sexual excess.[63] This argument represented their real break with previous British understandings of sex between men in the nineteenth century, because, unlike Krafft-Ebing, they did not connect nineteenth-century ideas of character and self-control to a man's ability to be considered both healthy and attracted to other men. Their formulation was the first in which middle-class notions of character seem to recede in importance.

Both class and the types of sexual acts performed were treated very differently in Sexual Inversion than in Psychopathia Sexualis. Working-class men were well represented in Sexual Inversion as protagonists, rather than just as objects available for sex. The subjects of case studies included a postman, a sports enthusiast, an actor, and a man employed in a workshop. Many of the men in both books expressed the idea that their feelings were normal for them, but in Sexual Inversion those designated as healthy engaged in a full range of sexual activities with other men that went beyond the forms of touch or mutual masturbation considered healthy in Psychopathia Sexualis.[64] Eschewing Krafft-Ebing's correlation between the sexual acts men performed and degrees of degeneration or effeminacy, Ellis and Symonds maintained that the types of physical contact engaged in were of little real significance. Although masturbation might enfeeble the sexual instinct in general, it did not cause inversion. Neither did any form of seduction or sexual contact with other men, as "the seed of suggestion can only develop when it falls on suitable soil."[65]

The work of Ellis and Symonds was not indicative of any shift in official British opinion. As Sean Brady has recently documented, Symonds, before collaborating with Ellis on the book, lived outside Britain for well over a decade in order to escape the repressive climate in Britain and explore his own sexual desires for other men in greater freedom.[66] After Symonds's death, Havelock Ellis could not find an English publisher for Sexual Inversion because of publishers' fears of prosecution under the English obscenity laws. The book was published first in Germany, as *Das konträre Geschlechtsgefühl,* and only later in English by an American company. At least some British authorities tried to suppress it when copies were brought to Britain, convicting one individual for selling a copy to an undercover police officer. Symonds's family also worked to ensure that all copies of the first edition of *Sexual Inversion,* bearing Symonds's name, were withdrawn from publication in order to protect the family's reputation.[67] More indicative of respectable opinion in Britain were the medical professionals who condemned the work and continued to print derogatory observations about Krafft-Ebing's theories into the early twentieth century.[68]

Nevertheless, Ellis and Symonds exemplified the increased willingness to challenge and change models of respectability and moral behavior. Scholars have recently emphasized the ways in which Ellis was a countercultural and maverick figure for his time.[69] In addition to conducting research on sexuality, both Ellis and Symonds were drawn to broader social-reform movements. Ellis was an early member of the Fellowship of the New Life, which was dedicated to the transformation of society by the example of "the cultivation of a perfect character in each and all."[70] From this group arose the Fabian Society, which played an influential role in shifting British government policy and social attitudes into the twentieth century.

Through the scientific analysis of social problems, the Fabians put forward policies that went against mid-Victorian notions of character involving self-help and charity. Their ideas had gained prominence after Britain's spectacularly flawed performance during the Boer War revealed the extent to which urban poverty could undermine Britain's national power and prestige.[71] Victorian arguments that industrial capitalism and the individual desire for self-improvement would eventually eliminate social problems, so long as the lower classes were not corrupted into indolence by handouts that would blunt their motivation to work, paled in the face of generations of intractable and growing poverty in the urban slums. It was with these radical reformers that Ellis and Symonds aligned.[72] The reformers' criticism of mid-Victorian values extended to sexuality but was not limited to it.

This association raises the question of whether the ideas of Ellis and Symonds are better considered in the context of sexology or among broader cultural developments that enabled individuals to challenge hegemonic notions of masculinity and character. Edward Carpenter wrote that same-sex love would break down the English class system.

In his writings democracy, socialism, and spiritualism are all linked with the acceptance of love between men as a model for a new society. But Carpenter probably had the causality of the situation reversed; more likely it was the larger cultural challenge to Victorian values already under way that allowed Carpenter's voice and voices like his to be heard.[73] Rather than change the world, Carpenter was able to exploit the ways that the world had changed.

The result of the late nineteenth-century medical writing on homosexuality was a cultural rhetoric that created space for the respectable homosexual in European society. This new understanding was only one of many ways an individual might incorporate his sexual desires into a positive self-image, but because it was tied into the powerful liberal rhetoric of middle-class respectability within the framework of liberal political philosophy, it had greater long-term potential for bringing about change than any previous formulations. It was in the name of liberal respectability, and the granting of rights based on actions, that Britain eased some of the restrictions on sex between men in 1967, making good at least in part on the promise of liberalism to recognize fundamental equalities—even as, in practice, its legacy has also been marked by the exclusions it has created.[74]

Jeffrey Weeks first labeled this respectable homosexual identity as the "modern" homosexual identity. The formulation has recently been criticized, but Weeks's original terminology is understandable given that so much of what we define as "modern" history stems from the time when the Enlightenment understanding of the self was directly tied to political consequences in the context of the French Revolution. Political subjectivity changed in that period in ways that individuals worldwide are still coming to terms with. For men motivated by same-sex desire, the analogous moment of modernity, when an Enlightenment discourse of rights became tied to political subjectivity incorporating sex between men, came later, at the point identified by Weeks. The first political right demanded was not for enfranchisement, which the respectable men concerned already had, but rather for the protection of privacy, which was also a fundamental tenet of liberal philosophy.

This late nineteenth-century development did not resolve or end the process of identity formation around acts of same-sex desire, but rather it established a politically powerful subject position that over time has gained ascendancy. Medical opinion remained fractured; respectability was compatible with some systems of understanding sex between men but not with others. Sigmund Freud attempted to change the terms of the conversation altogether, although the language of earlier sexology persisted into the 1950s and beyond.[75] Many who felt these desires continued to see homosexuality as a moral failing, and others, such as Edward Carpenter and the Bolton Whitman Fellowship analyzed by H. G. Cocks, saw it as the result of a higher level of intellectual and spiritual development. Some men were content to cruise the urinals, sleep with men casually, and make excuses to themselves for their behavior. Others continued to rouge their cheeks and roam the parks and other urban spaces of the city, forming their own positive interpretations of their actions based on the traditions of their neighborhoods and their friends. Men incorporated their sexual desires into their self-understandings in many different ways, but that range was clearly different from what it had been earlier in the century because the material and cultural elements through which individuals interpreted their experiences were also different. The self-understandings forged by any group or individual are always unique to their time.

Notes

INTRODUCTION

1. For a discussion of this methodology, see Anna Clark, "Anne Lister's Construction of Lesbian Identity," *Journal of the History of Sexuality* 7 (1996): 23–50.

2. Deposition of Samuel Patrick Lea, in the Petition of George Dawson Lowndes, February 1841. National Archive, London, HO 18 43/33.

3. Lowndes did make a countercharge, with the *Weekly Dispatch* reporting Lowndes as saying he would "make the young rascal know for making such a charge against him" (26 January 1840). After Lowndes was found guilty, Lord Chief Justice Thomas Denman castigated him for his "scandalous attempt to impute perjury to those persons by whom it was brought forward" (*Times*, 10 February 1841, 6f.).

4. Lowndes was accused of "la[ying] hold of [Lea's] person in an indecent manner." Such behavior more than met the legal criteria for indecent assault under the law. *Times*, 22 January 1840, 6f.; *Weekly Dispatch*, 26 January 1840.

5. For important early work in this area, see Randolph Trumbach, "London's Sodomites: Homosexual Behavior and Western Culture in the Eighteenth Century," *Journal of Social History* 2 (1977): 1–33; A.D. Harvey, "Prosecutions for Sodomy in England at the Beginning of the Nineteenth Century," *Historical Journal* 21 (1978): 939–48; Arthur Gilbert, "Sodomy and the Law in Eighteenth- and Early Nineteenth-Century Britain," *Societas* 8 (1978): 225–41. From the 1780s, sodomy and attempted-sodomy cases were no longer summarized in the Session Papers as were other trials: entries for "sodomitical assault" were followed by statements to the effect that "the court ordered the evidence to be suppressed, as too indecent for publication" (Session Papers, Old Bailey Proceedings: no. 7, part 10 (1785), 1125).

6. The eighteenth-century material has also been analyzed in Tim Hitchcock, *English Sexualities, 1700–1800* (New York: St. Martin's Press, 1997), 58–75; Rictor Norton, *Mother Clap's Molly House: The Gay Subculture in England, 1700–1830* (London: Gay Men's Press, 1992); and Netta Murray Goldsmith, *The Worst of Crimes: Homosexuality and the Law in Eighteenth-Century London* (Brookfield, Vt.: Ashgate, 1998). For details of some of the earliest raids, see Hitchcock, *English Sexualities,* 67–70.

7. For some of the earliest works on these "scandal trials," see H. Montgomery Hyde, ed., *The Three Trials of Oscar Wilde* (New York: University Books, 1956); H. Montgomery Hyde, *The Cleveland Street Scandal* (London: W. H. Allen, 1976); H. Montgomery Hyde, *The Love That Dared Not Speak Its Name* (Boston: Little, Brown, 1970). See also Holbrook Jackson, *The Eighteen-Nineties: A Review of Art and Ideas at the Close of the Nineteenth Century* (London: 1913; repr., New York: A. A. Knopf, 1922).

8. Jeffery Weeks, *Coming Out: Homosexual Politics in Britain from the Nineteenth Century to the Present* (New York: New Horizon Press, 1977), 3.

9. For influential scholarly works that have used the late nineteenth-century trials to build broader interpretive frameworks, see Eve Kosofsky Sedgwick, *Epistemology of the Closet* (Berkeley: University of California Press, 1990); Ed Cohen, *Talk on the Wilde Side* (New York: Routledge, 1993).

10. See, for example, Robert Gildea, *Barricades and Borders: Europe, 1800–1914* (New York: Oxford University Press, 2003), 335–36, 394–95; Lynn Hunt et. al., *The Making of the West: Peoples and Cultures* (New York: Bedford/St. Martin's, 2005), 965–66.

11. One example, printed at the conclusion of the police-court hearings for Ernest Boulton and Frederick William Park on 31 May 1870, explained that "the charges made by the prosecution are such as are seldom advanced in this country, except against the lowest, the most ignorant, and the most degraded. . . . We have been accustomed to associate such offences with the sensuous civilizations of antiquity, and with the barbarism or demoralization of certain races in our own day. But we were not prepared to find even the suspicion of them attached to youths of respectable family and position" (*Times,* 31 May 1870).

12. Neil Bartlett, *Who Was that Man? A Present for Mr. Oscar Wilde* (London: Serpent's Tail, 1988), 31–37; Alan Sinfield, *The Wilde Century: Effeminacy, Oscar Wilde, and the Queer Movement* (New York: Columbia University Press, 1994), 4–10; Cohen, *Talk on the Wilde Side,* 103–25.

13. Matt Cook, *London and the Culture of Homosexuality, 1885–1914* (Cambridge: Cambridge University Press, 2003), 7–22. This pattern is also apparent in Jeffrey Weeks, *Sex, Politics and Society: The Regulation of Sexuality Since 1800* (London: Longman, 1989), 100.

14. Sean Brady, *Masculinity and Male Homosexuality in Britain, 1861–1913* (New York: Palgrave, 2006); Morris B. Kaplan, *Sodom on the Thames: Sex, Love, and Scandal in Wilde Times* (Ithaca, N.Y.: Cornell University Press, 2005).

15. Cocks was not the first scholar to take note of the use of attempted-sodomy prosecutions, but he was the first to give them a central role in his

interpretation. Jeffrey Weeks noted that "forms of homosexual activity were subsumed under the major form either as assault or attempts at the major crime" (*Sex, Politics and Society,* 99). See also Harvey, "Prosecutions for Sodomy in England," 941.

16. There were just over 1,800 prosecutions for sodomy and 3,100 prosecutions for attempted sodomy in England and Wales between 1810 and 1870. No fewer than 600 separate reports of these cases between men appeared in the *Times* in the years between 1820 and 1870, with approximately half as many appearing in the *Weekly Dispatch*. Prosecution statistics gathered from the annual Criminal Offenders and Judicial Statistics returns in the Command Papers of the British Parliamentary Papers.

17. For a theoretical overview of the significance of this shift, see Michel Foucault, *Discipline and Punish: The Birth of the Prison,* trans. Alan Sheridan (New York: Vintage, 1979), 47–53.

18. For an analysis of the authors in these two camps, see Joseph Bristow, "Remapping the Sites of Modern Gay History: Legal Reform, Medico-legal Thought, Homosexual Scandal, Erotic Geography," *Journal of British Studies* 46 (January 2007): 116–42.

19. The historical relationship between homosexual acts and homosexual identity is contested. The work of historians following the methodologies associated with Michel Foucault's approach to the history of sexuality has discounted the possibility of a homosexual identity that extends back further than 130 years. Yet both a continuous subculture and a cultural stereotype of an adult man motivated by and identifying with feelings of same-sex desire seem evident in English society at least by the early eighteenth century, as indicated in the work of Randolph Trumbach and other scholars. For a broad discussion of this debate, see John Boswell, "Revolutions, Universals, and Sexual Categories," and David M. Halperin, "Sex Before Sexuality: Pederasty, Politics, and Power in Classical Athens," in *Hidden from History: Reclaiming the Gay and Lesbian Past,* ed. Martin Duberman, Martha Vicinus, and George Chauncey Jr. (New York: New American Library, 1989), 17–53. For discussions of the issue of identity in lesbian history and how it differs from the problem of analyzing men's experiences, see Judith M. Bennett, "'Lesbian-Like' and the Social History of Lesbianism," *Journal of the History of Sexuality* 9 (January–April 2000): 1–24; Martha Vicinus, "Lesbian History: All Theory and No Facts or All Facts and No Theory?" *Radical History Review* 60 (Fall 1994): 57–75; Adrienne Rich, "Compulsory Heterosexuality and Lesbian Existence," *Signs* 5 (1980): 631–60.

20. David M. Halperin, *How to Do the History of Homosexuality* (Chicago: University of Chicago Press, 2002), 28–29. In this assessment, Halperin mirrors Foucault's chronology.

21. See Arthur Burns and Joanna Innes, eds., *Rethinking the Age of Reform: Britain, 1780–1850* (New York: Cambridge University Press, 2003).

22. Roy Porter, *English Society in the Eighteenth Century* (New York: Penguin, 1990), 310–39, and John Gillis, *For Better, For Worse: British Marriages, 1600 to Present* (New York: Oxford University Press, 1985), 162–63.

23. See "The Moral Economy Reviewed" and "The Moral Economy of

the English Crowd in the Eighteenth Century," in E. P. Thompson, *Customs in Common: Studies in Traditional Popular Culture* (New York: New Press, 1993), 185–351.

24. Leonore Davidoff and Catherine Hall, *Family Fortunes: Men and Women of the English Middle Class, 1780–1850* (Chicago: University of Chicago Press, 1987), 21–26.

25. Linda Colley, *Britons: Forging the Nation, 1707–1837* (New Haven: Yale University Press, 1992), 308–19.

26. Michael Mason, *The Making of Victorian Sexuality* (New York: Oxford University Press, 1994); Roy Porter and Lesley Hall, *The Facts of Life: The Creation of Sexual Knowledge in Britain, 1650–1950* (New Haven: Yale University Press, 1995), 14–21; Colley, *Britons*, 151–59.

27. G. J. Barker-Benfield, *The Culture of Sensibility: Sex and Society in Eighteenth-Century Britain* (Chicago: University of Chicago Press, 1996), 321–42; Dror Wahrman, *The Making of the Modern Self: Identity and Culture in Eighteenth-Century England* (New Haven: Yale University Press, 2005), 69–72.

28. For the distinction between character and reputation as they relate to class, see John Tosh, *Manliness and Masculinities in Nineteenth-Century Britain: Essays on Gender, Family, and Empire* (Harrow: Pearson Longman, 2005), 61–83.

29. Anna Clark, *The Struggle for the Breeches: Gender and the Making of the British Working Class* (Berkeley: University of California Press, 1995), 42–43.

30. See Douglas Hay, Peter Linebaugh, J. Rule, E. P. Thompson, and C. Winslow, *Albion's Fatal Tree: Crime and Society in Eighteenth-Century England* (New York: Pantheon, 1975), 17–63; Clive Emsley, *Crime and Society in England, 1750–1900* (New York: Longman, 1996), 1–16; David Taylor, *Crime, Policing and Punishment in England, 1750–1914* (New York: St. Martin's Press, 1998), 1–6.

31. This pattern was especially evident during Robert Peel's effort to modify the laws regulating sex between men (see chapter 3).

32. In a 1974 article, A. D. Harvey mentions briefly that "it was standard practice to prosecute lesser forms of statutory felonies as misdemeanors, and this was the legal basis for the increasing number of non-capital prosecutions for homosexuality" (Harvey, "Prosecutions for Sodomy in England," 941). In 1985 the charge of attempted sodomy was briefly discussed in Louis Crompton's *Byron and Greek Love: Homophobia in 19th-Century England* (Swaffham: Gay Men's Press, 1985), 21. Nevertheless, scholars continued to emphasize 1885 as a transition point, as evidenced in work as recent as Morris Kaplan's "'Who's Afraid of John Saul?' Urban Culture and the Politics of Desire in Late Victorian London," *Gay and Lesbian Quarterly* 5 (1999): 267–314.

CHAPTER 1. FAMILIES AND SEX BETWEEN MEN

1. Anonymous urban space is important to the history of sex between men in modern Western Christian culture in part because that culture, unlike

those of ancient Greece and Rome, or of many other non-Western societies, made no provision for socially acceptable forms of sexual contact between men. For a survey of recent work on urban geography and homosexuality, see Joseph Bristow, "Remapping the Sites of Modern Gay History: Legal Reform, Medico-legal Thought, Homosexual Scandal, Erotic Geography." *Journal of British Studies* 46 (January 2007): 116–42.

2. For a discussion of the "twilight moment" as a useful concept for understanding same-sex desire in the early nineteenth century, see Anna Clark, "Twilight Moments," *Journal of the History of Sexuality* 14 (2005): 139–60.

3. John Gillis, *For Better, For Worse: British Marriages, 1600 to the Present* (New York: Oxford University Press, 1985), 56–62.

4. Leonore Davidoff and Catherine Hall, *Family Fortunes: Men and Women of the English Middle Class, 1780–1850* (Chicago: University of Chicago Press, 1987), 270–74.

5. David Cannadine, *The Rise and Fall of Class in Britain* (New York: Columbia University Press, 1999), 80–82.

6. F.M.L. Thompson, *The Rise of Respectable Society: A Social History of Victorian Britain: 1830–1900* (Cambridge, Mass.: Harvard University Press, 1988), 178–79.

7. Judith Walkowitz, *Prostitution and Victorian Society: Women, Class, and the State* (New York: Cambridge University Press, 1980), 14–31.

8. Raphael Samuel, "Workshop of the World: Steam-Power and Hand Technology in Mid-Victorian Britain," *History Workshop Journal* 3 (1977): 6–72.

9. Thompson, *Rise of Respectable Society*, 193–95.

10. Petition of Henry Franklin, Letter of Thomas Franklin, 14 November 1848, HO 18 226/6.

11. Letter of Thomas Franklin, 14 November 1848.

12. Letter of Thomas Franklin, 14 November 1848, HO 18 266/6.

13. The job was in a hatter's shop on Regent Street. Petition of Henry Franklin, HO 18 266/6.

14. Letter of Thomas Franklin, 14 November 1848, HO 18 266/6.

15. Thomas Franklin's letter to the Home Office indicates that family friends had told him of the sexual relationship between Geldart and their son before Henry's arrest. Henry confirmed in his confession that he had engaged in sexual acts with Geldart. HO 18 266/6.

16. Letter of Thomas Franklin, 14 November 1848, HO 18 266/6.

17. HO 18 226/6, emphasis in original. A curt "certainly not" was Undersecretary Waddington's written response to the idea of dropping the charge against Henry Franklin.

18. For another example of outside individuals brought in to help when acts of sex between men were involved, see CRIM 10/17, Second Session, 1842–43, case no. 293, 201–2.

19. Letter of Thomas Geldart, dated 8 July 1850, HO 18 300/5.

20. First letter of Thomas Geldart, Petition of Joseph Smith, HO 18 300/5.

21. Letter of Thomas Geldart, dated 14 April 1851, HO 18 300/5.

22. The name "Joseph Smith" was the only one that appeared in the *Morning Post*, although the newspaper report indicates that the judge believed the name to be a fake one. *Morning Post*, 12 July 1851, 8a. The official court record also listed only the alias "Joseph Smith." See CRIM 10/32, Central Criminal Court, New Court, Thursday, 11 July 1850, case no. 1307.

23. For a similar example, but one in which economic exploitation seemed more central, see the case of Henry Jones, a poor seventeen-year-old recently moved to London, and George Newman. CRIM 10/20, Eighth Session, 10 June 1844, 218.

24. Law Cases, the King vs. Seymour, Western Circuit Court, 12 March 1828. *Annual Register; Or, a View of the History and Politics of the Year 1828* (London: J. Dodsley, 1828), 323–37. This case was also the subject of at least ten separate reports in the *Times* between August 1827 and March 1831 and at least six separate reports in the *Weekly Dispatch* over the same period. For other newspaper coverage, both within and outside London, see *Examiner*, 5 August 1827, 492; *Morning Chronicle*, 17 March 1828; *Flying Post* (Exeter), 20 March 1828; *Ipswich Journal*, 22 March 1828; *Jackson Oxford Journal*, 22 March 1828; *Morning Post*, 7 July 1830, 3.

25. For another case in which a servant provided testimony against his former employer, stating that he had left that employer's service more than forty years before due to "practices he observed . . . of such a nature, that no man of character could live in his service," see *Weekly Dispatch*, 28 August 1825, 274–75.

26. *Annual Register, 1828*, 323. Similarly, Anna Clark has found that when servants brought charges against their masters for heterosexual sexual assaults, it was an upper servant in a large household staff who began the proceedings. See Clark, *Women's Silence, Men's Violence: Sexual Assault in England, 1770–1845* (New York: Pandora, 1987), 105.

27. *Annual Register, 1828*, 323. This level of detail, describing the sexual act and the methods the servants used to observe it, was not given in the *Weekly Dispatch* account, although it did appear in the *Times*. See *Weekly Dispatch*, 16 March 1828, 82; *Times*, 14 March 1828, 4.

28. For another case where the young male servant did not allow himself to be so quickly marginalized, see the prosecution of James Newbery by Edward Davis Protheroe. CRIM 10/24, Twelfth Session, 1845–46, case no. 2914, 859–63.

29. Ann Bailey refused to be intimidated, telling Mr. Seymour that "what I have seen would hang any two men in England" (*Annual Register, 1828*, 324). The same exchange appeared in the *Times* (14 March 1828, 4), but not in the *Weekly Dispatch* (16 March 1828, 84).

30. *Annual Register, 1828*, 336; *Times*, 14 March 1828, 4; *Weekly Dispatch*, 16 March 1828, 84.

31. *Annual Register, 1828*, 324; *Times*, 14 March 1828, 4; *Weekly Dispatch*, 16 March 1828, 84.

32. *Annual Register, 1828*, 328–29.

33. *Annual Register, 1828*, 329–30.

34. The degree to which upper-class men closed ranks even in the face of

legitimate charges of sex among their own number is discussed in H. G. Cocks, "Safeguarding Civility: Sodomy, Class and Moral Reform in Early Nineteenth-Century England," *Past and Present* 190 (February 2006): 121–46. Conforming to the pattern discussed by Cocks, three years later Seymour's conviction was overturned. He was acquitted after a new trial was granted and no one showed up to prosecute. See *Weekly Dispatch,* 13 March 1831, 88; *Morning Post,* 7 July 1830, 3e.

35. *Times,* 14 September 1853, 10d–e.

36. *Weekly Dispatch,* 25 September 1842, 458; *Times,* 21 September 1842, 6f. Both newspapers described John Webber as "a person of gentlemanly appearance."

37. *Times,* 21 September 1842, 6f. This phrasing did not appear in the *Weekly Dispatch* report, which was written more from the perspective of the boys (25 September 1842, 458).

38. *Times,* 21 September 1842, 6f; *Weekly Dispatch,* 25 September 1842, 458. A similar incident reported in the *Weekly Dispatch* seemed more premeditated. In it, Richard Marks Wittyall, "pretending that he was locked out from lodgings, received permission to sleep with the footman, when the attempt was made in the course of the night" (25 September 1825, 206).

39. *Times,* 21 September 1842, 6f; *Weekly Dispatch,* 25 September 1842, 458.

40. CRIM 10/12, Fourth Session, 1841, case no. 645, 464.

41. The *Weekly Dispatch* reported that the "occurrence having become known in the neighbourhood, the Court was throughout the sitting most inconveniently crowded" (25 September 1842, 458). The *Times* also reported that the court "was most inconveniently crowded throughout the whole period of the investigation" (21 September 1842, 6f).

42. *Times,* 27 October 1842, 6f; 21 September 1842, 6f. The *Weekly Dispatch* report contained similar wording (30 October 1842, 519).

43. For other examples in which a man began as the prosecutor of a wealthier man on charges of unnatural assault and ended up becoming prosecuted himself on the charge of attempted extortion, see the cases involving Joseph Stokes, William Peters, and a Mr. Baker, *Times,* 20 December 1844, 7e; the cases of James Button and J. F. Daniel, *Times,* 31 July 1846, 7f–8a; the cases involving Michael Tasburgh, Joseph Braznell, and John Wren, CRIM 10/32, Eleventh Session, 1849–50, case no. 1589, 626–29; and the case involving Joseph Softlaw and Jeremiah William Callan, *Times,* 14 May 1851, 7d; 16 May 1851, 8d; 19 May 1851, 7e; *Weekly Dispatch,* 9 July 1851, 435.

44. For further examples of the countercharge of attempted extortion being used to counter an initial and seemingly valid accusation of unnatural assault, see the prosecution of James Button by John Fielding, CRIM 10/24, Tenth Session, 1845–46, case no. 1584, 505–6; the prosecution of George Marsh by Private Thomas Gill, *Times,* 21 September 1846, 6e; the prosecution of William Jones, *Times,* 11 August 1847, 8b; the prosecution of Edward Peckham, *Times,* 27 October 1847, 7b; the dispute between the Rev. Henry Charles Sellers and a soldier guarding the Duchess of Kent, CRIM 10/29, Fifth Session, 1848–49, case no. 675, 464–70; the charge made by Charles Richards

against Police Constable David Patching, *Times*, 26 October 1858, 9c; and the prosecution of James Williams by Henry Welch, *Times*, 12 March 1864, 12f.

45. *Annual Register, 1853*, 262.

46. *Times*, 13 May 1833, 3d.

47. Further examples of a man's leaving the court with his reputation intact include the case where the presiding judge said that John Fielding Daniel "would leave the Court without the slightest stain upon his character" (*Times*, 24 August 1846, 7d). In a different case, a soldier proved innocent was told by the judge that "he leaves this Court without the slightest stain upon his character" (*Weekly Dispatch*, 16 November 1851, 722). Like statements were made in a similar court case reported in the *Times*, 19 January 1870, 11c. See also the trial of Captain Peter Craycroft, R.N., who after his acquittal on indecent assault charges "was instantly surrounded by his friends, who congratulated him most warmly" (*Times*, 1 March 1847, 8d).

48. Bankes was voted out of Parliament in 1835, the first time he faced voters after his 1833 trial. *Annual Register, 1855*, 266.

49. *Weekly Dispatch*, 5 September 1841, 423; 12 September 1841, 435; and Anonymous, *Don Leon; a poem by the late Lord Byron, author of Childe Harold, Don Juan, &c., &c., And forming part of the private journal of his Lordship, supposed to have been entirely destroyed by Thos. Moore . . .* (London: "Printed for the Booksellers," 1866), 58–59. Court documents were also saved from the 1841 prosecution of Bankes. See TS 11/897: 3060, Central Criminal Court, September Sessions, 1841. For a report on the earlier trial that is favorable to Bankes, see *Caledonian Mercury* (Edinburgh), 7 December 1833.

50. Petition for George Dawson Lowndes, February 1841, HO 18 43/33.

51. There were eighteen reports in the *Times* on the appearances of George Dawson Lowndes before the London courts between August 1838 and December 1843, and ten reports on him in the *Weekly Dispatch* in the same period. *Times*, 30 August 1838, 7e; 4 January 1839, 7e; 22 January 1840, 6f; 10 February 1841, 6f; 13 February 1841, 7a; 18 April 1843, 7b; 20 April 1843, 6f; 26 April 1843, 7c; 6 May 1843, 8d; 18 May 1843, 8d; 24 May 1843, 8d; 5 June 1843, 8d; 13 June 1843, 8b; 9 August 1843, 8c; 14 August 1843, 7e; 14 October 1843, 7a; 4 November 1843, 7a; 28 November 1843, 6f; 6 December 1843, 6f. See *Weekly Dispatch*, 2 September 1838, 411; 6 January 1839, 5; 26 January 1840; 23 April 1843, 194; 30 April 1843, 208; 21 May 1843, 243; 11 June 1843, 278; 13 August 1843, 391; 3 December 1843, 579; and 10 December 1843, 590.

52. This pattern of high acquittal rates before the Court of the Queen's Bench continued into the late nineteenth century. For the later period, Sean Brady argues that such acquittal rates were due to the refusal of upper-class men to acknowledge sodomy among men of their own class. See Sean Brady, *Masculinity and Homosexuality in Britain, 1861–1913* (New York: Palgrave Macmillan, 2006), 59–62.

53. Case heard before the Court of the Queen's Bench, February, 1841, HO 18 43/33.

54. Letter from George Dawson Lowndes to the home secretary, dated 12 March 1841, HO 18 43/33.

55. Petition for George Dawson Lowndes, February 1841, HO 18 43/33.

56. George Curtis's bail was also set high because of his social position, but his defense asked for a reduction because "there has been a want of cordiality between himself and his family" (*Times*, 12 July 1850, 8a; 11 July 1850, 7e).

57. *Annual Register, 1833*, 245–47. See also Heber's obituary in the *North Wales Chronicle*, 15 October 1833.

58. The statement that sparked the case appeared in the 14 May 1826 issue of *John Bull* (see chapter 5).

59. The bishop of Clogher was arrested at the St. Alban's Tavern, Charles Street, Haymarket. More than a decade later, this case was still being alluded to in the press, as seen in a similar 1832 case centering on a clergyman and a soldier. See *Morning Chronicle*, 25 August 1832, 4d.

60. For reports on the death of Jocelyn, see *Morning Post*, 3 January 1844, 4d; *Times*, 2 January 1844. Both stories contained extracts from the *Scotsman* of the preceding Saturday.

61. For a discussion of Evangelical beliefs regarding suffering, trial, and personal guilt and depravity as a stage for the demonstration of the availability of God's grace to all, see Boyd Hilton, *The Age of Atonement: The Influence of Evangelicalism on Social and Economic Thought, 1795–1865* (Oxford: Clarendon Press, 1988), 10–12.

62. Five letters of Johanna Carrington were preserved in the Petition for John Jones, alias Joyce, HO 18 281/14. The trial was held at the Central Criminal Court on 8 April 1850.

63. Letters of Johanna Carrington, HO 18 281/14. Joyce seems to be unique in the records for this period as an upper-class man who became involved in extorting money from other men with accusations of unnatural desire. Joyce's accomplices were all far below him in social status. See CRIM 10/31, Sixth Session, 1849–50, case no. 803, 699–711.

64. Letters of Johanna Carrington, HO 18 281/14.

65. Marginal notes written on a letter from the warden of the convict prison of Gibraltar, 2 April 1860, HO 18 281/14. John Joyce had been convicted four years earlier on similar charges and sentenced to six months' imprisonment. CRIM 10/20, Tenth Session, 1843–44, case no. 1946, 495–500.

66. Mrs. Seymour also gave a long statement in support of her husband at the trial, although after her testimony it was reported that she "dissolved in tears" (*Annual Register, 1822*, 212).

67. CRIM 10/31, Sixth Session, 1849–50, case no. 803, 700.

68. For the newspaper coverage of this case, see *Morning Post*, 14 March 1850, 8a; 15 April 1850, 7a; *Weekly Dispatch*, 17 March 1850, 162; 21 April, 1850, 248; *Times*, 14 March 1850, 8b. For the criminal court records, see CRIM 10/31, Sixth Session, 1849–50, case no. 803, 699–711.

69. CRIM 10/31, Sixth Session, 1849–50, case no. 803, 702.

70. Margaret Nugent wrote five letters on behalf of her son Edward between July 1848 and July 1849. HO 18 243/48.

71. Hannah Burton felt equally sure that similar workplace motivations

had led sailors to accuse her husband, a tidewaiter of customs in the Port of London, of unnatural acts. HO 17 Pz/1. See also *Times, 30* October 1838, 6b; *Weekly Dispatch,* 4 November 1838, 519.

72. Letter of Margaret Nugent, received 17 July 1848, HO 18 243/48.

73. *Weekly Dispatch,* 6 April 1862, 4; *Times,* 2 April 1862, 11f. The same quote appeared in both publications.

74. The Rev. Greaves stated that whether his father had a "sudden" or a "peaceful descent into the grave might depend upon the clemency of the court in this particular" (*Annual Register, 1803,* 460).

75. Margaret closed her letter by suggesting that "my husband his father may get his reason again when he will see his son out at liberty at home." Letter of Margaret Nugent, received 17 July 1848, HO 18 243/48.

76. Margaret Nugent's alerting the Home Office to her son's failing health, confirmed by a surgeon at the prison, led to Edward's release in July 1849. HO 18 243/48.

77. Letter of Mary Ann Campbell to the home secretary, received 24 August 1849, HO 18 234/38.

78. Henry Campbell, Mary Ann's son, was also sentenced to six months' imprisonment for his part in the incident. Trial of John Campbell, Kent Summer Assizes, 23 July 1849, "Unnatural Crime." HO 18 234/38.

79. Petition of John Campbell, HO 18 234/38.

80. Petition of John Campbell, HO 18 234/38.

81. HO 18 268/27; HO 18 234/38.

82. Letters from Mary Ann Campbell, 26 March 1851, 12 July 1851, HO 18 268/27.

83. Letter of Mary Ann Campbell, 1 April, 1851, HO 18 268/27.

84. Letter of Mary Ann Campbell, 5 June, 1851, HO 18 268/27.

85. The final note attached to the petition is in Undersecretary Waddington's hand, stating that while "this is one of those life sentences in which some commutation appears to be necessary," he felt that not enough of the sentence had yet been served for him to accede to the request. The HO 18 234/38 petition series records that John Campbell was not discharged until 9 June 1859.

86. Robert Holloway, *The Phoenix of Sodom, or the Vere Street Coterie* (London: J. Cook, 1813). See also Rictor Norton, *Mother Clap's Molly House: The Gay Subculture in England, 1700–1830* (London: Gay Men's Press, 1992), 187–98.

87. Only the reactions of women were singled out for special attention in the *Times* report (13 August 1833, 4b).

88. *The Infamous Life of John Church, the St. George's Preacher, from his infancy up to his trial and conviction . . .* (London: Hay and Turner, 1817).

89. Recounted in *Don Leon,* notes, 17. In the context of a report on a molly-house raid in 1830, the *Morning Chronicle* noted that one of the arrested men "has been long notorious. About fifteen years ago he resided at a village near London, from which he was driven by the indignation of the inhabitants, who burned his effigy" (19 April, 1830, 4d).

90. *Times,* 23 September 1822, 3c.

91. *Weekly Dispatch,* 21 September 1823, 303. In the same month, the

Times reported that men in custody on charges of engaging in sex between men needed "a strong escort to protect them from the indignation of the assembled multitude" (13 September 1823, 3).

92. *Times,* 4 September 1810, 3.

93. *Times,* 31 August 1843, 6e. The much shorter report in the *Weekly Dispatch* gave Allpress's name as "Richard Correll Allpress" (3 September 1843, 424).

94. *Times,* 24 December 1846, 7b.

95. See *Times,* 13 March 1828, 4a.

96. *Morning Chronicle,* 1 April 1848, 7.

97. *Times,* 9 May 1864, 13d.

98. For examples of statements to this effect by men in courtrooms, see *Times,* 24 September 1842, 5c; *Weekly Dispatch,* 9 July 1851, 435; *Times,* 24 September 1850, 7e. Quotation from *Times,* 16 May 1851, 8d.

99. Tosh differentiates between reputation, based on the opinion of others and more important for upper-class men, and character, which was seen as a reflection of an individual's inner essence, and most critical for the self-image of middle-class men. Serious divisions existed between upper- and middle-class forms of masculinity in the first half of the nineteenth century, yet Tosh also stresses the underlying unities. John Tosh, *Manliness and Masculinities in Nineteenth-Century Britain: Essays on Gender, Family, and Empire* (Harlow: Pearson Longman, 2005), 72–77.

100. Brady, *Masculinity and Male Homosexuality,* 26, 121–22, and George L. Mosse, *Nationalism and Sexuality: Respectability and Abnormal Sexuality in Modern Europe* (New York: Howard Fertig, 1985), 24–29.

CHAPTER 2. CLASS, MASCULINITY, AND SPACES

1. For the eighteenth century, see Randolph Trumbach, "Modern Sodomy: The Origins of Homosexuality, 1700–1800," in *A Gay History of Britain: Love and Sex between Men since the Middle Ages,* ed. Matt Cook, Randolph Trumbach, and H.G. Cocks (Oxford: Greenwood World Publishing, 2007), 78–94. For the persistence of such forms in the twentieth century, see Matt Houlbrook, *Queer London: Perils and Pleasures in the Sexual Metropolis, 1918–1957* (Chicago: University of Chicago Press, 2005), 144–49.

2. Anna Clark, "Anne Lister's Construction of Lesbian Identity," *Journal of the History of Sexuality* 7 (1996): 23–50.

3. Lewis Crompton, *Byron and Greek Love: Homophobia in Nineteenth-Century England* (Swaffham: Gay Men's Press, 1985), 87–95.

4. Craig Williams, *Roman Homosexuality: Ideologies of Masculinity in Classical Antiquity* (New York: Oxford University Press, 1999), 61–63; Kenneth James Dover, *Greek Homosexuality* (London: Duckworth, 1978), 192.

5. Michael Rocke, *Forbidden Friendships: Homosexuality and Male Culture in Renaissance Florence* (New York: Oxford University Press, 1996), 4, 47.

6. George L. Mosse, *Nationalism and Sexuality: Respectability and Abnormal Sexuality in Modern Europe* (New York: Howard Fertig, 1985),

32; quote from Graham Robb, *Strangers: Homosexual Love in the Nineteenth Century* (New York: W. W. Norton, 2003), 96.

7. Williams, *Roman Homosexuality*, 132–37.

8. Alan Bray, *Homosexuality in Renaissance England* (New York: Columbia University Press, 1982), 33–36, and Randolph Trumbach, *Sex and the Gender Revolution*, vol. 1, *Heterosexuality and the Third Gender in Enlightenment London* (Chicago: University of Chicago Press, 1998), 49–55.

9. Compton, *Byron and Greek Love*, 67–68, 185–86. Matt Houlbrook has also found this age-structured pattern among working-class men in twentieth-century Britain. See Houlbrook, *Queer London*, 167–74.

10. John Tosh, "The Old Adam and the New Man: Emerging Themes in the History of English Masculinities: 1750–1850," in John Tosh, *Manliness and Masculinities in Nineteenth-Century Britain: Essays on Gender, Family, and Empire* (Harlow: Pearson Longman, 2005), 72–77.

11. Roy Porter, *English Society in the Eighteenth Century* (New York: Penguin, 1990), 48–97.

12. Morris B. Kaplan, *Sodom on the Thames: Sex, Love, and Scandal in Wilde Times* (Ithaca, N.Y.: Cornell University Press, 2005), 186–201.

13. Linda Colley, *Britons: Forging the Nation, 1707–1837* (New Haven: Yale University Press, 1992), 151–77.

14. *John Halifax, Gentleman* was second only to *Uncle Tom's Cabin* in sales in the 1850s and 1860s. See Catherine Hall, *White, Male, and Middle Class: Explorations in Feminism and History* (New York: Routledge, 1992), 258–62.

15. Leonore Davidoff and Catherine Hall, *Family Fortunes: Men and Women of the English Middle Class, 1780–1850* (Chicago: University of Chicago Press, 1987), 108–18.

16. Tosh, *Manliness and Masculinities*, 74.

17. Porter, *English Society*, 163; Randolph Trumbach, *The Rise of the Egalitarian Family: Aristocratic Kinship and Domestic Relations in Eighteenth-Century England* (New York: Academic Press, 1978), 252–65; Lawrence Stone, *The Family, Sex and Marriage in England, 1500–1800*, abridged ed. (New York: Harper and Row, 1979), 322–23.

18. John Raymond de Symons Honey, *Tom Brown's Universe: The Development of the English Public School in the Nineteenth Century* (New York: Quadrangle, 1977), 1–26; Philip Mason, *The English Gentleman: The Rise and Fall of an Ideal* (London: A. Deutsch, 1982), 169–74.

19. Anonymous, *Don Leon; a poem by the late Lord Byron, author of Childe Harold, Don Juan, &c., &c., And forming part of the private journal of his Lordship, supposed to have been entirely destroyed by Thos. Moore . . .* (London: "Printed for the Booksellers," 1866), notes, 17.

20. For details of this case, see *Weekly Dispatch*, 27 May 1860, 4; 3 June 1860, 5; 15 July 1860, 5; *Times*, 26 May 1860, 12b; *Morning Post*, 12 July 1860, 7e; 13 July 1860, 7b.

21. *Times*, 22 September 1863, 9f.

22. *Times*, 4 October 1843, 5c.

23. The prosecutor "considered no punishment could be too severe for that man." *Morning Chronicle,* 4 December 1832, 4d; 29 December 1832, 4d.

24. *Weekly Dispatch,* 17 May 1857, 11; *Times,* 12 May 1857, 12d.

25. *Times,* 15 November 1842, 6a; 17 November 1842, 4d; *Weekly Dispatch,* 18 December 1842, 602. See also the petition of Patrick Leigh Strachan, 29 February 1844, HO 18 134/2.

26. *Times,* 17 November 1842, 4d; *Weekly Dispatch,* 18 December 1842, 602.

27. For a full discussion of this incident, see "Part Two: Love Stories," in Kaplan, *Sodom on the Thames,* 102–65.

28. For a brief discussion of letters "couched in very affectionate terms" that passed between teacher and pupil in a day school where unnatural acts were proved in court, see *Weekly Dispatch,* 3 June 1860, 5; *Times,* 2 June 1860, 11e–f; 26 May 1860, 12b.

29. *Times,* 15 October 1850, 8a. See also *Morning Post,* 11 October 1850, 2d; *Reynolds' Newspaper,* 13 October 1850; *Times,* 11 October 1850, 5e; 12 October 1850, 5e; 16 October 1850, 5b; *Weekly Dispatch,* 13 October 1850, 645; 20 October 1850, 655. This case was also discussed by the author of *Don Leon:* see *Don Leon,* notes, 16–17.

30. *Times,* 15 October 1850, 8a; *Morning Post,* 11 October 1850, 2d.

31. *Times,* 16 October 1850, 5b.

32. *Times,* 15 October 1850, 8a.

33. *Times,* 15 October 1850, 8a.

34. *Times,* 12 October 1850, 5e.

35. *Times,* 11 October 1850, 5e–f.

36. *Times,* 11 October 1850, 5e–f.

37. One letter to the editor argued that the expelled and dismissed boys had been "perverted and disgraced." *Times,* 15 October 1850, 8a.

38. *Weekly Dispatch,* 20 October 1850, 665.

39. Richard von Krafft-Ebing, *Psychopathia Sexualis: A Medico-forensic Study,* 12th ed., trans. F. J. Rebman (New York: Pioneer Publications, 1939), 446.

40. Havelock Ellis and John Addington Symonds, *Sexual Inversion* (London: Wilson and Macmillan, 1897; repr. New York: Arno Press, 1975), 37.

41. Lesley Hall, "Forbidden by God, Despised by Men: Masturbation, Medical Warnings, Moral Panic and Manhood in Great Britain, 1850–1950," *Journal of the History of Sexuality* 2 (1993): 374.

42. James Scott, *Domination and the Arts of Resistance: Hidden Transcripts* (New Haven: Yale University Press, 1990), 12–13.

43. John Tosh, *A Man's Place: Masculinity and the Middle-Class Home in Victorian England* (New Haven: Yale University Press, 1999), 127–29.

44. For the Mary Anne Clarke Affair, see Anna Clark, *Scandal: The Sexual Politics of the British Constitution* (Princeton: Princeton University Press, 2004), 148–57.

45. For an overview of the role of the language of respectability in British political reform movements in the long nineteenth century, see Matthew

McCormack, "Married Men and the Fathers of Families: Fatherhood and Franchise Reform in Britain," in *Gender and Fatherhood in the Nineteenth Century,* ed. Trev Lynn Broughton and Helen Rogers (New York: Palgrave Macmillan, 2007), 43–54.

46. John Gillis, *For Better, For Worse: British Marriages, 1600 to the Present* (New York: Oxford University Press, 1985), 110–16.

47. E.P. Thompson, "The Moral Economy of the English Crowd in the Eighteenth Century," *Past and Present* 50 (February 1971): 76–136.

48. Felix Driver, *Power and Pauperism: The Workhouse System, 1834–1884* (New York: Cambridge University Press, 1993), 22–26, 48–57.

49. Anna Clark, *Women's Silence, Men's Violence: Sexual Assault in England, 1770–1845* (New York: Pandora, 1987) 14–15, 39–43.

50. Anna Clark, *The Struggle for the Breeches: Gender and the Making of the British Working Class* (Berkeley: University of California Press, 1995), 197–99, 266–68.

51. Tosh, *Manliness and Masculinities,* 178–84.

52. Tosh, *Manliness and Masculinities,* 61–82; F.M.L. Thompson, *The Rise of Respectable Society: A Social History of Victorian Britain, 1830–1900* (Cambridge, Mass.: Harvard University Press, 1988), 318–28.

53. Houlbrook, *Queer London,* 167–77.

54. "Even in Europe to-day a considerable lack of repugnance to homosexual practices may be found among the lower classes" (Ellis and Symonds, *Sexual Inversion,* 9).

55. Thomas Hosier's wealth and position made it likely that he had experience of the conditions in Paris. He originally gave the name of William Hennesy. *Times,* 22 September 1840, 6c–d.

56. *Times,* 31 August 1843, 6e. For a shorter report on the same case, see *Weekly Dispatch,* 3 September 1843, 424.

57. *Weekly Dispatch,* 19 February 1843, 88; *Times,* 16 February 1843, 8d. Both newspapers carried the same quote.

58. *Times,* 4 November 1865, 11d.

59. Examples of this pattern include James Lawrence, who committed "an indelicate assault" on James Parsley, the son of the man to whom he was apprenticed, as the two men slept in the same bed. *Weekly Dispatch,* 11 September 1825, 290.

60. *Weekly Dispatch,* 1 December 1850, 754; *Times,* 27 November 1850, 7e.

61. CRIM 10/20, Tenth Session, 1843–44, case no. 1945, 495–500.

62. *Weekly Dispatch,* 23 November 1851, 738; 14 December 1851, 787; *Times,* 20 November 1851, 8c–d.

63. *Morning Chronicle,* 25 August 1832, 4d. For later developments in this case, see *Weekly Dispatch,* 23 September 1832, 309.

64. The constable returned to the house with a sergeant from the Portman barracks and caught the two men in Doyle's bedroom together in various stages of undress. The female servant who answered the door was unaware that a lodger had brought a soldier home. *Morning Chronicle,* 25 August 1832, 4d.

65. *Times,* 6 July 1850, 7d; 26 August 1850, 7d.

66. *Times,* 14 August 1843, 7e. For a similar case involving a constable observing two men in Hyde Park, see *Weekly Dispatch,* 24 October 1824, 347.

67. *Times,* 16 August 1841, 7b.

68. *Morning Chronicle,* 8 May 1848, 7; *Times,* 8 May 1848, 7e; 18 May 1848, 7e.

69. *Times,* 14 May 1851, 7e.

70. CRIM 10/34, New Court, Eleventh Session, 17 September 1851, case no. 1805; *Times,* 18 September 1851, 7b; *Weekly Dispatch,* 21 September 1851, 595.

71. *Times,* 21 December 1846, 6e.

72. *Times,* 27 June 1835, 4e. For a similar Hyde Park incident, see CRIM 10/31, Second Session, 1849–50, case no. 223, 206–7.

73. *Weekly Dispatch,* 31 October 1847, 518; *Times,* 27 October 1847, 7b.

74. Houlbrook, *Queer London,* 59–64.

75. All quotes from *Weekly Dispatch,* 20 August 1843, 399. For much shorter coverage of the same incident, see *Times,* 19 August 1843, 8e.

76. *Times,* 5 November 1844, 7c.

77. *Times,* 4 April, 1867, 11d. For another incident occurring in a urinal, see *Morning Post,* 31 July 1846, 7d; 31 July 1846, 7a.

78. *Times,* 24 October 1863, 11d–e. For a similar case involving a soldier in a urinal in Orange Street, see CRIM 10/20, Tenth Session, 1843–44, case no. 1916, 435–38; *Morning Post,* 21 August 1844, 4b.

79. CRIM 10/41, First Session 1854–55, case no. 47, 43–44.

80. *Times,* 30 November 1850, 7f.

81. *Weekly Dispatch,* 9 August 1840, 376; *Times,* 7 August 1840, 7c–d.

82. *Weekly Dispatch,* 30 October 1825, 349.

83. *Times,* 27 November 1862, 11e.

84. *Morning Post,* 26 October 1858, 7c. Exactly the same wording appears in *Times,* 26 October 1858, 9c. See also *Weekly Dispatch,* 31 October 1858, 5a.

85. *Times,* 12 November 1862, 12b; *Weekly Dispatch,* 16 November 1862, 5.

86. Private Bissett's friends testified that they saw nothing occur. *Times,* 21 September 1849, 8c–d.

87. *Times,* 11 August 1847, 8b.

88. *Weekly Dispatch,* 11 September 1825, 290.

89. The house was in Crescent Place, off the Hampstead Road. *Times,* 30 August 1853, 9d.

90. Aylmer tried using an assumed name, but cards he carried revealed his identity. *Morning Post,* 1 May 1844, 7b; *Times,* 1 May 1844, p 8d.

91. *Times,* 10 September 1864, 11e.

92. *Times,* 8 December 1842, 6f; *Weekly Dispatch,* 18 December 1842, 602. For the court records of the trial, see CRIM 10/13, Fourth Session, 1841, case no. 645, 460.

93. *Times,* 4 November 1865, 11d–e. For another similar case in front

of a picture-shop window in the Strand, see CRIM 10/17, Second Session, 1842–43, case no. 293, 201.

94. CRIM 10/32, Eleventh Session, 1849–50, case no. 1589, 627. The encounter was a prelude to an extortion attempt on Tasburgh.

95. Petition for John Pacey, HO 18 7/19.

96. *Weekly Dispatch*, 28 August 1825, 274–75.

97. *Times*, 7 September 1869, 9e. The *Morning Post* report related only that Wood acted "in an indecent manner," and it did not give the details found in the *Times*. *Morning Post*, 7 September 1869, 7b.

98. *Times*, 2 April, 1862, 11f. For a similar case, see *Morning Post*, 3 September 1846, 7b.

99. *Times*, 21 March 1864, 12f.

100. *Morning Post*, 31 July 1856, 7b; *Weekly Dispatch*, 31 July 1856, 2a; *Times*, 31 July 1856, 11d. For further similar examples, see *Morning Chronicle*, 2 March 1832, 4d; and CRIM 10/29, Fifth Session, 1848–49, case no. 675, 464.

101. *Weekly Dispatch*, 24 June 1833, 189; *Times*, 24 June 1833, 7c; *Morning Chronicle*, 24 June 1833, 4d.

102. It was the owner of the Beehive who became suspicious and watched the two men. *Times*, 16 February 1843, 8d; *Weekly Dispatch*, 19 February 1843, 88.

103. *Morning Post*, 21 August 1852, 7e. The phrase "a pretty sort of gentleman" was also reprinted in the *Times* but not in a detailed report in the *Weekly Dispatch*. *Times*, 21 August 1852, 7d; *Weekly Dispatch*, 22 August 1852, 531.

104. *Weekly Dispatch*, 2 October 1825, 315.

105. CRIM 10/31, Sixth Session, 1849–50, case no. 803, 700.

106. *Weekly Dispatch*, 12 July 1863, 5b; *Morning Post*, 8 July 1863, 7e; *Times*, 8 July 1863, 11.

107. CRIM 10/31, Second Session, 1849–50, case no. 223, 206–7.

108. CRIM 10/31, Second Session, 1849–50, case no. 223, 206–7.

109. Jeffrey Weeks, *Coming Out: Homosexual Politics in Britain from the Nineteenth Century to the Present* (New York: New Horizon Press, 1977), 36–40.

110. *Weekly Dispatch*, 30 July 1854, 482; *Times*, 27 July 1854, 12b–c.

111. *Morning Post*, 1 August 1854, 7e; *Times*, 1 August 1854, 12d.

112. *Times*, 1 August 1854, 12d; *Weekly Dispatch*, 6 August 1854, 498.

113. *Morning Post*, 1 August 1854, 7e; *Times*, 1 August 1854, 12d.

114. See Charles Upchurch, "Forgetting the Unthinkable: Cross-Dressers and British Society in the Case of the Queen vs. Boulton and Others," *Gender and History* 12 (April 2000): 127–57.

115. *Weekly Dispatch*, 23 October 1842, 506; *Times*, 20 October 1842, 7b.

116. *Morning Post*, 29 October 1846, 4a; *Weekly Dispatch*, 1 November 1846, 519.

117. CRIM 10/24, Twelfth Session, 1845–46, case no. 2014, 859–63.

118. CRIM 10/24, Twelfth Session, 1845–46, case no. 2014, 861.

119. One letter sent by Newbery read: "To the Gentlemen of the Travellers' Club. I wish to inform you, E.D. Protheroe is guilty of that crime which is forbidden by God and man . . . it is well known the steward of the other club which he belongs to lost his place, through accusing him of an unnatural offence, which I can prove he is guilty of." CRIM 10/24, Twelfth Session, 1845–46, case no. 2014, 862.

120. A defendant in another case four years later was also interrogated over his dealings with Protheroe. Henry Tiddiman was asked if he had "never taken persons to Mr. Protheroe; lads, youths, which Mr. Protheroe likes." CRIM 10/31, Sixth Session, 1849–50, case no. 803, 703.

CHAPTER 3. LAW AND REFORM IN THE 1820S

1. John Jacob Tobias, *Crime and Police in England, 1700–1900* (New York: St. Martin's Press, 1979), 32–33; Phillip Thurmond Smith, *Policing Victorian London: Political Policing, Public Order, and the London Metropolitan Police* (London: Greenwood Press, 1985), 19.

2. Douglas Hay, Peter Linebaugh, John G. Rule, E.P. Thompson, and Cal Winslow, *Albion's Fatal Tree: Crime and Society in Eighteenth-century England* (New York: Pantheon Books, 1975), 56–63; Robert Brink Shoemaker, *Prosecution and Punishment: Petty Crime and the Law in London and Rural Middlesex, c. 1660–1725* (New York: Cambridge University Press, 1991), 316–19.

3. See Randolph Trumbach, "Sodomy Transformed: Aristocratic Libertinage, Public Reputation and the Gender Revolution of the Eighteenth Century," *Journal of Homosexuality* 19 (1990): 105–24; Rictor Norton, *Mother Clap's Molly House: The Gay Subculture in England, 1700–1830* (London: Gay Men's Press, 1992), 55.

4. Tim Hitchcock, *English Sexualities, 1700–1800* (New York: St. Martin's Press, 1997), 70–72, and Netta Murray Goldsmith, *The Worst of Crimes: Homosexuality and the Law in Eighteenth-Century London* (Brookfield, Vt.: Ashgate, 1998), 8–9.

5. Goldsmith, *Worst of Crimes*, 9. On the increase in executions for sodomy from the 1790s to the 1830s, see Arthur Gilbert, "Sodomy and the Law in Eighteenth- and Early Nineteenth-Century Britain," *Societas* 8 (1978): 235.

6. For the cultural uses of the image of the sodomite in the eighteenth century, see Randolph Trumbach, "The Birth of the Queen: Sodomy and the Emergence of Gender Equality in Modern Culture, 1660–1750," in *Hidden From History: Reclaiming the Gay and Lesbian Past,* ed. Martin Duberman, Martha Vicinus, and George Chauncey Jr. (New York: New American Library, 1989), 129–40.

7. Michael Ignatieff, *A Just Measure of Pain: The Penitentiary in the Industrial Revolution, 1750–1850* (New York: Pantheon Books, 1978), 16.

8. David Taylor, *Crime, Policing and Punishment in England, 1750–1914* (New York: St. Martin's Press, 1998), 119.

9. Clive Emsley, *Crime and Society in England, 1750–1900* (New York:

Longman, 1996), 255; Taylor, *Crime, Policing and Punishment in England*, 142.

10. Taylor, *Crime, Policing and Punishment in England*, 120.

11. Leon Radzinowicz, *A History of English Criminal Law and Its Administration from 1750*, vol. 1, *The Movement for Reform, 1750–1833* (New York: Macmillan, 1948), 231–67.

12. Radzinowicz, *History of English Criminal Law*, 1: 268–300.

13. Radzinowicz, *History of English Criminal Law*, 1: 567–82.

14. The best that Peel could achieve at first was an assent to the creation of a uniformed day patrol for central London, staffed by a few dozen officers. Radzinowicz, *History of English Criminal Law*, 1: 588. See also *Hansard Parliamentary Debates*, 2nd ser., vol. 6 (1822), cols. 1165–66.

15. Taylor, *Crime, Policing and Punishment in England*, 148–49; Randall McGowen, "The Well-Ordered Prison: England, 1780–1865," in *The Oxford History of the Prison: The Practice of Punishment in Western Society*, ed. Norval Morris and David J. Rothman (New York: Oxford University Press, 1995), 89–97.

16. Taylor, *Crime, Policing and Punishment in England*, 145, 148–49.

17. Emsley, *Crime and Society in England*, 277–82; Taylor, *Crime, Policing and Punishment in England*, 147.

18. Taylor, *Crime, Policing and Punishment in England*, 149; McGowen, "Well-Ordered Prison," 99–103.

19. Norman Gash, *Aristocracy and People: Britain, 1815–1865* (Cambridge, Mass.: Harvard University Press, 1979), 113–28.

20. Radzinowicz, *History of English Criminal Law*, 1: 541–51.

21. *Hansard Parliamentary Debates*, 2nd ser., vol. 10 (1824), col. 1062.

22. Richard Follett, *Evangelicalism, Penal Theory and the Politics of Criminal Law Reform in England, 1808–30* (New York: Palgrave, 2001), 173, 182–83.

23. Henry Richard Dearsly and Thomas Bell, *Crown Cases Reserved for Consideration, and Decided by the Judges of England, with a Selection of Cases and Notes of Cases Relating to Indictable Offences*. vol. 1, parts 1–6 (London: Stevens & Norton; H. Sweet & W. Maxwell, 1858), 342.

24. Between 1799 and 1851, seven cases published in the *Crown Cases Reserved* series centered on sexual acts between men.

25. Anonymous, *Don Leon; a poem by the late Lord Byron, author of Childe Harold, Don Juan, &c., &c., And forming part of the private journal of his Lordship, supposed to have been entirely destroyed by Thos. Moore . . .* (London: "Printed for the Booksellers," 1866).

26. See Ed Cohen, "Legislating the Norm: From Sodomy to Gross Indecency," *South Atlantic Quarterly* 88 (1989): 181–217; Vern L. Bullough, "Homosexuality and the Medical Model," *Journal of Homosexuality* 1 (1974): 99–110.

27. Privy Council Papers, PC 1/3953.

28. Privy Council Papers, PC 1/3953.

29. The Criminal Law (India) Act of 1828 contained the English definition of "what shall be deemed an infamous crime." Similar legislation was passed

for Ireland in 1828 as the Larceny (Ireland) Act and supplemented in the following year by the Irish Offences against the Person Act of 1829. Section 7 of the British North America Act of 1840 listed the reasons for which a member of the Canadian Legislative Council might be removed, which included any infamous crime. This stipulation was renewed in the British North America Act of 1867, and a similar clause was included in the Newfoundland Act of 1842 and the Australian Constitutions Act of 1842. In England, the Parish Constables Act of 1842 disqualified any man from serving as an officer if he had been previously convicted of any infamous crime.

30. This change in language between the sixteenth and nineteenth centuries seems like an example of the shift in state power as described by Michel Foucault in *Discipline and Punish: The Birth of the Prison*, trans. Alan Sheridan (New York: Vintage Books, 1979), 135–69.

31. See the Criminal Offenders and Judicial Statistics in the Command Papers of the British Parliamentary Papers, and the HO 26 series of documents in the National Archive. Between 1730 and 1800, 101 cases of assault with intent to commit sodomy were heard before the Old Bailey and in the City of London Quarter Sessions.

32. In two exceptional cases, indicating the degree of discretion that judges had in setting sentences, John Fielding was convicted of attempted sodomy at the February 1827 Clerkenwell Sessions and given a sentence of only fourteen days, and in 1823 William Franklin was likewise given a fourteen-day sentence after being convicted for unnatural assault. HO 26/33; HO 26/29.

33. For a recent analysis of the Labouchère amendment to the Criminal Law Amendment Act of 1885 that stressed the protection of children as a primary motivation, see Louise A. Jackson, *Child Sexual Abuse in Victorian England* (New York: Routledge, 2000), 105. Sean Brady argues that the amendment may have been offered as a means to force the government to reconsider the bill. See Brady, *Masculinity and Male Homosexuality in Britain, 1861–1913* (New York: Palgrave Macmillan, 2006), 92–93. For an earlier interpretation, see F. B. Smith, "Labouchère's Amendment to the Criminal Law Amendment Bill," *Historical Studies* 17 (1976): 165–73.

34. H. G. Cocks, *Nameless Offences: Homosexual Desire in the Nineteenth Century* (London: I. B. Tauris, 2003), 31.

35. Magistrates had a wide discretion in determining who would be allowed to give evidence, and many allowed one involved party to testify against another. See Christopher Allen, *The Law of Evidence in Victorian England* (New York: Cambridge University Press, 1997), 43–49.

36. Sean Brady has also found another example of this pattern later in the century, when the 1861 Offences against the Person Act came into direct conflict with the 1891 Penal Servitude Act. "Asquith, like his predecessors, would rather have lived with the irritation of the Home Office officials who dealt with the administrative chaos of sentencing for sodomy, than risk a political scandal through attempting to clarify the Buggery laws" (Brady, *Masculinity and Male Homosexuality*, 110).

37. For England and Wales over the same period, attempted sodomy cases outnumbered those for sodomy by a ratio of less than two to one, indicating a

difference between the pattern of prosecution in the capital and that in the rest of the nation. Between 1810 and 1870 there were 3,183 trials for attempted sodomy in England and Wales and 1,887 trials for sodomy. Statistics compiled from Parliamentary Papers, Command Papers, Criminal Offender and Judicial Statistics annual returns.

38. CRIM 10/16, 1842, 1013; *Weekly Dispatch*, 25 September 1842, 459. For another example of a man given into custody solely on the word of another man, see Judges' Reports on Criminals, John Aves, HO 47/75.

39. CRIM 10/24, 1846, 551–52.

40. Omissions in original. CRIM 10/21, First Session, 1844, case no. 29, 34.

41. Taylor, *Crime, Policing and Punishment in England,* 31.

42. Examples include the 1778 extortion of a Mr. Chapman, *Annual Register, 1778,* 205; the extortion of the Hon. Charles Fielding, *Annual Register, 1779,* 208; the extortion of Edmund Lodge, *Annual Register, 1805,* 366; and the extortion of John Hodges, heard at the Old Bailey in March 1806, HO 26/12.

43. Anthony Simpson, "Masculinity and Control: the Prosecution of Sex Offenses in Eighteenth-Century London" (PhD diss., New York University, 1984), 526–27. See also Anthony Simpson, "Blackmail as a Crime of Sexual Indiscretion in Eighteenth-Century England," in *Crime, Gender and Sexuality in Criminal Prosecutions,* ed. Louis A. Knafla (Westport, Conn.: Greenwood Press, 2002), 61–86; Angus McLaren, *Sexual Blackmail: A Modern History* (Cambridge, Mass.: Harvard University Press, 2002), 10–29.

44. *Annual Register, 1779,* 209.

45. The 1754 revision of the law removed the stipulation that such letters must explicitly demand money, and the 1757 revision made it applicable to those who threatened to accuse another not only of a felony but of any "infamous crime." Prosecutors could still use the laws on perjury, libel, or conspiracy in these cases, but they rarely did so, as these charges were much harder to prove. Simpson, "Masculinity and Control," 536–37, 540.

46. Simpson, "Masculinity and Control," 578. For an additional source on eighteenth-century patterns of blackmail, see Norton, *Mother Clap's Molly House,* 227–51.

47. The repealed law was An Act for the More Effectual Punishment of Assaults with Intent to Commit Robbery, 7 Geo. 2, c. 21 (1734). Quote from Benefit of Clergy, etc. Act, 1823, 4 Geo. 4, c. 54, s. 5.

48. An alternative sentence of four years' domestic imprisonment in the house of correction was also possible under this law but rarely imposed in practice. Larceny (England) Act, 7 & 8 Geo. 4, c. 29, s. 8 (1827).

49. *Times,* 11 April 1825, 3. For the court record of this trial, see Old Bailey Session Papers: PCOM 1/21, 4th session, 1825, case no. 68, 291–94. See also *Weekly Dispatch,* 10 April 1825, 117; 17 April 1825, 122.

50. Trials involving sex between men covered by the *Annual Register* before 1820 can be found in the volumes for 1761, 166; 1763, 67; 1778, 205–7; 1779, 199–200, 208–9; 1803, 460; 1805, 366; 1806, 438–39; 1807, 496, 500–501; 1810, 280–81, 293–94; and 1811, 28.

51. The *Weekly Dispatch* reported that Holder and Gardener "were indicted on the statute 4 Geo. 4. c. 54" but gave no details of the case, only reporting that the prisoners were found guilty. *Weekly Dispatch*, 3 April 1825, 107. The *Times* gave this case almost a full column of coverage (28 March 1825, 6d).

52. *Annual Register, 1825,* Law Cases, 6.

53. *Annual Register, 1825,* Law Cases, 7.

54. Castlereagh reportedly said to George IV, "I am accused of the same crime as the Bishop of Clogher" (H. Montgomery Hyde, *The Strange Death of Lord Castlereagh* [London: Heinemann, 1959], 51–52).

55. For another example where the accusation of attempted extortion was used as a countercharge against an accusation of unnatural assault, see *Times,* 24 July 1845, 8c.

56. The opening of the 1825 legislation specifically states that it is meant to be a modification of the 1823 Act. Threatening Letters Act, 1825, 6 Geo. 4, c. 19.

57.

And Whereas it is expedient to enact that not only every Crime now by Law deemed infamous by reason of the Person convicted thereof being thereby rendered incompetent to give Evidence, but also that each of the several Offences hereinafter mentioned shall be deemed and taken to be an infamous Crime. . . . That as well every Crime now by Law deemed infamous, as also every Assault with Intent to commit any Rape, or the abominable Crimes of Sodomy or Buggery, or either of those Crimes, and every Attempt or Endeavour to commit any Rape, or the said abominable Crimes or either of them, and also every Solicitation, Persuasion, Promise, Threat or Menace, offered or made to any Person, whereby to move or induce such Person to commit or to permit the said abominable Crimes or either of them, shall be deemed and taken to be an infamous Crime within the Meaning of the said recited Act.

Threatening Letters Act, 1825, 6 Geo. 4, c. 19.

58. Dearsly and Bell, *Crown Cases Reserved,* 1: 36.

59. *Hansard Parliamentary Debates,* 2nd ser., vol. 12 (1825), col. 1163.

60. This pattern of avoiding debate on bills related to sex between men continued into the late nineteenth century. See Smith, "Labouchère's Amendment," 165–73. See also Brady's discussion of the defeated 1896 Halsbury Bill, designed to make it a criminal offense to report details of gross indecency trials, in *Masculinity and Homosexuality,* 42.

61. Parliamentary Papers, Command Papers, Criminal Offender and Judicial Statistics, Annual Returns. Statistics gathered for 1838–70.

62. *Times,* 4 August 1825, 2f–3a. The *Weekly Dispatch* also noted the most recent change in the law in its report (7 August 1825, 251).

63. Parliamentary Papers, Command Papers, Criminal Offender and Judicial Statistics, Annual Returns. Statistics gathered for 1810–70. One example of an unnatural-assault case in which the bill of indictment was "not found" involved an instance in which a soldier's word was given against that of a clergyman. See CRIM 10/29, Fifth Session, 1848–49, case no. 675, 466.

64. *Times,* 30 March 1830, 4b.

65. *Weekly Dispatch,* 20 July 1851, 450.

66. *Times,* 7 April 1830, 6b.

67. David Taylor cites the discretion of the prosecutor as well as the magistrate in his discussion of the reduction of charges. Taylor, *Crime, Policing and Punishment in England,* 30–31.

68. See M. J. D. Roberts, "Public and Private in Early Nineteenth-Century London: The Vagrancy Act of 1822 and its Enforcement," *Social History* 13 (May 1988): 273–94; H. G. Cocks, "Abominable Crimes: Sodomy Trials in English Law and Culture, 1830–1889" (PhD diss., University of Manchester, 1998), 87; Penelope J. Corfield, "Walking the City Streets: The Urban Odyssey in Eighteenth-Century England," *Journal of Urban History* 16 (February 1990): 132–74.

69. Anna Clark, *Women's Silence, Men's Violence: Sexual Assault in England, 1770–1845* (New York: Pandora, 1987), 74. See also Susan Edwards, *Female Sexuality and the Law* (Oxford: Martin Robertson, 1981), 55–57.

70. *Weekly Dispatch,* 2 October 1825, 315.

71. See Daily Reports from Metropolitan Police Offices, HO 62/5, HO 62/6, HO 62/17, and HO 62/18.

72. Jeffrey Merrick and Bryant T. Ragan Jr., *Homosexuality in Modern France* (New York: Oxford University Press, 1996), 82–89; Gert Hekma, "Wrong Lovers in the Nineteenth Century Netherlands," *Journal of Homosexuality* 13 (Winter 1986–Spring 1987): 43–55; Theo van der Meer, "Sodomy and the Pursuit of a Third Sex in the Early Modern Period," in *Third Sex, Third Gender: Beyond Sexual Dimorphism in Culture and History,* ed. Gilbert Herdt (New York: Zone Books, 1994), 137–211.

73. Jeremy Bentham's utilitarianism led him to conclude that the state had no role to play in the regulation of sex between men, although Bentham kept this conclusion for fear of discrediting the whole of his philosophy. See Lewis Crompton, *Byron and Greek Love: Homophobia in Nineteenth-Century England* (Swaffham: Gay Men's Press, 1985), 251–57.

74. William Peniston, *Pederasts and Others: Urban Culture and Sexual Identity in Nineteenth-Century Paris* (New York: Harrington Park Press, 2004), 32–34; Isabel V. Hull, *Sexuality, State, and Civil Society in Germany, 1700–1815* (Ithaca, N.Y.: Cornell University Press, 1996), 340–42, 361–62.

75. Hay stresses that 90 percent of the laws concerned preserving the existing distribution of property, a situation that led to glaring differences in the ways the rich and the poor experienced the law. Hay, et al., *Albion's Fatal Tree,* 32–35.

76. For a case where the plaintiff and the defendant immediately changed places in the courtroom after the first defendant was acquitted by the jury, see *Morning Post,* 29 October 1863, 7c.

CHAPTER 4. PUBLIC MEN

1. See CRIM 10/7, 1838, case no. 980, 880–85.

2. CRIM 10/7, 1838, case no. 980, 880–85. Omissions in original.

3. For another case showing the anger and violence that a community could focus on a policeman, in this case an individual felt to be a "special,"

or policeman in plain clothes, see CRIM 10/28, Eighth Session, 1847–48, case no. 1530, 212.

4. Robert D. Storch, "The Plague of the Blue Locusts: Police Reform and Popular Resistance in Northern England, 1840–1857," *International Review of Social History* 20 (1975): 61–90.

5. CRIM 10/7, 1838, case no. 980, 884. For a further discussion of the contentious relationship between the Metropolitan Police and the magistrates, see Stephan Petrow, *Policing Morals: The Metropolitan Police and the Home Office, 1870–1914* (Oxford: Clarendon Press, 1994), 43–44.

6. John Jacob Tobias, *Crime and Police in England: 1700–1900* (New York: St. Martin's Press, 1979), 32–33; Phillip Thurmond Smith, *Policing Victorian London: Political Policing, Public Order, and the London Metropolitan Police* (London: Greenwood Press, 1985), 19.

7. Because of the workload involved and in an effort to improve the educational background of the men in these positions, London's stipendiary magistrates were paid by the government starting in 1792, and expected to achieve the level of barrister before taking the post. Tobias, *Crime and Police*, 45–47.

8. Elaine A. Reynolds, *Before the Bobbies: The Night Watch and Police Reform in Metropolitan London, 1720–1830* (Stanford, Calif.: Stanford University Press, 1998), 1–6; Elaine A. Reynolds, "St. Marylebone: Local Police Reform in London, 1755–1829," *Historian* 51 (1989): 446–66; Douglas Hay, Peter Linebaugh, John G. Rule, E.P. Thompson, and Cal Winslow, *Albion's Fatal Tree: Crime and Society in Eighteenth-Century England* (New York: Pantheon Books, 1975), 15–16.

9. *Times,* 13 September 1823, 3.

10. *Times,* 18 October 1826, 3e. The constable followed Brewer because of "his previous knowledge of the prisoner's character." For a similar case in which a suspicious man was followed in Hyde Park, see *Weekly Dispatch,* 24 October 1824, 347.

11. Four men were subsequently arrested at the house "for unlawfully assembling and conspiring together, with the intention of committing an abominable offense" (*Times,* 23 September 1822, 3c).

12. *Times,* 22 October 1824, 3. Green was admonished in the courtroom for walking arm in arm with Barnard after the alleged unnatural assault had occurred. For other examples of constables following or secretly observing suspicious men, see *Morning Chronicle,* 25 August 1832, 4d; *Times,* 21 December 1850, 6f.

13. PCOM 1/21, 133. Other examples of constables' being brought in after alleged sexual assaults can be found in HO 47/75 and CRIM 10/20, Tenth Session, case no. 1946, 495–500.

14. PCOM 1/21, 191–94. For newspaper coverage of this trial, see *Weekly Dispatch,* 10 April 1825, 117; *Times,* 2 April 1825, 3d; *Weekly Dispatch,* 17 April 1825, 122.

15. PCOM 1/22, 6–7.

16. *Times,* 16 August 1825, 3.

17. For Tosier, see HO 26/39 (1833). For Wack, see *Weekly Dispatch,* 14 December 1851, 787; 23 November 1851, 738.

18. *Weekly Dispatch,* 25 November 1827, 370; *Times,* 24 November 1827, 3; *Weekly Dispatch,* 20 January 1828, 18; *Times,* 15 January 1828, 3.

19. For the earlier conviction, see *Weekly Dispatch,* 2 October 1825, 314; *Times,* 26 September 1825, 3e.

20. Bail was set at five hundred pounds from Hayes and two hundred pounds each from two sureties. *Times,* 1 June 1824, 4.

21. *Times,* 23 July 1850, 7e; 10 March 1846, 8d; 16 July 1851, 7e; *Weekly Dispatch,* 29 July 1851, 450. See also the report of Thomas Strange's indecent assault on a police constable in a railway carriage, for which he was only fined five pounds, *Times,* 10 June 1856, 11f; and the case of Benjamin Pool, whose charge was reduced to "insure some punishment . . . the full penalty of 5l." (*Times,* 13 November 1846, 7c).

22. Randall McGowen, "Civilizing Punishment: The End of the Public Execution in England," *Journal of British Studies* 33 (July 1994): 257–82.

23. Michel Foucault, *Discipline and Punish: The Birth of the Prison,* trans. Alan Sheridan (New York: Vintage Books, 1979), 222. Philip Smith also argues that "applied liberalism would extend formal political rights but would sharply reduce the scope for 'deviant' behavior" (*Policing Victorian London,* 18).

24. Hay et al., *Albion's Fatal Tree,* 61–63. See also E.P. Thompson, "The Moral Economy of the English Crowd in the Eighteenth Century," *Past and Present* 50 (February 1971): 76–136.

25. Jennifer Davis, "A Poor Man's System of Justice: The London Police Courts in the Second Half of the Nineteenth Century," *Historical Journal* 27 (1984): 328, 315.

26. Parliamentary Papers, Command Papers, Criminal Offender and Judicial Statistics, Annual Returns.

27. Petition of James Pratt and John Smith, HO 17/120 Xv 13.

28. *Annual Register,* 1833, 314–19; *Weekly Dispatch,* 28 April 1833, 125; 12 May 1833, 143; *Times,* 13 May 1833, 3c.

29. A special jury was composed primarily of men of the rank of esquire or above. Bankers and merchants who met a substantial property qualification were also eligible. David Bentley also notes "the backgrounds of special jurors meant that they could usually be relied upon to find for the Crown in political cases." See Bentley, *English Criminal Justice in the Nineteenth Century* (London: Hambledon Press, 1998), 89–90.

30. *Times,* 13 May 1833, 3c. Two and a half newspaper columns were taken up with the story.

31. *Annual Register,* 1833, 319; *Weekly Dispatch,* 12 May 1833, 143; *Times,* 13 May 1833, 3f.

32. For examples of contradictions within prosecution cases that led to the collapse of unnatural-assault trials, see *Times,* 16 May 1851, 8d; 15 September 1851, 7e.

33. H.G. Cocks, "Trials of Character: The Use of Character Evidence in Victorian Sodomy Trials," in *The Trial in History,* vol. 2, *Domestic and International Trials, 1700–2000,* ed. R.A. Melikan (Manchester: University of Manchester Press, 2003), 36–53. See also Ivan Crozier, "Nineteenth-Century

British Psychiatric Writing about Homosexuality before Havelock Ellis: The Missing Story," *Journal of the History of Medicine and Allied Sciences* 63 (2008): 71–74.

34. Judges' Reports on Criminals, Letter to Robert Peel, Home Secretary, 22 December 1829, HO 47/75. For another example in which these two criteria are mentioned as significant in cases involving charges of sexual assaults between men, see *Times,* 18 April 1850, 7f.

35. Judges' Reports on Criminals, Letter to Robert Peel, 22 December 1829, HO 47/75.

36. *Annual Register, 1833,* 315; *Times,* 13 May 1833, 3c.

37. *Morning Post,* 3 May 1845, 7; *Times,* 3 May 1854, 11d–e; 16 March 1854, 9f.

38. *Times,* 1 November 1836, 4c. For other examples of a police constable's being approached on the street for sex, see Thomas Hosier's sexual advance on Constable Reilly, *Times,* 22 September 1840, 6c–d; Arthur Hume Plunkett's sexual advance on a constable, *Times,* 20 October 1842, 7b; William Wilson's sexual advance on a constable, *Times,* 21 May 1849, 8f, 19 June 1849, 7c–d; George Sharp's indecent assault on Constable Ivatts, *Times,* 6 July 1850, 7d; the trial of Joseph Hanyams for indecently assaulting Constable William Todman, *Times,* 5 February 1853, 7c; the trial of George Manton, steward of St. Mark's College, for indecently assaulting Constable Alfred Carter, *Times,* 31 December 1853, 9f; Edward Park's sexual advance on a constable, *Times,* 2 April 1862, 11f; an indecent assault on a constable by "a gentleman whose name we omit," *Times,* 4 April 1867, 11d; and an indecent assault on Constable James Cooper, *Times,* 19 January 1870, 11c.

39. *Times,* 3 March 1865, 11f. For further reports on the situation involving Constable Teehan, see *Weekly Dispatch,* 5 December 1869, 4c; *Times,* 30 November 1869, 9d; 1 December 1869, 12c; 6 December 1869, 11e; 11 December 1869, 11e.

40. *Morning Post,* 6 December 1869, 7e; *Times,* 1 December 1869, 12c; *Weekly Dispatch,* 5 December 1869, 4c.

41. *Morning Post,* 11 December 1869, 7d; *Times,* 11 December 1869, 11e.

42. *Times,* 11 December 1869, 11e.

43. *Times,* 4 April 1867, 11d.

44. *Times,* 15 June 1850, 7d.

45. CRIM 10/21, First Session, 1846, case no. 29, 34–36.

46. CRIM 10/21, First Session, 1846, case no. 29, 34–35.

47. CRIM 10/29, Fifth Session, 1848–49, case no. 675, 464–70.

48. CRIM 10/29, Fifth Session, 1848–49, case no. 675, 468–70.

49. *Times,* 25 October 1837, 6e.

50. David Taylor also notes that of more than 3,400 men who joined the Metropolitan Police in 1829–30, only one-quarter remained in their posts four years later. Taylor, *The New Police in Nineteenth-Century England: Crime, Conflict, and Control* (Manchester: Manchester University Press, 1997), 44–47.

51. All recruits had to be under the age of thirty, at least five feet seven

inches tall, and able to provide at least two character recommendations, which were always checked. See Petrow, *Policing Morals,* 37; Smith, *Policing Victorian London,* 39, 45.

52. A certain number of constables "if so ordered, must sleep in their clothes, to be in complete readiness when called on" (MEPO 8/1, *Metropolitan Police: Instructions, Orders, &c. &c.* Metropolitan Police Office, Whitehall Place [London: W. Clowes & Sons, 1836], 4–5). See also Taylor, *New Police,* 49–51.

53. On the training of officers, an article in the *Quarterly Review* noted that "a wild young fellow, who perhaps only a few months before [knew] no restraint, should become a machine, moving, thinking, and speaking only as his instruction-book directs" (*Quarterly Review* 99 [June 1856]: 171). See also Smith, *Policing Victorian London,* 40.

54. Smith, *Policing Victorian London,* 49–50.

55. Smith, *Policing Victorian London,* 48; Taylor, *New Police,* 50.

56. See Smith, *Policing Victorian London,* 37.

57. Tobias, *Crime and Police,* 86.

58. The class gulf between the commissioners and the divisional super-intendents was seen by some as a weakness in the police hierarchy. Smith, *Policing Victorian London,* 43–44.

59. CRIM 10/42, 1855, case no. 558, 44.

60. CRIM 10/13, 1841, case no. 645, 462.

61. Lord Hawkesbury to Lord Sydney, 8 November 1808, HO 79/1/66.

62. *The Boudoir: A Magazine of Scandal, Facetiae, &c.,* nos. 1–6 (London: H. Smith, 1860), 97–98.

63. *Times,* 30 March 1830, 4b.

64. The *Morning Post* had much more limited coverage; see e.g., *Morning Post,* 26 April 1830, 2c.

65. *Times,* 30 March 1830, 4b.

66. *Times,* 30 March 1830, 4b; 21 May 1830, 4c; 5 April 1830, 4c; 2 April 1830, 4f.

67. *Times,* 5 April 1830, 4c; 2 April 1830, 4f.

68. *Times,* 30 March 1830, 4b.

69. *Times,* 30 March 1830, 4b.

70. *Times,* 21 May 1830, 4c. For another case in which a man offered a constable first one sovereign and then two to let him go, see *Weekly Dispatch,* 27 May 1860, 4.

71. *Times,* 26 April 1830, 3f; see also *Morning Post,* 26 April, 2c.

72. One article began: "Two persons, James Bryan and Frederick Symonds, who were recently apprehended in Hyde Park, for indecent practices, were yesterday tried at the Westminster Sessions. It was proved that the police disguised themselves on the occasion" (*Sun,* 29 April 1830, as quoted in Anonymous, *Don Leon; a poem by the late Lord Byron, author of Childe Harold, Don Juan, &c., &c., And forming part of the private journal of his Lordship, supposed to have been entirely destroyed by Thos. Moore . . .* [London: "Printed for the Booksellers," 1866], notes, 2).

73. *Times,* 21 May 1830, 4c.

74. *Times,* 21 May 1830, 4c.

75. *Times,* 26 April 1830, p 3f. The *Morning Post* used almost exactly this same wording in a much shorter report. *Morning Post,* 26 April 1830, 2c.

76. *Times,* 21 May 1830, 4c.

77. *Times,* 26 April 1830, 3f.

78. *Papers of Sir Robert Peel,* vol. 220, General Correspondence, January–June 1830, British Library, Manuscript Collection, MS 40,400 ff. 177–182. Letter to Col. Rowan, 20 May 1830.

79. *Papers of Sir Robert Peel,* vol. 220, General Correspondence, Letter from Col. Rowan to Sir Robert Peel, 21 May 1830. It was also stated several times in court that the cases began with individuals in the S Division.

80. Dror Wahrman, *Imagining the Middle Class: The Political Representation of Class in Britain, c. 1780–1840* (New York: Cambridge University Press, 1995), 190–99.

81. Tobias, *Crime and Police,* 86; Taylor, *New Police,* 45.

CHAPTER 5. UNNATURAL-ASSAULT REPORTING IN THE LONDON PRESS

1. *Times,* 11 July 1842, 7c.

2. *Morning Post,* 11 July 1842, 4.

3. *Weekly Dispatch,* 17 July 1842, 340.

4. For an introduction to the debates surrounding the new journalism, see Laurel Brake, "The Old Journalism and the New: Forms of Cultural Production in London in the 1880s," and Joel H. Wiener, "How New Was the New Journalism?" in *Papers for the Millions: The New Journalism in Britain, 1850s to 1914,* ed. Joel H. Wiener (New York: Greenwood Press, 1988), 1–22, 47–65.

5. Hannah Barker, *Newspapers, Politics, and English Society, 1695–1895* (New York: Longman, 2000), 44.

6. First published in 1867, Walter Bagehot's analysis of the English government still proves insightful. Before the increase in party discipline after 1867, parliamentary debate enjoyed perhaps its greatest potential for actually affecting the outcome of votes. See Walter Bagehot, *The English Constitution* (Ithaca, N.Y.: Cornell University Press, 1963).

7. Anna Clark, *Women's Silence, Men's Violence: Sexual Assault in England, 1770–1845* (New York: Pandora, 1987), 75.

8. Clark, *Women's Silence, Men's Violence,* 44.

9. To the Royal Court of the King's (or Queen's) Bench at Westminster and the Central Criminal Court in the Old Bailey were added the New Court, the Third Court, and the Fourth Court in the following decades. The number of London police courts more than doubled between 1792 and the 1850s.

10. *Times,* 13 October 1827, 3e.

11. Jennifer Davis, "A Poor Man's System of Justice: The London Police Courts in the Second Half of the Nineteenth Century," *Historical Journal* 27 (1984): 317.

12. Sean Brady, *Masculinity and Male Homosexuality in Britain, 1861–1913* (New York: Palgrave Macmillan, 2006), 54.

13. *Times,* 20 August 1838, 7a.

14. *Morning Post,* 22 June 1844, 7d.

15. Barker, *Newspapers, Politics, and English Society,* 30.

16. Barker, *Newspapers, Politics, and English Society,* 39; Ivon Asquith, "The Structure, Ownership, and Control of the Press, 1780–1850," in *Newspaper History From the Seventeenth Century to the Present Day,* ed. George Boyce, James Curran, and Pauline Wingate (Beverly Hills, Calif.: Sage Publications, 1978), 22–23.

17. Barker, *Newspapers, Politics, and English Society,* 33.

18. Charles Mitchell, *The Newspaper Press Directory: Containing Full Particulars Relative to Each Journal Published in the United Kingdom and the British Isles* (London: C. Mitchell, 1846).

19. Barker, *Newspaper, Politics, and English Society,* 57–59.

20. See Roger Schofield, "Dimensions of Illiteracy in England, 1750–1850," in *Literacy and Social Development in the West: A Reader,* ed. Harvey J. Graff (New York: Cambridge University Press, 1981), 207.

21. Barker, *Newspapers, Politics, and English Society,* 37.

22. Barker, *Newspapers, Politics, and English Society,* 68, 71.

23. The *Black Dwarf* was edited, printed, and published by T. J. Wooler between 1817 and 1824.

24. *Black Dwarf,* 27 February 1822, 313.

25. The letter was signed "Jack Wild." *Black Dwarf,* 27 February 1822, 313.

26. *Black Dwarf,* 27 February 1822, 314–15.

27. *Black Dwarf,* 9 October 1822, 517–19. Emphasis in original. For other newspaper coverage, see *Examiner,* 3 August 1822, 475; 4 August 1822, 491.

28. *Black Dwarf,* 9 October 1822, 517.

29. *Black Dwarf,* 4 September 1822, 337–38.

30. By contrast, the *Times* gave very scant coverage to George Kelly's case and made no allusions to the bishop of Clogher. *Times,* 19 October 1822, 3.

31. *Black Dwarf,* 4 September 1822, 338.

32. *Black Dwarf,* 4 September 1822, 337.

33. The *Dublin Herald* countered by arguing "Very happy man, the convicts at present under sentence of death in London, for Jocelynism would be very likely to pronounce his right worshipful reverence." See *Black Dwarf,* 9 October 1822, 518.

34. The stories of the trials associated with Coldbath Fields, which filled nearly six pages of the thirty-two page issue, quoted the jury's opinion that "the conduct of *the police was ferocious, brutal,* and *unprovoked* by the people." *Cobbett's Weekly Register,* 25 May 1833, 488, emphasis in original.

35. The second arrest in September 1841 of William Bankes, the former MP, on unnatural-assault charges occurred during the run of the *London Phalanx,* but the events were not discussed. For details of this case, see *Times,* 3 September 1841, 7c; 8 September 1841, 7a; 9 September 1841, 6f; 11 September 1841, 7c; 25 September 1841, 7d.

36. *The Man: A Rational Advocate,* 18 August 1833, 54.

37. The full scope of these men's activities remains unclear. The most tragic reports came on 14 March 1833, after a thirteen-year-old boy was found in Regent's Canal in Regent's Park. The *Morning Chronicle* report noted that "an unnatural offence had been recently committed on the deceased." *Times,* 14 March 1833, 3d; *Morning Chronicle,* 14 March 1833, 1d.

38. For that shorter report, see *Weekly Dispatch,* 28 September 1851, 610.

39. The soldier in the bed with the man's nephew had been invited to spend the night by a servant in the house. *Weekly Dispatch,* 16 November 1851, 722.

40. *John Bull,* 14 May 1826, 158. Emphasis in original.

41. A similar case occurred in 1833, when the *Windsor Express* published an insinuation that John Bailey, a clergyman and tutor, was thought by his students to be disposed toward unnatural acts. Bailey won the case and was awarded one hundred pounds in damages. *Times,* 30 March 1833, 4b.

42. Anna Clark, *Scandal: The Sexual Politics of the British Constitution* (Princeton: Princeton University Press, 2004), 189.

43. Mitchell, *Newspaper Press Directory.*

44. Sean Brady has recently argued that "throughout the 1850s and 1860s, the *Times,* almost exceptionally among mainstream newspapers, continued to report and comment upon unnatural crimes between men that came to attention through the police and the criminal courts." Brady also underestimates the coverage in the *Times* for the 1860s, speculating that "unnatural crime in its pages numbered no more than three incidents in any given year." Brady's larger argument, that the *Times* curtailed its coverage after the 1870–71 Boulton and Park case, is generally correct. Brady, *Masculinity and Male Homosexuality,* 55, 233 n. 34.

45. *Times,* 13 August 1842, 7b. "Stringer" was actually referred to by his alias "Fitzgerald" for the first days of the proceedings. The real Fitzgerald, who was Stringer's close friend of many years, was also arrested and tried in the same series of cases for extorting money in a similar fashion. For clarity, I refer to Stringer always by his real name.

46. *Times,* 13 August 1842, 7b.

47. *Times,* 15 August 1842, 7c.

48. *Times,* 17 August 1842, 3f.

49. *The Satirist; Or the Censor of the Times,* 28 August 1842, 279. The *Satirist* article also described the alleged prejudice of the magistrate against Churchill at the first hearing.

50. *Weekly Dispatch,* 24 August 1842, 412. For almost exactly the same wording, see *Times,* 23 August 1842, 7b. John Ellis Churchill was the nephew of Wynn Ellis, a member of Parliament.

51. *Times,* 23 August 1842, 7b.

52. *Times,* 23 August 1842, 7b.

53. In addition to Fitzgerald, Stringer's aliases included Skinner and Kales Bill. Stringer had originally been convicted in July 1838 and sentenced to seven years' transportation. *Times,* 23 August 1842, 7b.

54. "Eliza Fitzgerald . . . was an old widow who made a precarious living selling lace and the like on the street. She knew Stringer well and . . . he was living in an abandoned public-house with her son." *Times,* 23 August 1842, 7b.

55. *Times,* 27 August 1842. 7d; see also *Morning Chronicle,* 27 August 1842, 4e.

56. *Times,* 29 August 1842, 7e. Watson worked as a hairdresser.

57. *Times,* 29 August 1842, 7e; *Morning Chronicle,* 31 August 1842, 4; *Morning Post,* 29 August 1842, 4c; *Weekly Dispatch,* 4 September 1842, 422.

58. *Times,* 29 August 1842, 7e; *Weekly Dispatch,* 4 September 1842, 422.

59. *Times,* 30 August 1842, 3b.

60. *Times,* 31 August 1842, 6; *Morning Post,* 31 August 1842, 4; *Weekly Dispatch,* 9 September 1842, 422, 424. Mr. Bodkin, one of the prosecutors, described the case as "one of the greatest public importance" (*Morning Chronicle,* 31 August 1842, 4c).

61. The *Morning Chronicle* used the phrase "but it was immediately checked."

62. *Times,* 31 August 1842, 6.

63. See *Times,* 2 September 1842, 7d; 22 September 1842; and, for the final letter to the editor, 24 September 1842, 5c.

64. The *Morning Chronicle* most frequently published reports from the police courts at Bow Street, Mansion House, and Queen Square.

65. The *Morning Chronicle* coverage opened with this sentence: "The persons who were apprehended in Hyde-park by the policemen in disguise, for certain practices, were this day placed at the bar for trial" (26 April 1830, 4c).

66. *Morning Chronicle,* 19 April 1830, 4d; *Morning Chronicle,* 17 April 1830; *Morning Post,* 19 April 1830, 2d.

67. *Morning Chronicle,* 19 April 1830, 4d.

68. *Morning Chronicle,* 20 April 1830, 4c; *Times,* 20 April 1830, 3c.

69. Examples include the prosecution of the Rev. Thomas Reynolds by Daniel Collins, *Times,* 26 April 1861, 12f; 27 April 1861, 11e; the prosecution of the Rev. Timothy Crowther by a workman, *Times,* 17 December 1863, 11f; the prosecution of William Wilson for an indecent assault on Constable Martin Palmer, *Times,* 19 June 1849, 7 c–d; the prosecution of Edward Peckham by Private Robert Precious, *Times,* 27 October 1847, 7b; the prosecution of George Marsh by Private Thomas Gill, *Times,* 21 September 1846, 6e; the prosecution of Thomas Hosier for a sexual advance on Constable Reilly, *Times,* 22 September 1840, 6c; the prosecution of David Burton by a sailor, *Times,* 30 October 1838, 6d; the prosecution of Benjamin Smith, a "well-dressed man," by John Taylor, *Times,* 4 November 1865, 11d–e; the Rev. Thomas Gray's sexual assault on Thomas Lloyd, *Times,* 23 July 1868, 9c; Edward Wood's indecent assault on a fishmonger, *Times,* 7 September 1869, 9e; and George Middleditch's prosecution of Frederick Thackeray, *Times,* 22 June 1844, 8c–d.

70. Brian Fothergill, *Beckford of Fonthill* (London: Faber and Faber, 1979),

168–72. Beckford's newspaper clippings are held in the manuscript collection of the Bodleian Library, MS Beckford, c. 75, 83.

71. Anonymous, *Don Leon; a poem by the late Lord Byron, author of Childe Harold, Don Juan, &c., &c., and forming part of the private journal of his Lordship, supposed to have been entirely destroyed by Thos. Moore . . .* (London: "Printed for the Booksellers," 1846).

72. To find positive literary representations of sex between men, the author cites passages from Plutarch and other ancient authors, as well as from Dante and Shakespeare.

73. *Don Leon*, notes, 41.

74. The story was originally in the *Ledger,* quoted in *Don Leon* from *Galignani's Messenger,* 28 May 1836. *Don Leon*, notes, 46–47.

75. *Don Leon,* 50, ll. 1377–80.

76. On the issue of a reader's response to a text, Jonathan Rose argues that "we should forswear the critical habit of pronouncing that texts reinforce or subvert existing social and political structures." Rose calls instead for "a history of audiences" in which the actual response of readers from the historical period is used as a guide to the meaning of a text. Jonathan Rose, "Rereading the English Common Reader: A Preface to a History of Audiences," *Journal of the History of Ideas* 53 (January–March 1992): 65.

77. *Times,* 12 November 1862, 12b.

78. CRIM 10/31, Sixth Session, 1849–50, case no. 803, 703; see also *Weekly Dispatch,* 17 March 1850, 162; 21 April 1850, 248.

79. CRIM 10/31, Sixth Session, 1849–50, case no. 803, 705.

80. *Weekly Dispatch,* 28 September 1851, 610; *Times,* 24 September 1851, 7c.

81. John Tosh, *A Man's Place: Masculinity and the Middle-Class Home in Victorian England* (New Haven: Yale University Press, 1999), 125; Leonore Davidoff and Catherine Hall, *Family Fortunes: Men and Women of the English Middle Class, 1780–1850* (Chicago: University of Chicago Press, 1987), 400–402. For a review of the literature on this topic, see Dror Wahrman, "'Middle-Class' Domesticity Goes Public: Gender, Class, and Politics from Queen Caroline to Queen Victoria," *Journal of British Studies* 32 (October 1993): 396–432.

82. Davidoff and Hall, *Family Fortunes,* 410–13.

83. Walter Edwards Houghton, *The Victorian Frame of Mind* (New Haven: Yale University Press, 1985), 5–12.

84. Oliver Woods and James Bishop, *The Story of the* Times: *Bicentenary Edition, 1785–1985* (London: Michael Joseph, 1985), 47.

85. James Grant, *The Newspaper Press: Its Origin, Progress, and Present Position,* vol. 1 (London: Tinsley Brothers, 1871), 141–52. See also Grant, *Newspaper Press,* vol. 2, 36–39.

86. Woods and Bishop, *Story of the* Times, 57.

87. Catherine Hall, *White, Male, and Middle Class: Explorations in Feminism and History* (New York: Routledge, 1992), 151–69.

88. *Times,* 25 January 1853, 4e. See also George Robb, *White-Collar*

Crime in Modern England: Financial Fraud and Business Morality, 1845–1929 (New York: Cambridge University Press, 1992).

89. Barker, *Newspapers, Politics, and English Society*, 69.

90. Barker, *Newspapers, Politics, and English Society*, 95.

91. Patricia Hollis, *The Pauper Press: A Study in Working-Class Radicalism of the 1830s* (London: Oxford University Press, 1970), 136.

92. Quoted in Tom Morley, "'The Times' and the Concept of the Fourth Estate: Theory and Practice in Mid-nineteenth Century Britain," *Journal of Newspaper and Periodical History* 3 (1985): 12–13.

93. On the influence of the new journalism and new political actors, see Judith R. Walkowitz, *City of Dreadful Delight: Narratives of Sexual Danger in Late Victorian London* (Chicago: University of Chicago Press, 1992), 68–72, 84–85, 95–97. See also Wiener, "How New Was the New Journalism?" 47–65.

94. Morris B. Kaplan, *Sodom on the Thames: Sex, Love, and Scandal in Wilde Times* (Ithaca, N.Y.: Cornell University Press, 2005), 167–79; Wiener, "How New Was the New Journalism?" 12–22.

95. H.G. Cocks, *Nameless Offences: Homosexual Desire in the Nineteenth Century* (London: I.B. Tauris, 2003), 139–44.

96. Kaplan, *Sodom on the Thames*, 248; Michael S. Foldy, *The Trials of Oscar Wilde: Deviance, Morality, and Late Victorian Society* (New Haven: Yale University Press, 1997), 21–30. The Boulton and Park scandal of 1870 seems to have followed a different dynamic, which I discuss in the following chapter.

97. Lewis Crompton, *Byron and Greek Love: Homophobia in Nineteenth-Century England* (Swaffham: Gay Men's Press, 1985), 251–83.

98. Hall, *White, Male, and Middle Class*, 264–76; Catherine Hall, Keith McClelland, and Jane Rendall, eds., *Defining the Victorian Nation: Class, Race, Gender and the Reform Act of 1867* (New York: Cambridge University Press, 2000), 136–38, 150.

CHAPTER 6. PATTERNS WITHIN THE CHANGES

1. *Times*, 3 April 1833, 4c; *Weekly Dispatch*, 7 April 1833, 187b. Edward Berry was a thirty-two-year-old shoemaker.

2. *Weekly Dispatch*, 7 April 1833, 187b; *Times*, 3 April 1833, 4c.

3. Christopher Allen, *The Law of Evidence in Victorian England* (New York: Cambridge University Press, 1997), 111–19.

4. The proceedings of the Central Criminal Court list the names of all individuals bringing cases during this period and the results of their trials. No other woman's name appears. HO 26/20–26/45 and CRIM 10/1–10/60 reviewed.

5. In the 1716 case of *Rex v. Wiseman*, Judge Fortescue ruled explicitly that the term *mankind* used in the sixteenth-century sodomy law included women as well as men. This decision became the precedent for later eighteenth-century cases. Arthur Gilbert, "Sodomy and the Law in Eighteenth- and Early Nineteenth-Century Britain," *Societas* 8 (1978): 226.

6. *Times*, 19 April 1830, 3f; *Weekly Dispatch*, 28 August 1825, 274; *Morning Post*, 19 April 1830, 2d; *Weekly Dispatch*, 25 September 1825, 306. Also raided in 1827 was the Rose and Crown in St. Martin's Lane, another molly house patronized by soldiers. See *Weekly Dispatch*, 15 July 1827, 219a.

7. *Weekly Dispatch*, 28 August 1825, 274.

8. *Weekly Dispatch*, 25 September 1825, 306.

9. H.G. Cocks, *Nameless Offences: Homosexual Desire in the Nineteenth Century* (London: I.B. Tauris, 2003), 51; Sean Brady, *Masculinity and Male Homosexuality in Britain, 1861–1913* (New York: Palgrave Macmillan, 2006), 102.

10. Jeffrey Weeks, "Inverts, Perverts, and Mary-Annes: Male Prostitution and the Regulation of Homosexuality in England in the Nineteenth and Early Twentieth Centuries," *Journal of Homosexuality* 6 (1980–81): 113–34.

11. *Yokel's Preceptor; or, More Sprees in London! Being a . . . show-up of all the rigs and doings of the flash cribs in this great metropolis . . . to which is added a Joskin's vocabulary . . .* (London: H. Smith, [1855]), 5–7.

12. *Yokel's Preceptor*, 5.

13. *Yokel's Preceptor*, 6.

14. *Yokel's Preceptor*, 6.

15. Letter from "an Advocate of Police Reform" to Robert Peel, 27 May 1827, HO 4418 ff. 426–27.

16. *Yokel's Preceptor*, 6.

17. *Morning Post*, 17 March 1846, 7d; *Weekly Dispatch*, 22 March 1846, 135; *Times*, 17 March 1846, 8c.

18. *Weekly Dispatch*, 22 March 1846, 135; *Times*, 17 March 1846, 8c; *Morning Post*, 17 March 1846, 7d.

19. *Weekly Dispatch*, 22 March 1846, 135; *Morning Post*, 17 March 1846, 7d; *Times*, 17 March 1846, 8c.

20. *Weekly Dispatch*, 22 March 1846, 135; *Morning Post*, 17 March 1846, 7d; *Times*, 17 March 1846, 8c.

21. *Weekly Dispatch*, 22 March 1846, 135; *Times*, 17 March 1846, 8c.

22. Cross-dressing for theatricals, carnivals or festivals, and social protest was well known in this period. Female cross-dressing in the nineteenth century followed different patterns, including "passing" as a man for economic and social advantages. See Martha Vicinus, "Lesbian History: All Theory and No Facts or All Facts and No Theory?" *Radical History Review* 60 (Fall 1994): 57–75.

23. *Times*, 19 October 1841, 7c. For a similar case not covered by the *Times*, see *Lloyd's Weekly Newspaper*, 22 January 1865, 12c.

24. *Weekly Dispatch*, 15 April 1855, 2a; *Times*, 11 April 1855, 9f.

25. *Morning Post*, 9 August 1858, 7d; *Times*, 9 August 1858, 9f.

26. *Times*, 19 October 1841, 7c.

27. *Weekly Dispatch*, 15 April 1855, 2a; *Times*, 11 April 1855, 9f.

28. *Morning Post*, 9 August 1858, 7d; *Times*, 9 August 1858, 9f.

29. *Weekly Dispatch*, 15 April 1855, 2a; *Times*, 11 April 1855, 9f.

30. *Morning Post*, 9 August 1858, 7d; *Times*, 9 August 1858, 9f.

31. *Morning Post*, 24 September 1850, 7e; *Times*, 24 September 1850, 7e;

Weekly Dispatch, 29 September 1850, 612; *Lloyd's Weekly London Newspaper,* 29 September 1850.

32. *Times,* 24 September 1850, 7e; *Morning Post,* 24 September 1850, 7e.

33. *Weekly Dispatch,* 29 September 1850, 612; *Times,* 24 September 1850, 7e.

34. *Times,* 24 September 1850, 7e; *Weekly Dispatch,* 29 September 1850, 612.

35. *Times,* 24 September 1850, 7e; *Weekly Dispatch,* 29 September 1850, 612.

36. *Times,* 25 October 1837, 6e. The issue in this case was whether the constable had entrapped a man based on assumptions about his style of clothing.

37. *Times,* 24 September 1850, 7e; *Weekly Dispatch,* 29 September 1850, 612.

38. *Times,* 26 October 1850, 7c. Unlike the *Times,* the *Weekly Dispatch* devoted only six lines to Scott's later criminal trial. *Weekly Dispatch,* 27 October 1850, 675.

39. See James H. Sweet, "Male Homosexuality and Spiritualism in the African Diaspora: The Legacies of a Link," *Journal of the History of Sexuality* 7 (1996): 184–202. See also Harriet Whitehead, "The Bow and the Burden Strap: A New Look at Institutionalized Homosexuality in Native North America," in *The Lesbian and Gay Studies Reader,* ed. Henry Abelove, Michèle Aina Barale, and David M. Halperin (New York: Routledge, 1993), 498–527.

40. Sweet, "Male Homosexuality and Spiritualism," 195.

41. *Times,* 24 September 1850, 7e.

42. *Times,* 26 October 1850, 7c.

43. George L. Mosse, *The Image of Man: The Creation of Modern Masculinity* (New York: Oxford University Press, 1996), 65–66. See also Mrinalini Sinha, *Colonial Masculinity: The "Manly Englishman" and the "Effeminate Bengali" in the Late Nineteenth Century* (Manchester: Manchester University Press, 1995), 17–22.

44. *Times,* 16 April 1849, 7.

45. Petition of Hassan, HO 18 231/18.

46. Letter from Viscount Palmerston, foreign secretary, to Earl Grey, home secretary, 1 May 1849, HO 18 231/18.

47. Letter from Palmerston, 1 May 1849, HO 18 231/18.

48. Letter from Judge N. W. Cope to the Home Office, dated 17 April 1849, HO 18 231/18.

49. Letter of Hafiz Bey to the Home Office, 18 June 1849, HO 18 231/18.

50. Letter of Hafiz Bey, 18 June 1849.

51. Such notes were often written in the margins of the preserved letters. The home secretary and Undersecretary Waddington initialed their comments, making it possible to follow their individual opinions on this and other similar cases.

52. Letter from Palmerston, 1 May 1849, HO 18 231/18.

53. They were sentenced to six months' imprisonment rather than the more common two-year sentence for unnatural assault. *Times,* 12 January 1829, 3e; for a less detailed report, see *Weekly Dispatch,* 11 January 1829, 13a.

54. This analysis is based on a sample of 152 police-court hearings held in London between 1810 and 1870 and reported in the *Times* for which the location of the hearing was readily identified. Forty-eight such cases were heard before the Marlborough Street court and 19 at Marylebone. Guildhall and Bow Street had 18 and 17 cases, respectively. Thirteen other police courts were represented in the sample, with total hearings as follows: Clerkenwell, 8; Thames, 7; Mansion House, 6; Westminster, 5; Worship Street, 5; Southwark, 5; Queen Square, 4; Union Hall, 2; Hatton Garden, 2; Hammersmith, 2; Woolwich, 2; Kensington, 1; and Wandsworth, 1.

55. Sean Brady has noted that the press gave a disproportionate amount of attention to the crimes committed by the middle and upper classes. Brady, *Masculinity and Male Homosexuality*, 59.

56. *Times*, 5 November 1862, 9f; *Weekly Dispatch*, 9 November 1862, 11.

57. *Times*, 5 November 1862, 9f; *Weekly Dispatch*, 9 November 1862, 11. The *Morning Post* did not cover the Whitehurst case.

58. *Times*, 7 November 1862, 5d.

59. *Times*, 12 November 1862, 12b; *Weekly Dispatch*, 16 November 1862, 5.

60. *Weekly Dispatch*, 9 November 1862, 11; *Times*, 5 November 1862, 9f.

61. *Times*, 8 November 1862, 12c.

62. *Times*, 19 November 1862, 6d; *Weekly Dispatch*, 23 November 1862, 11.

63. *Times*, 12 November 1862, 12b; *Weekly Dispatch*, 16 November 1862, 5.

64. *Morning Post*, 27 November 1863, 7a; *Weekly Dispatch*, 29 November 1863, 5a.

65. *Times*, 28 November 1863, 9a.

66. *Times*, 28 November 1863, 9b.

67. *Times*, 19 November 1862, 6e; *Weekly Dispatch*, 23 November 1862, 11.

68. *Weekly Dispatch*, 21 August 1864, 5a; *Times*, 18 August 1864, 11c–d.

69. *Times*, 18 August 1864, p 11c–d; *Weekly Dispatch*, 21 August 1864, 5a.

70. *Times*, 30 August 1853, 9d; *Weekly Dispatch*, 4 September 1853, 562.

71. *Weekly Dispatch*, 23 July 1826, 238d. The older man took the other's hand "and pressed it against his person" as the two strangers walked down Oxford Street at night. *Times*, 19 July 1826, 3d.

72. *Times*, 27 November 1850, 7e; *Weekly Dispatch*, 1 December 1850, 754.

73. CRIM 10/17, Second Session, 1842–43, case no. 292, 196–201. The *Weekly Dispatch* published two paragraphs on the trial, indicating that "Nathan had charged Mountain with being addicted to unnatural practices"

(18 December 1842, 602). See also *Morning Chronicle,* 15 December 1842, 4c; *Times,* 15 December 1842, 6c.

74. CRIM 10/17, Second Session, 1842–43, case no. 292, 196–201.

75. CRIM 10/17, Second Session, 1842–43, case no. 292, 196–201.

76. Anna Clark, "Twilight Moments," *Journal of the History of Sexuality* 14 (2005): 139–60.

77. *Times,* 21 April 1866, 11f.

78. *Times,* 22 September 1866, 11d–e; *Weekly Dispatch,* 23 September 1866, 12; *Morning Post,* 22 September 1866, 7a–b.

79. Petition for John Pacey, 1839, HO 18 7/19.

80. *Times,* 19 July 1851, 8b. See also *Weekly Dispatch,* 20 July 1851, 450.

81. Daniel Collins was fifteen years old. *Times,* 26 April 1861, 12f; 27 April 1861, 11e; *Weekly Dispatch,* 28 April 1861, 5c.

82. *Times,* 4 September 1835, 4c.

83. *Times,* 19 June 1849, 7c–d. For another case in which a man claimed intoxication as his excuse for indecently assaulting another man, see *Morning Post,* 29 August 1832, 4d.

84. *Weekly Dispatch,* 20 July 1851, 450.

85. *Times,* 20 June 1851, 7c; *Weekly Dispatch,* 22 June 1851, 387.

86. *Times,* 10 September 1864, 11e; *Weekly Dispatch,* 9 October 1864, 5a.

CHAPTER 7. CONCLUSION

1. Foucault, *The History of Sexuality: Volume 1, an Introduction,* trans. Robert Hurley (New York: Vintage Books, 1990).

2. Chris Waters, "Sexology," in *Palgrave Advances in the Modern History of Sexuality,* ed. H.G. Cocks and Matt Houlbrook (New York: Palgrave Macmillan, 2006), 43–47.

3. Harry Oosterhuis, *Stepchildren of Nature: Krafft-Ebing, Psychiatry, and the Making of Sexual Identity* (Chicago: University of Chicago Press, 2000).

4. Oosterhuis, *Stepchildren of Nature,* 164–70.

5. For a discussion of the need to connect sexology to the actions of individuals, see Laura Doan, *Fashioning Sapphism: The Origins of a Modern English Lesbian Culture* (New York: Columbia University Press, 2001), 127–30.

6. Sean Brady, *Masculinity and Male Homosexuality in Britain, 1861–1913* (New York: Palgrave Macmillan, 2006) 15–17, 187–90.

7. In the letter, Wilde claimed he suffered "from a mental illness, an erotomania" (quoted in Morris B. Kaplan, *Sodom on the Thames: Sex, Love, and Scandal in Wilde Times* [Ithaca, N.Y., Cornell University Press, 2005], 268–69). See also Matt Cook, *London and the Culture of Homosexuality, 1885–1914* (Cambridge: Cambridge University Press, 2003), 76, and H.G. Cocks, *Nameless Offences: Homosexual Desire in the Nineteenth Century* (London: I.B. Tauris, 2003), 90–95.

8. Oosterhuis, *Stepchildren of Nature,* 37–42; William Peniston, *Pederasts and Others: Urban Culture and Sexual Identity in Nineteenth-Century Paris*

(New York: Harrington Park Press, 2004), 55–56; Graham Robb, *Strangers: Homosexual Love in the Nineteenth Century* (New York W.W. Norton and Co., 2003), 66–70.

9. For certain characteristics of bourgeois masculinity common across borders in nineteenth-century Europe, and especially between Britain and the Protestant German states, see George Mosse, *Nationalism and Sexuality: Respectability and Abnormal Sexuality in Modern Europe* (New York: Howard Fertig, 1985), 20–22.

10. TS 11/506, no. 1660 Sussex County, Lent Assizes, 1806.

11. See HO 18 141/32, July 1844. In this 1844 case, the doctor was also asked to determine if a fluid found was semen. For a further example, see *Weekly Dispatch*, 25 September 1842, 458.

12. *Times*, 23 August 1825, 3d; 25 August 1825, 3d; 22 October 1825, 3c.

13. *Weekly Dispatch*, 28 August 1825, 274–75. See also *Morning Chronicle*, 22 October 1825; *Age*, September 1825.

14. For a discussion of how an individual's mental state affected outcomes in the nineteenth-century courtroom, see H.G. Cocks, "Trials of Character: The Use of Character Evidence in Victorian Sodomy Trials" in *The Trial in History*, vol. 2, *Domestic and International Trials, 1700–2000*, ed. R.A. Melikan (Manchester: University of Manchester Press, 2003): 37–40.

15. Robb, *Strangers*, 46–47. For a contemporary English-language work that explores similar themes, see William Acton, *The Functions and Disorders of the Reproductive Organs*, 7th ed. (London: John Churchill and Sons, 1865), 256–60.

16. Robb, *Strangers*, 46–47; Peniston, *Pederasts and Others*, 53–54.

17. *Times*, 21 May 1870, 11; *Morning Post*, 21 May 1870, 7; *Weekly Dispatch*, 22 May 1870, 16.

18. *Times*, 30 May 1870; 16 May 1871, 11; *Morning Post*, 30 May 1870, 3; *Weekly Dispatch*, 5 June 1870, 12.

19. George Mosse, *The Image of Man: The Creation of Modern Masculinity* (New York: Oxford University Press, 1996), 60–61.

20. Quoted from CRIM 10/31, Sixth Session, 1849–50, case no. 803, 700.

21. Mosse, *Image of Man*, 70–71; Peniston, *Pederasts and Others*, 53–54.

22. Thomas Laqueur, *Solitary Sex: A Cultural History of Masturbation* (New York: Zone Books, 2003), 37–44; Peniston, *Pederasts and Others*, 52.

23. Anonymous, *My Secret Life*, ed. James Kincaid (New York: Penguin, 1996); Anonymous, *The Pearl: A Journal of Facetive and Voluptuous Reading* (New York: Ballantine Books, 1996).

24. *The Boudoir: A Magazine of Scandal, Facetiae, &c.*, nos. 1–6 (London: H. Smith, 1860).

25. *Boudoir*, 97–98.

26. Similar treatments can be found in mainstream eighteenth-century literature. See Tobias Smollett's novels *Peregrine Pickle* and *Roderick Random*, published in 1751 and 1748 respectively. Netta Murray Goldsmith, *The Worst*

of Crimes: Homosexuality and the Law in Eighteenth-Century London
(Brookfield, Vt.: Ashgate, 1998), 16–17.

27. *Boudoir*, 178.

28. *Boudoir*, 180.

29. For an example of a defense claiming an "involuntary spasm" as the
reason for a same-sex advance, see the petition of Charles Carter, February
1846, HO 18 167/22. For the more frequent claim that a man's unfamiliar-
ity with alcohol made him more susceptible to its effects, see the petition of
Thomas Price, HO 18 246/45, and the petition of William Thomson, HO 18
3/32.

30. *Boudoir*, 180–81.

31. *Boudoir*, 181–82.

32. *Boudoir*, 182.

33. Mosse, *Image of Man*, 65–70.

34. For an analysis of mid-nineteenth-century British medical opinion on
this topic, see Mason, *Making of Victorian Sexuality*, 179, 226–27. On the
concept of "moral insanity" in the medical literature of this period, see Ivan
Crozier, "Nineteenth-Century British Psychiatric Writing about Homosexuality before Havelock Ellis: The Missing Story," *Journal of the History of Medicine and Allied Sciences* 63 (2008): 71–74.

35. *Weekly Dispatch*, 31 October, 1847, 518. The soldier, Robert Precious,
said that Peckham "approached him in an indecent manner, and made disgusting proposals to him." See also *Times*, 27 October 1847, 7b.

36. *Times*, 4 November 1865, 11d–e.

37. *Times*, 4 April 1867, 11d.

38. *Weekly Dispatch*, 20 June 1852, 386; *Times*, 15 June 1852, 8d.

39. Cook, *London and the Culture of Homosexuality*, 76; Waters, "Sexology," 46–47.

40. Crozier, "Nineteenth-Century British Psychiatric Writing," 98.

41. Cocks, "Trials of Character," 39–40; Waters, "Sexology," 46–47.

42. Oosterhuis, *Stepchildren of Nature*, 185–88.

43. Oosterhuis, *Stepchildren of Nature*, 47.

44. Oosterhuis, *Stepchildren of Nature*, 48.

45. Brady, *Masculinity and Male Homosexuality*, 119.

46. In a 1879 letter to Ulrichs, Krafft-Ebing wrote that "it was the knowl-
edge of your writings alone which led to my studies in this highly important
field" (quoted in Vern L. Bullough, *Science in the Bedroom: A History of
Sex Research* [New York: Basic Books, 1994], 38). See also Hubert Kennedy,
*Ulrichs: The Life and Works of Karl Heinrich Ulrichs, Pioneer of the Modern
Gay Movement* (Boston: Alyson Publications, 1988), 15–17.

47. Richard von Krafft-Ebing, *Psychopathia Sexualis: A Medico-Forensic
Study*, 12th ed., trans. F. J. Rebman (New York: Pioneer Publications, 1939),
case 137, "Mr. X."

48. Krafft-Ebing, *Psychopathia Sexualis*, 364.

49. Krafft-Ebing, *Psychopathia Sexualis*, 370.

50. Krafft-Ebing, *Psychopathia Sexualis*, 241–42.

51. Krafft-Ebing, *Psychopathia Sexualis*, 382.

52. Krafft-Ebing, *Psychopathia Sexualis*, 366.

53. Krafft-Ebing, *Psychopathia Sexualis*, case studies 147–51.

54. Krafft-Ebing, *Psychopathia Sexualis*, 391.

55. Krafft-Ebing, *Psychopathia Sexualis*, 392.

56. Krafft-Ebing, *Psychopathia Sexualis*, case studies 138–46.

57. Havelock Ellis and John Addington Symonds, *Sexual Inversion* (London: Wilson and Macmillan, 1897; repr. New York, Arno Press, 1975), 1–14.

58. Cook, *London and the Culture of Homosexuality*, 29–31, 54.

59. Matt Houlbrook, *Queer London: Perils and Pleasures in the Sexual Metropolis, 1918–1957* (Chicago: University of Chicago Press, 2005), 254–63.

60. Randolph Trumbach, "Modern Sodomy: The Origins of Homosexuality, 1700–1800," in *A Gay History of Britain: Love and Sex between Men Since the Middle Ages*, ed. Matt Cook, Randolph Trumbach, and H.G. Cocks (Oxford: Greenwood World Publishing, 2007), 82–87.

61. Catherine Hall, Keith McClelland, and Jane Rendall, eds., *Defining the Victorian Nation: Class, Race, Gender and the Reform Act of 1867* (New York: Cambridge University Press, 2000), 83–85.

62. Ellis and Symonds, *Sexual Inversion*, 40.

63. Ellis and Symonds, *Sexual Inversion*, 41.

64. Ellis and Symonds, *Sexual Inversion*, 117.

65. Ellis and Symonds, *Sexual Inversion*, 110.

66. Brady, *Masculinity and Male Homosexuality*, 183–84.

67. Brady, *Masculinity and Male Homosexuality*, 194.

68. Crozier, "Nineteenth-Century British Psychiatric Writing ," 93–101; Robb, *Strangers*, 52.

69. Brady, *Masculinity and Homosexuality*, 14; Oosterhuis, *Stepchildren of Nature*, 70–72.

70. Martha Vicinus, *Intimate Friends: Women Who Loved Women, 1778–1928* (Chicago: University of Chicago Press, 2004), 204–7; Oosterhuis, *Stepchildren of Nature*, 70.

71. Ellen Ross, *Love and Toil: Motherhood in Outcast London, 1870–1918* (New York: Oxford University Press, 1993), 198–202.

72. A.M. McBriar, *Fabian Socialism and English Politics, 1884–1918* (Cambridge: Cambridge University Press, 1962), 24–28.

73. See chapter 2, "Contested Terrain: New Social Actors," in Walkowitz, *City of Dreadful Delight: Narratives of Sexual Danger in Late Victorian London* (Chicago: University of Chicago Press, 1992), 48–80; J.W. Burrow, *The Crisis of Reason: European Thought, 1848–1914* (New Haven: Yale University Press, 2000), 136–46, 181–90.

74. Frederick Cooper and Ann Laura Stoler, *Tensions of Empire: Colonial Cultures in a Bourgeois World* (Berkeley: University of California Press, 1997), 35–37, 59–61.

75. Chris Waters, "Disorders of the Mind, Disorders of the Body Social: Peter Wildeblood and the Making of the Modern Homosexual," in *Moments of Modernity: Reconstructing Britain, 1945–1964*, ed. Becky Conekin, Frank Mort, and Chris Waters (New York: Rivers Oram Press, 1999), 121–50.

Select Bibliography

PRIMARY SOURCES

Government Documents

Central Criminal Court: After Trial Calendars of Prisoners. National Archive, CRIM 9. Full contents surveyed for the years 1855–75.
Central Criminal Court: Minutes of Evidence. National Archive, CRIM 10. Full contents surveyed 1835–70.
Central Criminal Court: CRIM 10/7, 1838, case no. 980, 880–85.
Central Criminal Court: CRIM 10/13, 1841, case no. 645, 460–66.
Central Criminal Court: CRIM 10/16, 1842, case no. 2780.
Central Criminal Court: CRIM 10/17, 1842–43, case no. 292, 196–201.
Central Criminal Court: CRIM 10/17, 1842–43, case no. 293, 201–2.
Central Criminal Court: CRIM 10/20, 10 June 1844, 218.
Central Criminal Court: CRIM 10/20, 1843–44, case no. 1916, 435–38.
Central Criminal Court: CRIM 10/20, 1843–44, case no. 1946, 495–500.
Central Criminal Court: CRIM 10/21, 1844, case no. 29, 34–36.
Central Criminal Court: CRIM 10/24, 1845–56, case no. 1584, 505–6.
Central Criminal Court: CRIM 10/24, 1846, 551–52.
Central Criminal Court: CRIM 10/24, 1845–46, case no. 2014, 859–63.
Central Criminal Court: CRIM 10/24, 1845–46, case no. 2914, 859–63.
Central Criminal Court: CRIM 10/28, 1847–48, case no. 1530, 212.
Central Criminal Court: CRIM 10/29, 1848–49, case no. 675, 464–70.
Central Criminal Court: CRIM 10/31, 1849–50, case no. 223, 206–7.
Central Criminal Court: CRIM 10/31, 1849–50, case no. 803, 699–711.
Central Criminal Court: CRIM 10/32, case no. 1307.
Central Criminal Court: CRIM 10/32, 1849–50, case no. 1589, 626–29.
Central Criminal Court: CRIM 10/34, 17 September 1851, case no. 1805.

Central Criminal Court: CRIM 10/36, case no. 977, 566–67.

Central Criminal Court: CRIM 10/39, 1854, case no. 201, 266.

Central Criminal Court: CRIM 10/41, 1854–55, case no. 47, 43–44.

Central Criminal Court: CRIM 10/42, 1855, case no. 558, 43–48.

Central Criminal Court: CRIM 10/52, 1863, 568.

Central Criminal Court: CRIM 10/55, 1866, 499.

Central Criminal Court, Depositions: The Queen on the Prosecution of Edward Norman against Henry Benham. CRIM 1/2/20.

Home Office: Criminal Petitions, Series I. National Archive, HO 17 Pz/1.

Home Office: Criminal Petitions, Series I, HO 17/120 Xv 13.

Home Office: Criminal Petitions, Series II. National Archive, HO 18 3/32.

Home Office: Criminal Petitions, Series II, HO 18 7/19

Home Office: Criminal Petitions, Series II, HO 18 43/33.

Home Office: Criminal Petitions, Series II, HO 18 134/2.

Home Office: Criminal Petitions, Series II, HO 18 141/32.

Home Office: Criminal Petitions, Series II, HO 18 167/22.

Home Office: Criminal Petitions, Series II, HO 18 226/6.

Home Office: Criminal Petitions, Series II, HO 18 231/18.

Home Office: Criminal Petitions, Series II, HO 18 234/38.

Home Office: Criminal Petitions, Series II, HO 18 236/20.

Home Office: Criminal Petitions, Series II, HO 18 243/48.

Home Office: Criminal Petitions, Series II, HO 18 246/45.

Home Office: Criminal Petitions, Series II, HO 18 266/6.

Home Office: Criminal Petitions, Series II, HO 18 268/27.

Home Office: Criminal Petitions, Series II, HO 18 281/14.

Home Office: Criminal Petitions, Series II, HO 18 300/5.

Home Office: Registers of Criminal Petitions, HO 17. Full contents surveyed 1797–1853.

Home Office: Annual returns for the Criminal Courts of London and Middlesex, HO 26/1 through HO 26/44. Full contents surveyed 1791–1838.

Home Office: Domestic Correspondence. HO 44/16, 19.

Home Office: Judges' Reports on Criminals, 10 47/75.

Home Office: Domestic Correspondence. HO 44/18, 426.

Home Office: Domestic Correspondence. HO 44/20, 205–7.

Home Office: Daily Reports from Metropolitan Police Offices, HO 62. Full contents surveyed 1828–39.

Home Office: Private and Secret Entry Books. HO 79/1/66.

Home Office: Registered Papers, Supplementary, Petition for Robert Watson. HO 144/8/21080.

London Metropolitan Archive: Registers of Convictions and Depositions in Police Courts and Petty Sessions. MSJ/CR/1–7.

Metropolitan Police, Office of the Commissioner, Confidential Books and Instructions. MEPO 8/1, *Metropolitan Police. Instructions, Orders, &c. &c.*

Old Bailey Session Papers: PCOM 1/21, 1825, case no. 68, 291–94.

Parliamentary Papers: Command Papers, Criminal Offender and Judicial Statistics, Annual Returns. Statistics gathered from 1805 to 1880.

Papers of Sir Robert Peel: General Correspondence, British Library Manuscript
    Collection. MS 40, 400.
Privy Council Papers. PC 1/3953, 1811.
Session Papers: Old Bailey Proceedings, PCOM 1. Surveyed 1800–34.
Session Papers: Old Bailey Proceedings, PCOM 1/21, 1825, 133.
Session Papers: Old Bailey Proceedings, PCOM 1/21, 1825, 191–4.
Session Papers: Old Bailey Proceedings, PCOM 1/22, 1825, 6–7. Treasury
    Solicitor, Papers: Regina vs. W. J. Bankes; Brief for the Prosecution, Central
    Criminal Court, September Sessions, 1841. TS 11/897 (3060).
Treasury Solicitor, Papers: Regina against Robert William Cook and George
    Wakeham, Maidstone Spring Assizes, 1841. TS 11/897 (3058).

Newspapers and Periodicals

The Annual Register; Or, a View of the History and Politics of the Year.
    London.
Bell's Life in London and Sporting Chronicle. London.
The Black Dwarf. London.
Cobbett's Weekly Political Register. London.
The Daily Telegraph. London.
The Examiner. London.
Galignani's Messenger, Paris.
Gentleman's Magazine and Historical Review. London.
The Globe. London.
Hansard Parliamentary Debates, House of Commons. London.
The Illustrated London News. London.
John Bull. London.
Lloyd's Weekly Newspaper. London.
The London Phalanx. London.
*The Man: A Rational Advocate for Universal Liberty, Free Discussion, and
    Equality of Conditions.* London.
The Morning Chronicle. London.
The Morning Post. London.
The Observer. London.
The Patriot. Dublin.
Quarterly Review. London.
The Satirist; or, the Censor of the Times. London.
The Sun. London.
The Times. London.
The Weekly Dispatch. London.

Other Primary Sources

Acton, William. *The Functions and Disorders of the Reproductive Organs in
    Childhood, Youth, Adult Age, and Advanced Life,* 7th ed. London: John
    Churchill and Sons, 1865.

————. *Prostitution, Considered in Its Moral, Social, and Sanitary Aspects, in London and Other Large Cities, and Garrison Towns, with Proposals for the Control and Prevention of Its Attendant Evils.* 2nd ed. London: J. Churchill, 1870; repr., London, Cass, 1972.

Anderson, Christopher. *The Genius and Design of the Domestic Constitution: With Its Untransferrable Obligations and Peculiar Advantages.* Edinburgh: Oliver & Boyd, 1826.

Anonymous. *Don Leon; a poem by the late Lord Byron, author of Childe Harold, Don Juan, &c., &c., And forming part of the private journal of his Lordship, supposed to have been entirely destroyed by Thos. Moore . . .* London: "Printed for the Booksellers," 1866.

Anonymous. *My Secret Life.* Edited by James Kincaid. New York: Penguin, 1996.

Anonymous. *The Pearl.* Ballantine Books, 1996.

Arthur, Timothy Shay. *Advice to Young Men on Their Duties and Conduct in Life.* Reprint, Boston: Elias Howe, 1848. In History of Women microform series, New Haven: Research Publications, Inc., 1975 reel 189, no. 1247.

Bagehot, Walter. *The English Constitution.* Ithaca, N.Y.: Cornell University Press, 1963.

Blackwell, Elizabeth. *Counsel to Parents on the Moral Education of Their Children.* New York: Brentano's Literary Emporium, 1879. In History of Women microform series, New Haven: Research Publications, Inc., 1975 reel 367, no. 2544.

The Boudoir: A Magazine of Scandal, Facetiae, &c., nos. 1–6 London: H. Smith, 1860.

Bushnell, Horace. *Views of Christian Nurture, and of Subjects Adjacent Thereto . . .* 2nd. ed. Hartford: Edwin Hunt, 1848.

Cobbett, William. *Advice to Young Men: and (incidentally) to Young Women in the Middle and Higher Ranks of Life, in a Series of Letters Addressed to a Youth, a Bachelor, a Lover, a Husband, a Father, and a Citizen or a Subject.* Reprint. New York: Oxford University Press, 1980.

Crown Cases Reserved for Consideration, and Decided by the Judges of England, with a Selection of Cases and Notes of Cases Relating to Indictable Offences. Vol. 1, pts. 1–6, ed. Henry Richard Dearsly and Thomas Bell. London: Stevens & Norton; H. Sweet & W. Maxwell, 1858.

Crown Cases Reserved for Consideration, and Decided by the Judges of England. From Hilary Term, 1861, to Trinity Term, 1865, pt. 7. The Hon. E. Chandos Leigh, and Lewis W. Cave. London: Stevens & Sons, 1866.

The Delicious Chanter, and Exciting Warbler . . . London: W. West, 1834.

Ellis, Havelock, and John Addington Symonds. *Sexual Inversion.* London: Wilson and Macmillan, 1897; repr. New York: Arno Press, 1975.

Grant, James. *The Newspaper Press; Its Origin, Progress, and Present Position.* Vols. 1 and 2. London: Tinsley Brothers, 1871.

Holloway, Robert. *The Phoenix of Sodom, or the Vere Street Coterie, etc.* London: J. Cook, 1813.

The Infamous Life of John Church . . . from his infancy up to his trial and Conviction. London: Hay and Turner, 1817.

James, John Angell. *The Family Monitor, or a Help to Domestic Happiness.* Birmingham: n.p., 1828.

Knight, Charles. *Knight's Cyclopaedia of London.* London: George Woodfall and Son, 1851.

Krafft-Ebing, Richard von. *Psychopathia Sexualis: A Medico-Forensic Study.* 12th ed. Trans. F. J. Rebman. New York: Pioneer Publications, 1939.

Leeves, Edward. *Leaves from a Victorian Diary, with an Introduction by John Sparrow.* London: Alison Press/Secker and Warburg, 1985.

Life in London: Or the Sprees of Tom and Jerry; Attempted in Cuts and Verse. London: Jas Catnach, 1822. Broadsheet no. 97, Miscellaneous Collections of Broadside Ballads, etc. 1–108 British Library.

Mayhew, Henry. *London Labour and the London Poor: A Cyclopedia of the Condition and Earnings of Those That Will Work, Those That Cannot Work, and Those That Will Not Work.* London: Griffin, Bohn, and Co, 1861–62.

Mitchell, Charles. *The Newspaper Press Directory: Containing Full Particulars Relative to Each Journal Published in the United Kingdom and the British Isles.* London: C. Mitchell, 1846.

The Nobby Songster, Or a prime selection as now singing at Offley's Cider Celler: Coal Hole &c. London: W. West, 1842.

O'Donnoghue, H. C. *Marriage: The Source, Stability and Perfection of Social Happiness and Duty.* London: n.p., 1828.

Papers of Sir Robert Peel. Vol. 220, General Correspondence, Jan.–June 1830, British Library, Manuscript Collection.

Papers of Henry Pelham, Fourth Duke of Newcastle. Estate and Personal Papers, Nottingham University Library, Department of Manuscripts and Special Collections.

Religion and Morality Vindicated against Hypocracy and Polution; Or, an Account of the Life and Character of John Church . . . London: 1813.

Roberts, William. *The Portraiture of a Christian Gentleman.* London: Hatchard, 1829.

Routledge's Guide to London and its Suburbs: Comprising Description of all its Points of Interest, Including the Most Recent Improvements and Public Buildings. London: George Routledge and Sons, 1877.

Ryan, Michael. *Prostitution in London: With a Comparative View of that of Paris and New York: as Illustrative of the Capitals and Large Towns of all Countries: And Proving Moral Depravation to be the Most Fertile Source of Crime, and of Personal and Social Misery: with an Account of the Nature and Treatment of the Various Diseases, Caused by the Abuses of the Reproductive Function.* London: H. Baillière, 1839.

Saul, Jack. *Sins of the Cities of the Plain, or the Confessions of a Mary-Anne: With Short Essays on Sodomy and Tribalism.* London: privately printed, 1881.

Tavern Anecdotes and Reminiscences of the Origins of Signs, Clubs, Coffee Houses, . . . &c. intended as a lounge-book for Londoners and their Country Cousins, by one of the Old School. London: W. West, Bookseller, 1825.

Taylor, Alfred Swaine. *Medical Jurisprudence* Philadelphia: Blanchard and
    Lea, 1853.
Taylor, Isaac. *Advice to the Teens: Or Practical Helps Towards the Formation
    of One's Own Character.* London: Rest Fenner, 1818.
Timbs, John. *Curiosities of London: Exhibiting the Most Rare and Remark-
    able Objects of Interest in the Metropolis with Nearly Sixty Years of Per-
    sonal Recollections.* London: J. S. Virtue, 1885.
Ulrichs, Karl Heinrich. *Forschungen über das Rätsel der Mannmännlichen
    Liebe.* Leipzig: M. Spohr, 1898.
Ulrichs, Karl Heinrich. *The Riddle of "Man-Manly" Love: The Pioneering
    Work on Male Homosexuality.* Translated by Michael A. Lombardi-Nash
    Buffalo, N.Y.: Prometheus Books, 1994.
Venn, Henry. *The Complete Duty of Man: or, A System of Doctrinal and
    Practical Christianity* . . . Reprint, New Brunswick, N.J.: J. Simpson;
    L. Deare, 1811.
Yokel's Preceptor: Or, More Sprees in London! Being a . . . *show-up of all the
    rigs and doings of the flash cribs in this great metropolis* . . . *to which is
    added a Joskin's vocabulary* . . . London: H. Smith, [1855].

SECONDARY SOURCES

Monographs and Dissertations

Adams, James Eli. *Dandies and Desert Saints: Styles of Victorian Masculinity.*
    Ithaca, N.Y.: Cornell University Press, 1995.
Allen, Christopher. *The Law of Evidence in Victorian England.* New York:
    Cambridge University Press, 1997.
Barker, Hannah. *Newspapers, Politics, and English Society, 1695–1895.* New
    York: Longman, 2000.
Barker-Benfield, G. J. *The Culture of Sensibility: Sex and Society in Eighteenth-
    Century Britain.* Chicago: University of Chicago Press, 1996.
Bartlett, Neil. *Who Was that Man? A Present for Mr. Oscar Wilde.* London:
    Serpent's Tail, 1988.
Bentley, David. *English Criminal Justice in the Nineteenth Century.* London:
    Hambledon Press, 1998.
Boswell, John. *Christianity, Social Tolerance, and Homosexuality: Gay People
    in Western Europe from the Beginning of the Christian Era to the
    Fourteenth Century.* Chicago: University of Chicago Press, 1980.
Boyce, George, James Curran, and Pauline Wingate, eds. *Newspaper History
    from the Seventeenth Century to the Present Day.* Beverly Hills, Calif.:
    Sage Publications, 1978.
Brady, Sean. *Masculinity and Male Homosexuality in Britain, 1861–1913.*
    New York: Palgrave Macmillan, 2006.
Bray, Alan. *Homosexuality in Renaissance England.* New York: Columbia
    University Press, 1982.
Bristow, Edward. *Vice and Vigilance: Purity Movements in Britain since 1700.*
    Totowa, N.J.: Rowman and Littlefield, 1977.

Broughton, Trev Lynn, and Helen Rogers, eds. *Gender and Fatherhood in the Nineteenth Century*. New York: Palgrave Macmillan, 2007.

Brown, Ford K. *Fathers of the Victorians; the Age of Wilberforce*. Cambridge: Cambridge University Press, 1961.

Brown, Lucy. *Victorian News and Newspapers*. Oxford: Clarendon Press, 1985.

Bullough, Vern L. *Science in the Bedroom: A History of Sex Research*. New York: Basic Books, 1994.

Burns, Arthur and Joanna Innes, eds. *Rethinking the Age of Reform: Britain, 1780–1850*. New York: Cambridge University Press, 2003.

Burrow, John W. *The Crisis of Reason: European Thought, 1848–1914*. New Haven: Yale University Press, 2000.

Butler, Judith. *Bodies that Matter: On the Discursive Limits of Sex*. New York: Routledge, 1993.

Butler, Judith. *Gender Trouble: Feminism and the Subversion of Identity*. New York: Routledge, 1990.

Cannadine, David. *The Rise and Fall of Class in Britain*. New York: Columbia University Press, 1999.

Cecil, Henry. *The English Judge*. London: Stevens and Sons, 1970.

Chandos, John. *Boys Together: English Public Schools, 1800–1864*. New Haven: Yale University Press, 1984.

Chauncey, George. *Gay. New York: Gender, Urban Culture, and the Makings of the Gay Male World, 1890–1940*. New York: Basic Books, 1994.

Chesney, Kellow. *The Victorian Underworld*. London: Maurice Temple Smith Ltd., 1970.

Clark, Anna. *Scandal: The Sexual Politics of the British Constitution*. Princeton: Princeton University Press, 2004.

———. *The Struggle for the Breeches: Gender and the Making of the British Working Class*. Berkeley: University of California Press, 1995.

———. *Women's Silence, Men's Violence: Sexual Assault in England, 1770–1845*. New York: Pandora, 1987.

Clawson, Mary Anne. *Constructing Brotherhood: Gender, Class, and Fraternalism*. Princeton: Princeton University Press, 1989.

Cocks, H. G. "Abominable Crimes: Sodomy Trials in English Law and Culture, 1830–1889." PhD diss., University of Manchester, 1998.

———. *Nameless Offences: Homosexual Desire in the Nineteenth Century*. London: I. B. Tauris, 2003.

Cocks, H.G., and Matt Houlbrook, eds. *Palgrave Advances in the Modern History of Sexuality*. New York: Palgrave Macmillan, 2006.

Cohen, Ed. *Talk on the Wilde Side*. New York: Routledge, 1993.

Cohen, William A. *Sex Scandal: The Private Parts of Victorian Fiction*. Durham, N.C.: Duke University Press, 1996.

Colley, Linda. *Britons: Forging the Nation, 1707–1837*. New Haven: Yale University Press, 1992.

Collins, Irene. *The Government and the Newspaper Press, 1814–1881*. New York: Oxford University Press, 1959.

Conekin, Becky, Frank Mort, and Chris Waters, eds. *Moments of Modernity: Reconstructing Britain, 1945–1964*. New York: Rivers Oram Press, 1999.

Cook, Hera. *The Long Sexual Revolution: English Women, Sex, and Contraception, 1800–1975*. New York: Oxford University Press, 2004.

Cook, Matt. *London and the Culture of Homosexuality, 1885–1914*. Cambridge: Cambridge University Press, 2003.

Cook, Matt, Randolph Trumbach, and H. G. Cocks, eds. *A Gay History of Britain: Love and Sex between Men Since the Middle Ages*. Oxford: Greenwood World Publishing, 2007.

Cornish, William Randolph. *The Jury*. London: Penguin Press, 1968.

Cornish, W. R., J. Hart, A. H. Manchester, and J. Stevenson. *Crime and Law in Nineteenth-Century Britain*. Dublin: Irish University Press, 1978.

Craft, Christopher. *Another Kind of Love: Male Homosexual Desire in English Discourse, 1850–1920*. Berkeley: University of California Press, 1994.

Crompton, Lewis. *Byron and Greek Love: Homophobia in Nineteenth-Century England*. Swaffham: Gay Men's Press, 1985.

Davidoff, Leonore, and Catherine Hall. *Family Fortunes: Men and Women of the English Middle Class, 1780–1850*. Chicago: University of Chicago Press, 1987.

Doan, Laura. *Fashioning Sapphism: The Origins of a Modern English Lesbian Culture*. New York: Columbia University Press, 2001.

Dollimore, Jonathan. *Sexual Dissidence: Augustine to Wilde, Freud to Foucault*. Oxford: Clarendon Press, 1991.

Donzelot, Jacques. *The Policing of Families*. New York: Pantheon Books, 1979.

Dover, Kenneth James. *Greek Homosexuality*. London: Duckworth, 1978.

Dowling, Linda. *Hellenism and Homosexuality in Victorian Oxford* Ithaca, N.Y.: Cornell University Press, 1994.

Driver, Felix. *Power and Pauperism: The Workhouse System, 1834–1884*. New York: Cambridge University Press, 1993.

Duberman, Martin, Martha Vicinus, and George Chauncey Jr., eds. *Hidden From History: Reclaiming the Gay and Lesbian Past*. New York: New American Library, 1989.

Edwards, J. L. J. *The Law Officers of the Crown: A Study of the Offices of Attorney-General and Solicitor-General of England with an Account of the Office of the Director of Public Prosecutions of England*. London: Sweet & Maxwell, 1964.

Edwards, Susan. *Female Sexuality and the Law*. Oxford: Martin Robertson, 1981.

Emsley, Clive. *Crime and Society in England, 1750–1900*. New York: Longman, 1996.

Evans, Eric J. *The Forging of the Modern State: Early Industrial Britain, 1783–1870*. New York: Longman, 1983.

Follett, Richard. *Evangelicalism, Penal Theory and the Politics of Criminal Law Reform in England, 1808–30*. New York: Palgrave, 2001.

Fothergill, Brian. *Beckford of Fonthill*. London: Faber and Faber, 1979.

Foucault, Michel. *Discipline and Punish: The Birth of the Prison.* Translated by Alan Sheridan. New York: Vintage Books, 1979.

———. *The History of Sexuality: An Introduction, Volume 1.* Translated by Robert Hurley. New York: Vintage Books, 1990.

Gash, Norman. *Aristocracy and People: Britain, 1815–1865.* Cambridge, Mass.: Harvard University Press, 1979.

Gibson, Mary. *Born to Crime: Cesare Lombroso and the Origins of Biological Criminology.* London: Praeger Publishers, 2002.

Gilbert, Alan D. *Religion and Society in Industrial England: Church, Chapel, and Social Change, 1740–1914.* London: Longman, 1976.

Gillis, John. *For Better, For Worse: British Marriages, 1600 to the Present.* New York: Oxford University Press, 1985.

———. *A World of Their Own Making: Myth, Ritual, and the Quest for Family Values.* Cambridge, Mass.: Harvard University Press, 1996.

———. *Youth and History: Tradition and Change in European Age Relations, 1770—Present.* New York: Academic Press, 1974.

Gilmore, David D. *Manhood in the Making: Cultural Concepts of Masculinity.* New Haven: Yale University Press, 1990.

Goldsmith, Netta Murray. *The Worst of Crimes: Homosexuality and the Law in Eighteenth-Century London.* Brookfield, Vt.: Ashgate, 1998.

Graff, Harvey J. *Literacy and Social Development in the West: A Reader.* New York: Cambridge University Press, 1981.

de Grazia, Victoria, and Ellen Furlough, eds. *The Sex of Things: Gender and Consumption in Historical Perspective.* Berkeley: University of California Press, 1996.

Hall, Catherine. *White, Male, and Middle Class: Explorations in Feminism and History.* New York: Routledge, 1992.

Hall, Catherine, Keith McClelland, and Jane Rendall, eds. *Defining the Victorian Nation: Class, Race, Gender and the Reform Act of 1867.* New York: Cambridge University Press, 2000.

Halperin, David. *How to Do the History of Homosexuality.* Chicago: University of Chicago Press, 2002.

Harling, Phillip. *The Waning of "Old Corruption": The Politics of Economical Reform in Britain, 1779–1846.* Oxford: Clarendon Press, 1996.

Hay, Douglas, Peter Linebaugh, John G. Rule, E.P. Thompson, and Cal Winslow. *Albion's Fatal Tree: Crime and Society in Eighteenth-century England.* New York: Pantheon Books, 1975.

Hekman, Susan J., ed. *Feminist Interpretations of Michel Foucault.* University Park: Pennsylvania State University Press, 1996.

Herd, Harold. *The March of Journalism: The Story of the British Press from 1622 to the Present Day.* Westport, Conn.: Greenwood Press, 1973.

Herdt, Gilbert, ed. *Third Sex, Third Gender: Beyond Sexual Dimorphism in Culture and History.* New York: Zone Books, 1994.

Hilton, Boyd. *The Age of Atonement: The Influence of Evangelicalism on Social and Economic Thought, 1795–1865.* Oxford: Clarendon Press, 1988.

Hitchcock, Tim. *English Sexualities: 1700–1800*. New York: St. Martin's Press, 1997.

Hollis, Patricia. *Class and Conflict in Nineteenth-Century England, 1815–1850*. London: Routledge, 1973.

———. *The Pauper Press: A Study in Working-Class Radicalism of the 1830s*. London: Oxford University Press, 1970.

Honey, John Raymond de Symons. *Tom Brown's Universe: the Development of the Victorian Public School*. London: Millington, 1977.

Houghton, Walter Edwards. *The Victorian Frame of Mind*. New Haven: Yale University Press, 1985.

Houlbrook, Matt. *Queer. London: Perils and Pleasures in the Sexual Metropolis, 1918–1957*. Chicago: University of Chicago Press, 2005.

Hull, Isabel V. *Sexuality, State, and Civil Society in Germany, 1700–1815*. Ithaca, N.Y.: Cornell University Press, 1996.

Hunt, Lynn, ed. *The Invention of Pornography*. New York: Zone Books, 1993.

Hunter, Tera W. *To 'Joy My Freedom: Southern Black Women's Lives and Labors after the Civil War*. Cambridge, Mass.: Harvard University Press, 1997.

Hyam, Ronald. *Empire and Sexuality: the British Experience*. New York: Manchester University Press, 1990.

Hyde, H. [Harford] Montgomery. *The Cleveland Street Scandal*. London: W.H. Allen, 1976.

———. *A History of Pornography*. London: Heinemann, 1964.

———. *The Love That Dared Not Speak Its Name*. Boston: Little, Brown, 1970.

———. *The Strange Death of Lord Castlereagh*. London: Heinemann, 1959.

———, ed. *The Three Trials of Oscar Wilde*. New York: University Books, 1956.

Ignatieff, Michael. *A Just Measure of Pain: The Penitentiary in the Industrial Revolution, 1750–1850*. New York: Pantheon Books, 1978.

Jackson, Louise A. *Child Sexual Abuse in Victorian England*. New York: Routledge, 2000.

Jenkyns, Richard. *The Victorians and Ancient Greece*. Cambridge, Mass.: Harvard University Press, 1980.

Jones, Aled. *Powers of the Press: Newspapers, Power and the Public in Nineteenth-Century England*. Brookfield, Vt.: Ashgate Publishing Co., 1996.

Kaplan, Morris B. *Sodom on the Thames: Sex, Love, and Scandal in Wilde Times*. Ithaca, N.Y.: Cornell University Press, 2005.

Kennedy, Hubert. *Ulrichs: the Life and Works of Karl Heinrich Ulrichs, Pioneer of the Modern Gay Movement*. Boston: Alyson Publications, 1988.

Kift, Dagmar. *The Victorian Music Hall: Culture, Class, and Conflict*. New York: Cambridge University Press, 1996.

Knafla, Louis A., ed. *Crime, Gender and Sexuality in Criminal Prosecutions*. Westport, Conn.: Greenwood Press, 2002.

Koven, Seth. *Slumming: Sexual and Social Politics in Victorian London.* Princeton: Princeton University Press, 2004.

Lambert, Royston. *Beloved and God: The Story of Hadrian and Antinous.* London: Weidenfeld and Nicolson, 1984.

Laqueur, Thomas. *Making Sex: Body and Gender from the Greeks to Freud.* Cambridge, Mass.: Harvard University Press, 1990.

———. *Solitary Sex: A Cultural History of Masturbation.* New York: Zone Books, 2003.

Lauritsen, John, and David Thorstad. *The Early Homosexual Rights Movement.* New York: Times Change Press, 1974.

Leps, Marie-Christine. *Apprehending the Criminal: The Production of Deviance in Nineteenth-Century Discourse.* Durham, N.C.: Duke University Press, 1992.

Lewis, John Royston. *The Victorian Bar.* London: Robert Hale, 1982.

Lovell, Colin Rhys. *English Constitutional and Legal History: A Survey.* New York: Oxford University Press, 1962.

McBriar, A. M. *Fabian Socialism and English Politics, 1884–1918.* Cambridge: Cambridge University Press, 1962.

McBride, Theresa M. *The Domestic Revolution: The Modernization of Household Service in England and France, 1820–1920.* New York: Holmes and Meier, 1976.

McCalman, Iain. *Radical Underworld: Prophets, Revolutionaries and Pornographers in London, 1795–1840.* New York: Cambridge University Press, 1988.

McConville, Seán. *A History of English Prison Administration,* vol. 1, *1750–1877.* Boston: Routledge & Kegan Paul, 1981.

McLaren, Angus. *Sexual Blackmail: A Modern History.* Cambridge, Mass.: Harvard University Press, 2002.

McLeod, Hugh. *Religion and the People of Western Europe, 1789–1970.* New York: Oxford University Press, 1981.

Mangan, J. A., and James Walvin, eds. *Manliness and Morality: Middle Class Masculinity in Britain and America, 1800–1940.* Manchester: Manchester University Press, 1987.

Mason, Michael. *The Making of Victorian Sexuality.* New York: Oxford University Press, 1994.

Mason, Philip. *The English Gentleman: The Rise and Fall of an Ideal.* London: A. Deutsch, 1982.

Merrick, Jeffrey, and Bryant T. Ragan Jr. *Homosexuality in Modern France.* New York: Oxford University Press, 1996.

Miller, Wilbur R. *Cops and Bobbies: Police Authority in New York and London, 1830–1870.* Chicago: University of Chicago Press, 1973.

Morris, Norval, and David J. Rothman, eds. *The Oxford History of the Prison: The Practice of Punishment in Western Society.* New York: Oxford University Press, 1995.

Mosse, George L. *The Image of Man: The Creation of Modern Masculinity.* New York: Oxford University Press, 1996.

——. *Nationalism and Sexuality: Respectability and Abnormal Sexuality in Modern Europe*. New York: Howard Fertig, 1985.

Murray, Stephen O., and Will Roscoe, eds. *Islamic Homosexualities: Culture, History, and Literature*. New York: NYU Press, 1997.

Nead, Lynda. *Victorian Babylon: People, Streets and Images in Nineteenth-Century London*. New Haven: Yale University Press, 2000.

Nord, Deborah Epstein. *Walking the Victorian Streets: Women, Representation, and the City*. Ithaca, N.Y.: Cornell University Press, 1995.

Norton, Rictor. *Mother Clap's Molly House: The Gay Subculture in England, 1700–1830*. London: Gay Men's Press, 1992. Rev. 2nd ed., Stroud: Chalford Press, 2006.

Olsen, Donald J. *The Growth of Victorian London*. New York: Holmes & Meier, 1976.

Oosterhuis, Harry. *Stepchildren of Nature: Krafft-Ebing, Psychiatry, and the Making of Sexual Identity*. Chicago: University of Chicago Press, 2000.

Peniston, William. *Pederasts and Others: Urban Culture and Sexual Identity in Nineteenth-Century Paris*. New York: Harrington Park Press, 2004.

Petrow, Stefan. *Policing Morals: The Metropolitan Police and the Home Office, 1870–1914*. Oxford: Clarendon Press, 1994.

Pflugfelder, Gregory. *Cartographies of Desire: Male-Male Sexuality in Japanese Discourse, 1600–1950*. Berkeley: University of California Press, 1999.

Porter, Roy. *English Society in the Eighteenth Century*. New York: Penguin, 1990.

Porter, Roy, and Lesley Hall. *The Facts of Life: The Creation of Sexual Knowledge in Britain, 1650–1950*. New Haven: Yale University Press, 1995.

Radzinowicz, Leon. *A History of English Criminal Law and Its Administration from 1750*. Vol. 1, *The Movement for Reform, 1750–1833*. New York: Macmillan, 1948.

Reynolds, Elaine A. *Before the Bobbies: The Night Watch and Police Reform in Metropolitan London, 1720–1830*. Stanford, Calif.: Stanford University Press, 1998.

Robb, George. *White-Collar Crime in Modern England: Financial Fraud and Business Morality, 1845–1929*. New York: Cambridge University Press, 1992.

Robb, Graham. *Strangers: Homosexual Love in the Nineteenth Century*. New York: W. W. Norton and Co., 2003.

Rocke, Michael. *Forbidden Friendships: Homosexuality and Male Culture in Renaissance Florence*. New York: Oxford University Press, 1996.

Roper, Michael, and John Tosh, eds. *Manful Assertions: Masculinities in Britain since 1800*. New York: Routledge, 1991.

Ross, Ellen, *Love and Toil: Motherhood in Outcast London, 1870–1918*. New York: Oxford University Press, 1993.

Roughead, William. *Bad Companions*. Edinburgh: W. Green and Son, 1930.

Rowell, George. *The Victorian Theatre, 1792–1914: A Survey*. New York: Cambridge University Press, 1978.

Rumbelow, Donald. *I Spy Blue: The Police and Crime in the City of London from Elizabeth I to Victoria*. London: Macmillan, 1971.

Scott, James C. *Domination and the Arts of Resistance: Hidden Transcripts*. New Haven: Yale University Press, 1990.

Scott, Joan. *Gender and the Politics of History*. New York: Columbia University Press, 1988.

Sedgwick, Eve Kosofsky. *Between Men: English Literature and Male Homosexual Desire*. New York: Columbia University Press, 1985.

————. *Epistemology of the Closet*. Berkeley: University of California Press, 1990.

Shoemaker, Robert Brink. *Prosecution and Punishment: Petty Crime and the Law in London and Rural Middlesex, c. 1660–1725*. New York: Cambridge University Press, 1991.

Simpson, Anthony. "Masculinity and Control: the Prosecution of Sex Offenses in Eighteenth-Century London." PhD dissertation, New York University, 1984.

Simpson, Colin. *The Cleveland Street Affair*. Boston: Little, Brown, 1976.

Sinfield, Alan. *The Wilde Century: Effeminacy, Oscar Wilde, and the Queer Movement*. New York: Columbia University Press, 1994.

Sinha, Mrinalini. *Colonial Masculinity: The "Manly Englishman" and the "Effeminate Bengali" in the Late Nineteenth Century*. Manchester: Manchester University Press, 1995.

Smith, Bonnie. *Ladies of the Leisure Class: The Bourgeoises of Northern France in the Nineteenth Century*. Princeton: Princeton University Press, 1981.

Smith, Phillip Thurmond. *Policing Victorian London: Political Policing, Public Order, and the London Metropolitan Police*. London: Greenwood Press, 1985.

Steakley, James D. *The Homosexual Emancipation Movement in Germany*. New York: Arno Press, 1975.

Stone, Lawrence. *The Family, Sex and Marriage in England, 1500–1800*. Abridged ed. New York: Harper and Row, 1979.

Taylor, David. *Crime, Policing and Punishment in England, 1750–1914*. New York: St. Martin's Press, 1998.

————. *The New Police in Nineteenth-Century England: Crime, Conflict, and Control*. New York: Manchester University Press, 1997.

Taylor, George. *Players and Performances in the Victorian Theatre*. New York: Manchester University Press, 1989.

Thompson, E. P. *Customs in Common: Studies in Traditional Popular Culture*. New York: New Press, 1993.

————. *The Making of the English Working Class*. New York: Vintage Books, 1966.

Thompson, F. M. L. *The Rise of Respectable Society: A Social History of Victorian Britain, 1830–1900*. Cambridge, Mass.: Harvard University Press, 1988.

Tobias, John Jacob. *Crime and Police in England: 1700–1900*. New York: St. Martin's Press, 1979.

Tobin, Robert. *Warm Brothers: Queer Theory and the Age of Goethe*. Philadelphia: University of Pennsylvania Press, 2000.

Tosh, John. *Manliness and Masculinities in Nineteenth-Century Britain: Essays on Gender, Family, and Empire*. Harlow: Pearson Longman, 2005.

——. *A Man's Place: Masculinity and the Middle-Class Home in Victorian England*. New Haven: Yale University Press, 1999.

Trumbach, Randolph. *The Rise of the Egalitarian Family: Aristocratic Kinship and Domestic Relations in Eighteenth-Century England*. New York: Academic Press, 1978.

——. *Sex and the Gender Revolution*, vol. 1, *Heterosexuality and the Third Gender in Enlightenment London*. Chicago: University of Chicago Press, 1998.

Vernon, James. *Re-reading the Constitution: New Narratives in the Political History of England's Long Nineteenth Century*. New York: Cambridge University Press, 1996.

Vicinus, Martha. *Intimate Friends: Women Who Loved Women, 1778–1928*. Chicago: University of Chicago Press, 2004.

Waddams, S. M. *Sexual Slander in Nineteenth-Century England: Defamation in the Ecclesiastical Courts, 1815–1855*. Toronto: University of Toronto Press, 2000.

Wahrman, Dror. *Imagining the Middle Class: The Political Representation of Class in Britain, c. 1780–1840*. New York: Cambridge University Press, 1995.

——. *The Making of the Modern Self: Identity and Culture in Eighteenth-Century England*. New Haven: Yale University Press, 2005.

Walkowitz, Judith R. *City of Dreadful Delight: Narratives of Sexual Danger in Late Victorian London*. Chicago: University of Chicago Press, 1992.

——. *Prostitution and Victorian Society: Women, Class, and the State*. New York: Cambridge University Press, 1980.

Weeks, Jeffery. *Coming Out: Homosexual Politics in Britain from the Nineteenth Century to the Present*. New York: New Horizon Press, 1977.

——. *Sex, Politics and Society: The Regulation of Sexuality since 1800*. London: Longman, 1981.

Wiener, Joel H., ed. *Papers for the Millions: The New Journalism in Britain, 1850s to 1914*. New York: Greenwood Press, 1988.

Williams, Craig. *Roman Homosexuality: Ideologies of Masculinity in Classical Antiquity*. New York: Oxford University Press, 1999.

Winfield, Percy Henry. *The History of Conspiracy and Abuse of Legal Procedure*. Cambridge: Cambridge University Press, 1921.

Woods, Oliver, and James Bishop. *The Story of the* Times: *Bicentenary Edition, 1785–1985*. London: Michael Joseph, 1985.

Journal Articles and Book Chapters

Bennett, Judith M. "'Lesbian-Like' and the Social History of Lesbianism." *Journal of the History of Sexuality* 9 (January–April 2000): 1–24.

Bristow, Joseph. "Remapping the Sites of Modern Gay History: Legal Reform, Medico-legal Thought, Homosexual Scandal, Erotic Geography." *Journal of British Studies* 46 (January 2007): 116–42.

Bullough, Vern L. "Homosexuality and the Medical Model." *Journal of Homosexuality* 1 (1974): 99–110.

Calder, Marshall. "Havelock Ellis and Company." *Encounter* 37 (1974): 8–23.

Chauncey, George Jr. "From Sexual Inversion to Homosexuality: Medicine and the Changing Conceptualization of Female Deviance." *Salmagundi* 58/9 (1982): 114–46.

Clark, Anna. "Anne Lister's Construction of Lesbian Identity." *Journal of the History of Sexuality* 7 (1996): 23–50.

———. "Twilight Moments." *Journal of the History of Sexuality* 14 (2005): 139–60.

Cocks, H.G. "Safeguarding Civility: Sodomy, Class and Moral Reform in Early Nineteenth-Century England." *Past and Present* 190 (2006): 121–46.

Cocks, H.G. "Trials of Character: The Use of Character Evidence in Victorian Sodomy Trials." In *The Trial in History*, vol. 2, *Domestic and International Trials, 1700–2000*, ed R.A. Melikan, 36–53. Manchester: University of Manchester Press, 2003.

Cohen, Ed. "Legislating the Norm: From Sodomy to Gross Indecency." *South Atlantic Quarterly* 88 (1989): 181–217.

Compton, Lewis. "Gay Studies: From the French Revolution to Oscar Wilde." *Nineteenth-Century Contexts* 11 (1987): 23–32.

Cooper, Robert Allen. "Ideas and Their Execution: English Prison Reform." *Eighteenth-Century Studies* 10 (1976–77): 73–93.

Corfield, Penelope J. "Walking the City Streets: The Urban Odyssey in Eighteenth-Century England." *Journal of Urban History* 16 (February 1990): 132–74.

Crozier, Ivan. "Nineteenth-Century British Psychiatric Writing about Homo-sexuality before Havelock Ellis: The Missing Story." *Journal of the History of Medicine and Allied Sciences* 63 (2008): 65–102.

Davis, Jennifer. "A Poor Man's System of Justice: The London Police Courts in the Second Half of the Nineteenth Century." *Historical Journal* 27 (1984): 309–35.

Davis, Natalie Zemon. "'Women's History' in Transition: the European Case." *Feminist Studies* 3–4 (Spring–Summer 1976): 83–103.

Francis, Martin. "The Domestication of the Male? Recent Research on Nineteenth-and Twentieth- Century British Masculinity." *Historical Journal* 45 (2002): 637–52.

Gibson, William. "Homosexuality, Class and the Church in Nineteenth-Century England: Two Case Studies." *Journal of Homosexuality* 21 (1991): 45–54.

Gilbert, Arthur, "The 'Africaine' Court Martial: A Study of Buggery in the British Navy." *Journal of Homosexuality* 1 (Fall 1974): 111–22.

———. "Buggery and the British Navy, 1700–1861." *Journal of Social History* 10 (1976): 72–98.

———. "Social Deviance and Disaster during the Napoleonic Wars." *Albion* 9 (1977): 98–113.

———. "Sodomy and the Law in Eighteenth- and Early Nineteenth-Century Britain." *Societas* 8 (1978): 225–41.

Gillis, John. "Servants, Sexual Relations and the Risks of Illegitimacy in London, 1801–1900." *Feminist Studies* 5 (Spring 1975): 143–73.

Harvey, A.D. "Prosecutions for Sodomy in England at the Beginning of the Nineteenth Century." *Historical Journal* 21 (1978): 939–48.

Hekma, Gert. "A History of Sexology: Social and Historical Aspects of Sexology." In *From Sappho to Sade: Moments in the History of Sexuality,* ed. Jan Bremmer. London: Routledge, 1989.

———. "Homosexual Behavior in the Nineteenth-Century Dutch Army." *Journal of the History of Sexuality* 2 (1991): 266–88.

———. "Wrong Lovers in the Nineteenth-Century Netherlands." *Journal of Homosexuality* 13 (Winter 1986–Spring 1987): 43–55.

Hilliard, David. "UnEnglish and Unmanly: Anglo-Catholicism and Homosexuality." *Victorian Studies* 25 (1982): 181–210.

Kaplan, Morris B. "Who's Afraid of John Saul? Urban Culture and the Politics of Desire in Late Victorian London." *Gay and Lesbian Quarterly* 5 (1999): 267–314.

McClelland, Keith. "Rational and Respectable Men: Gender, the Working Class and Citizenship in Britain, 1850–1867." In *Gender and Class in Modern Europe,* ed. Laura Frader and Sonya Rose, 280–89. Ithaca, N.Y.: Cornell University Press, 1996.

McGowen, Randall. "Civilizing Punishment: The End of the Public Execution in England." *Journal of British Studies* 33 (July 1994): 257–82.

Meer, Theo van der. "The Persecutions of Sodomites in Eighteenth-Century Amsterdam: Changing Perceptions of Sodomy." *Journal of Homosexuality* 16 (1988): 263–307.

———. "Tribades on Trial: Female Same-Sex Offenders in Late Eighteenth-Century Amsterdam." *Journal of the History of Sexuality* 3 (1991): 424–45.

Moodie, T. Dunbar, with Vivienne Ndatshe and British Sibuyi. "Migrancy and Male Sexuality on the South African Gold Mines." In *Hidden From History: Reclaiming the Gay and Lesbian Past,* ed. Martin Duberman, Martha Vicinus, and George Chauncey Jr., 411–25. New York: New American Library, 1989.

Morley, Tom. "'The Times' and the Concept of the Fourth Estate: Theory and Practice in Mid-nineteenth-Century Britain." *Journal of Newspaper and Periodical History* 3 (1985): 11–23.

Nash, David S. "Unfettered Investigation: The Secularist Press and the Creation of Audience in Victorian England." *Victorian Periodicals Review* 28 (Summer 1995): 123–35.

Nye, Robert A. "The History of Sexuality in Context: National Sexological Traditions." *Science in Context* 4 (1991): 387–406.

Rey, Michel. "Paris Homosexuals Create a Lifestyle, 1700–1750: The Police Archives." *Eighteenth-Century Life* 9 (1985): 179–91.

Reynolds, Elaine A. "St. Marylebone: Local Police Reform in London, 1755–1829." *Historian* 51 (1989): 446–66.

Rich, Adrienne. "Compulsory Heterosexuality and Lesbian Existence." *Signs* 5 (1980): 631–60.

Roberts, M.J.D. "Public and Private in Early Nineteenth-Century London: The Vagrancy Act of 1822 and Its Enforcement." *Social History* 13 (May 1988): 273–94.

Rose, Jonathan. "Rereading the English Common Reader: A Preface to a History of Audiences." *Journal of the History of Ideas* 53 (January–March 1992): 47–70.

Rosenberg, Carol Smith. "The Female World of Love and Ritual: Relations between Women in Nineteenth-Century America." *Signs* 1 (1975): 1–29.

Samuel, Raphael. "Workshop of the World: Steam-Power and Hand Technology in Mid-Victorian Britain." *History Workshop Journal* 3 (1977): 6–72.

Savage, Gail. "Erotic Stories and Public Decency: Newspaper Reporting of Divorce Proceedings in England." *Historical Journal* 41 (1998): 511–28.

Schofield, Roger. "Dimensions of Illiteracy in England, 1750–1850." In *Literacy and Social Development in the West: A Reader,* ed. Harvey J. Graff. New York: Cambridge University Press, 1981.

Scott, Joan. "Deconstructing Equality-versus-Difference: Or the Uses of Poststructuralist Theory for Feminism." *Feminist Studies* 14 (Spring 1988): 33–50.

———. "The Evidence of Experience." *Critical Inquiry* 17 (1991): 773–97.

———. "Gender: A Useful Category of Historical Analysis." *American Historical Review* 91 (1986): 1053–75.

Sindall, Rob. "Middle-Class Crime in Nineteenth-Century England." *Criminal Justice History* 4 (1983): 23–40.

Smith, F.B. "Labouchère's Amendment to the Criminal Law Amendment Bill." *Historical Studies* 17 (1976): 165–73.

Soderlund, Richard. "Crime, Policing, and Punishment in Nineteenth-Century England." *Criminal Justice History* 7 (1986): 155–66.

Sprague, Gregory. "Male Homosexuality in Western Culture: The Dilemma of Identity and Subculture in Historical Research." *Journal of Homosexuality* 10 (1984): 29–44.

Storch, Robert D. "The Plague of the Blue Locusts: Police Reform and Popular Resistance in Northern England, 1840–1857." *International Review of Social History* 20 (1975): 61–90.

Sweet, James H. "Male Homosexuality and Spiritualism in the African Diaspora: The Legacies of a Link." *Journal of the History of Sexuality* 7 (1996): 184–202.

Thomas, Keith. "The Double Standard." *Journal of the History of Ideas* 20 (1959): 197–224.

Thompson, E.P. "The Moral Economy of the English Crowd in the Eighteenth Century." *Past and Present* 50 (February 1971): 76–136.

Trumbach, Randolph. "The Birth of the Queen: Sodomy and the Emergence of Gender Equality in Modern Culture, 1660–1750." In *Hidden From History: Reclaiming the Gay and Lesbian Past,* ed. Martin Duberman, Martha Vicinus, and George Chauncey Jr., 129–40. New York: New American Library, 1989.

Trumbach, Randolph. "London's Sodomites: Homosexual Behavior and Western Culture in the Eighteenth Century." *Journal of Social History* 11 (1977): 1–33.

———. "Sex, Gender, and Sexual Identity in Modern Culture: Male Sodomy and Female Prostitution in Enlightenment London." *Journal of the History of Sexuality* 2 (1991–92): 186–203.

———. "Sodomy Transformed: Aristocratic Libertinage, Public Reputation and the Gender Revolution of the Eighteenth Century." *Journal of Homosexuality* 19 (1990): 105–24.

Tuss, Alex J. "Divergent and Conflicting Voices: Victorian Images of the Male." *Journal of Men's Studies* 44 (August 1995): 43–57.

Upchurch, Charles. "Forgetting the Unthinkable: Cross-Dressers and British Society in the Case of the Queen vs. Boulton and Others." *Gender and History* 12 (April 2000): 127–57.

Vicinus, Martha. "Helpless and Unfriended: Nineteenth-Century Domestic Melodrama." *New Literary History* 13 (1981): 127–43.

———. "Lesbian History: All Theory and No Facts or All Facts and No Theory?" *Radical History Review* 60 (Fall 1994): 57–75.

———. "Lesbian Perversity and Victorian Marriage: The 1864 Codrington Divorce Trial." *Journal of British Studies* 36 (January 1997): 70–98.

Vickery, Amanda. "Historiographical Review: Golden Age of Separate Spheres? A Review of the Categories and Chronology of English Women's History." *Historical Journal* 36 (1993): 383–414.

Wahrman, Dror. "'Middle-Class' Domesticity Goes Public: Gender, Class, and Politics from Queen Caroline to Queen Victoria." *Journal of British Studies* 32 (October 1993): 396–432.

Weeks, Jeffrey. "Inverts, Perverts, and Mary-Annes: Male Prostitution and the Regulation of Homosexuality in England in the Nineteenth and Early Twentieth Centuries." *Journal of Homosexuality* 6 (Fall 1980–Winter 1981): 113–34.

———. "'Sins and Diseases': Some Notes on Homosexuality in the Nineteenth Century." *History Workshop Journal* 1 (1976): 211–19.

Whitehead, Harriet. "The Bow and the Burden Strap: A New Look at Institutionalized Homosexuality in Native North America." In *The Lesbian and Gay Studies Reader,* ed. Henry Abelove, Michèle Aina Barale, and David M. Halperin, 498–527. New York: Routledge, 1993.

Index

Text:	10/13 Sabon
Display:	Sabon
Compositor:	BookMatters, Berkeley
Indexer:	Sharon Sweeney
Printer and binder:	Thomson-Shore, Inc.